THE VISUAL STORY

THE VISUAL STORY
SEEING THE STRUCTURE OF
FILM, TV, AND NEW MEDIA

Bruce Block

Focal Press

An Imprint of Elsevier

Boston   Oxford   Auckland   Johannesburg   Melbourne   New Delhi

Focal Press

An Imprint of Elsevier

∞ This book is printed on acid-free paper.

Library of Congress Cataloging-in-Publication Data
Block, Bruce A.
 The visual story : seeing the structure of film, TV, and new media / Bruce A. Block
  p. cm.
 Includes bibliographical references and index.
 ISBN 0-240-80467-8 (pbk. : alk. paper)
 1. Cinematography. 2. Video recording. I. Title.
 TR850 .B514 2001
 778.5--dc21   00-068126

British Library Cataloguing-in-Publication Data
A catalogue record for this book is available from the British Library.

The publisher offers special discounts on bulk orders of this book.
For information, please contact:
Manager of Special Sales
Elsevier
200 Wheeler Road
Burlington, MA 01803
Tel: 781-313-4700
Fax: 781-313-4802

For information on all Focal Press publications available, contact our World Wide Web homepage at http://www.focalpress.com

10 9 8 7 6
Printed in the United States of America

This book is dedicated to my parents
Stanley and Helene Block

CONTENTS

ACKNOWLEDGMENTS

I would like to thank my students at the University of Southern California and the thousands of other students and working professionals who have attended my classes and seminars at various universities, design firms, and motion picture studios. It is only through our interaction that this book has emerged.

No one finds their way alone. My teachers Word Baker, Lawrence Carra, Sulie and Pearl Harand, Dave Johnson, Bernard Kantor, Eileen Kneuven, Mordecai Lawner, William Nelson, Lester Novros, Woody Omens, Gene Peterson, Mel Sloan, Glenn Voltz, Jewell Walker, and Mort Zarkoff have inspired me and continue to do so.

The practical aspects of making pictures that I discuss here are the outgrowth of working with talented professionals on commercials, documentaries, animated films, television shows, and feature films. The experiences we shared have been critical to the maturation of the ideas presented in this book. I am particularly grateful to Billy Fraker, Neal Israel, and long time compadre Charles Shyer who all gave me my start in Hollywood.

Thanks to Dr. Rod Ryan for his detailed examination and astute comments about Chapter 6, "Color," and to Alan Mandel for the dialogue scene used in the Appendix.

Much encouragement and support has come from all of these people as well as Richard Jewell at USC, Billy Pittard of Pittard-Sullivan Design, Ronnie Rubin of the UCLA Extension Program, Chris Huntley of Screenplay Systems, my dear friends Alan Dressler, Eric Sears, Heidi Boren, and my brother David Block.

Bruce A. Block
Los Angeles, California, 2000

INTRODUCTION

On an icy Russian winter night in 1928, an eager group of film students gathered in a poorly heated classroom at the Soviet GIK. The building, located on the Leningrad Chaussée, had once been the exclusive restaurant Yar but was now the Russian Film Institute. Its main room with floor-to-ceiling mirrors and tall white columns had become a lecture hall for one of the first, and perhaps most famous film teachers of his time: Sergei Eisenstein. Eisenstein, considered by his Soviet government to be a brash, wildly talented filmmaker, along with Vsevolod Pudovkin and Alexander Dovchenko were the first to develop formal theories of film based not only upon their own ideas but on their practical experience making films. Eisenstein developed his montage theories during this period and was by far Russia's brightest film director and teacher.

Eisenstein's dual talents would take him all over the world. In 1933 he spoke at The Motion Picture Academy in Hollywood and lectured at the University of Southern California (USC). He was only 50 when he died in 1948. Had Eisenstein lived, he might have met Slavko Vorkapich, a Yugoslavian filmmaker, who had been directing Hollywood montages at MGM, RKO, and Warner Bros. and headed the film department at USC in 1951. Vorkapich, also a teacher, had taken Eisenstein's filmic ideas further and developed groundbreaking theories about movement and editing. Vorkapich's charming, humorous teaching style taught fundamental cinematic concepts to a new generation of filmmakers. He lectured internationally until his death in 1976.

In the 1940s Lester Novros, a painter and Disney animator, began teaching a class at USC about the visual aspects of motion pictures. Novros' class was based on fine art theories, and the writing of Eisenstein and Vorkapich. I was a student of Novros a few years before he retired in 1978 and took over teaching the course. I decided to delve into the writings of Eisenstein, Vorkapich, and Novros, their source material, plus dozens of other books on visual perception, theatre, photography, art history, and psychology. It was my goal to bring the class and visual theory into the present, make it practical, and link it with story structure. I wanted to remove the wall between theory and practice and make visual structure easy to use.

This book is the result of my research, teaching, and practice of film and video production. What you'll read in these pages can be used immediately in the preparation, production, and editing of theatrical motion pictures, television shows, short films, documentaries, music videos, and commercials be it live action, animated, or computer-generated. Whether you shoot on film or video, for a large screen or small screen, the visual structure of your pictures is usually overlooked yet it's as important as your script.

You will learn how to structure your visuals as carefully as a writer structures a story or a composer structures music. Understanding visual structure allows you to communicate moods and emotions, give your production visual variety, unity and style, and most importantly, reveals the critical relationship between story structure and visual structure.

Here, perhaps for the first time, you'll see how important the visual principles are to practical production. Some of these principles are thousands of years old; others are the result of new, emerging technologies.

The concepts in this book will benefit writers, directors, photographers, production designers, art directors, and editors who are always confronted by the same visual problems that has faced every picture maker in the past, present, and future. The students who sat in Eisenstein's cold Russian classroom had the same basic goal as the picture makers of today: "How to make a good picture." This book will teach you how to find that goal.

C H A P T E R   1

THE VISUAL COMPONENTS

THE CAST OF VISUAL CHARACTERS

Everywhere we go, we're confronted by pictures. We go to the movies, watch television, play video games, surf the Internet, look at pictures in books, magazines, and on billboards. We attend plays and concerts, take videos and snapshots, and visit museums and look at works of art. It's all pictures—big, little, moving, still, color, or black and white, but they're all pictures.

In this book we're going to learn how to understand and control these pictures.

Every picture is comprised of things like a story (an idea, a message, or a script), dialogue or printed words, possibly music and sounds, people (or actors), costumes, and scenery. If the picture is of quality, each of these things will be carefully controlled to have an effect on the viewer. If the picture is an advertisement, we may become interested and buy the item. If the picture is part of a computer game, we might find it exciting and decide to play. If the picture is a movie, we can become involved in its story.

Our first challenge is to examine pictures and break them down into fundamental building blocks. We can look at four main areas for building blocks:

1. The Script. Building blocks of plot, character, and dialogue.
2. The Music. Building blocks of instruments, notes, and melody.
3. The Sound. Building blocks of volume, bass and treble, sound effects, and other elements.
4. The Visuals. What are the building blocks of the visuals? Scenery? Props? Costumes? No. The building blocks for all visuals are the basic visual components.

THE BASIC VISUAL COMPONENTS

The basic visual components are *space, line, shape, tone, color, movement,* and *rhythm*. These visual components are found in every picture we see. Actors, locations, props, costumes, and scenery are made up of visual components. A visual component communicates moods, emotions, ideas, and, most importantly, gives visual structure to what we're watching. In this book we're going to discuss these components in relation to television, computer, and movie screens, although the basic visual components are used in creating any type of picture.

Each chapter of this book is devoted to the study of a single component, but let's introduce each of them now.

SPACE

What do we mean when we say space? We're not talking about outer space or "giving someone their space." The visual component of space refers to three things:

1. The physical space in front of the camera when we're shooting.
2. The difference between the actual space where we shot and the same space as it appears on a screen.
3. The characteristics of the screen where we watch our pictures.

LINE

Line doesn't exist. It's a perceptual fact. It only exists in our heads. Line is the result of other visual components that allow us to perceive lines, but none of the lines are real.

SHAPE

Shape goes hand in hand with line because all shapes appear to be constructed from lines. The shape of an object is revealed when we reduce the object to a silhouette.

TONE

Tone refers to black & white and the gray scale. Tone doesn't refer to the tone of a scene (happy, angry, etc.), or the audio terms (treble and bass). We deal with tone visually when we work in black & white, but we must also consider tone when we use color because tone is a component of color.

COLOR

One of the most powerful visual components is also the most misunderstood. We're going to simplify the complex component of color and make it easy to understand and use.

MOVEMENT

We make *motion* pictures, and although some great films and videos have been produced without any real movement (using only still photographs), we usually rely on movement as a key ingredient in our pictures. Since movement is the component that first attracts an audience's eye, it will play a major role in visual structure.

RHYTHM

We're most familiar with rhythm we can hear, but there's also rhythm we can see. We find rhythm in stationary (nonmoving) objects and moving objects. We also use rhythm extensively in that important tool we called editing.

So this is our cast of characters: *space, line, shape, tone, color, movement,* and *rhythm*. We may be more familiar with the other cast of characters called actors, but both casts are critical to producing great work. Once production begins, the cast of characters called visual components will show up on the set every day. The visual components will be in front of the camera in every shot, and they will be communicating with the audience as much as the other cast called actors. That's why understanding these components is so important. Although each component is given its own chapter, you'll see that they overlap and that an understanding of one component will only be complete after you understand the others.

Since the actor has been introduced here, let's take a moment and discuss an actor. An actor is a very unique object we can place on the screen. It is the actor's personality and talent that attracts an audience. The actor communicates by talking, making facial expressions, and using body language, but an actor is also a collection of spaces, lines, shapes, tones, colors, movements, and rhythms. In that respect, there's no difference between an actor and any other object. Actors and objects all share the same building blocks that we call the basic visual components. Because of this, on one level, an audience relates to all of them in the same way.

I'm not suggesting that actors be treated like inanimate objects (or, as Alfred Hitchcock allegedly suggested, like cattle), because an actor's performance can be an extraordinary experience for the audience. The audience should never be aware of the manipulative aspects of the actor's performance just as they should not be aware of the manipulative values of the visual components. The audience unconsciously reacts to the actor's performance, the music, and the visual components all the time. The components constantly feed the audience visual information, and that information will always affect their moods, emotions, and feelings. The audience cannot escape the effects of the visual components.

Let's look at an example of how a musical component communicates. If we watch Hitchcock's *Psycho* (1960) or Spielberg's *Jaws* (1975) we'll learn how a music cue signals "terror" for the audience. In both films, a music cue warns the audience that the murdering mother or the carnivorous shark are nearby. In *Psycho* it's the screech of the violins and in *Jaws* it's the pounding notes of a bass. In both cases, the filmmaker introduces the musical theme when the murderous character first appears, and then by playing a few bars of that theme, reminds the audience of the threat and keeps them on the edge of their seats. In this case, a musical component communicates fear.

We can do the same thing with a visual component. Color, for example, can signal danger. It can be any color. Blue can mean "murder" to an audience if you define it as such. If every murder in a story occurs in blue light, the audience will expect a murder whenever blue light is presented to them. This is the concept used in Sidney Lumet's *Murder on the Orient Express* (1974). Once you establish a color and its meaning, the audience will accept the idea and react accordingly.

Certain visual components have emotional characteristics already associated with them, although most of these visual stereotypes are easy to break. For example, a longstanding stereotype in movie westerns was the color of the cowboy's hat. Traditionally the hero wore a white hat and the villain wore a black hat. Does white always communicate the identity of the hero? Of course not. Any color can stand for good, evil, happy, sad, honest, dishonest, and so on. Although stereotypes effectively prove that visual components can communicate with an audience, they're also the weakest, perhaps least creative use of the visual components. You'll see why visual stereotypes are often wrong or inappropriate, and how you can use the visual components in more skillful ways.

Can we decide in the planning stages of a production not to use the visual components in our production? If we ignore the visual components, won't they simply go away? No. Color is the only visual component we can eliminate by shooting in black & white. Otherwise, it's impossible to eliminate any other component.

We can never remove the visual components from a shot because they exist in everything we place on the screen. If a viewer looks at a blank screen it still contains the visual components of rhythm, space, line, shape, tone, and movement. So the screen isn't really blank at all. Even still photos display the components of rhythm and movement.

Defining the visual components opens the door to understanding visual structure, which will be your guide in the selection of locations, set dressing, props, wardrobe, lenses, camera positions, lighting, actor staging, and editorial choices. It will be the basis for your answer to questions about every visual aspect of your pictures.

Remember, though, that any study, if rigidly adhered to, can be misleading. It's not the purpose of this book to leave you with a set of textbook definitions and ironclad rules. If visual structure was that predictable and precise, anyone could pull out a calculator and produce perfect pictures. Visual structure isn't math. It isn't that predictable. Fortunately, there are definitions and guidelines, even some rules, that will help us wrestle with the problems of producing a great visual production. The key is in the visual components.

In this book, I'm going to define each visual component and break it down into smaller subcomponents that I'll also define. Sometimes I'll even divide those subcomponents into smaller sub-subcomponents. In every case, no matter how subordinate our component, I'll describe it, define it, illustrate it, and show you how to use it. The purpose of this book is to enable you to understand and use visual structure so that you can make better pictures.

TERMS

This book will introduce many new ideas and terms that will help you understand visual picture-making. Here are a few terms that need defining now.

THE SCREEN

The *screen* refers to the two-dimensional screens where we watch pictures. This includes movie screens, television and computer screens, the proscenium of a theater stage, the canvases hanging in museums, and the pictures in books and magazines. All of these flat, two-dimensional surfaces are screens.

REAL WORLD/SCREEN WORLD

The *real world* is the environment we live in. It's the three-dimensional world we inhabit. The *screen world* is created by images on screens. Sometimes the two different worlds will follow the same visual rules, other times they will not.

FOREGROUND, MIDGROUND, AND BACKGROUND

A group of terms we'll use are *foreground* abbreviated as FG (objects close to the viewer or camera), *midground* or MG (objects that are further away from the viewer or camera), and *background* or BG (objects that are farthest away or at least more distant than the FG and MG objects).

VISUAL PROGRESSION

Whenever we talk about any kind of structure, we have to talk about progressions. A progression begins as one thing and changes to something else. Music can make a progression from quiet to loud or slow to fast, for example. A story can have a progression as a character learns and grows. We can also have visual progressions. Let's look at an example of a *visual progression*. This progression is going to begin with something visually simple and change towards something visually complex.

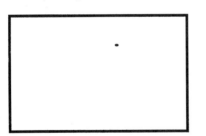

Here's the simplest object we can place on a screen, a *point*. From here, we'll begin a visual progression that will gain complexity.

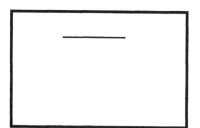

We can take the point, drag it across the frame, and create a *line*. The line is visually more complicated than the point, so things have progressed from simple to a little more complex.

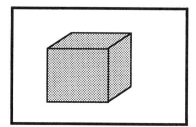

If we take the line and pull it down, we create a *plane*. The two-dimensional plane is more complex than the line.

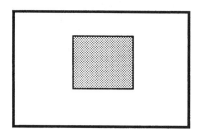

If we take the plane and pull it out into space, we create the final and most complex level of this visual progression: a cube or *volume*.

That is a progression. From a point, to a line, to a plane, to a volume. From the simple to the complex. Visual structure, like any type of structure, uses progressions. We'll come back to the concept of progressions as we deal with each of the visual components.

THE PICTURE PLANE

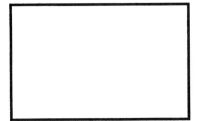

Whenever we discuss anything visual in the screen world, we'll surround it with frame lines. These frame lines create a *picture plane*.

The picture plane is the "window" within which the picture will exist. These frame lines represent the height and width of this window or screen. The proportions of the screen will vary depending on whether we're using a motion picture, television, or computer screen, but every screen is a picture plane.

In a museum, the picture plane is defined by the actual frame around the painting. The picture plane of a camera is the viewfinder and the aperture of the film plane. The picture plane of a television or computer is the edges of the screen. When we hold our hands up in front of our eye to frame a shot, we make a window with our hands. That, too, is a picture plane.

PRACTICE, NOT THEORY

Right now you might be thinking that this book has made a sudden turn off the path of practicality. The Introduction promised a book that would help you plan and shoot a movie. So what's all this "point, line, plane" stuff? Asking an actor to be more of a visual progression doesn't sound very helpful.

Wait. Don't let these terms scare you away. Don't think that theory is bad because it might ruin creative instincts, become impractical, or kill spontaneity. It's actually going to help your visual ideas become reality. Look at the film *Raging Bull* (1980) and you'll see that each new boxing ring sequence is part of a progression that builds in dramatic, visual, and sound intensity throughout the film. Scorsese's fight sequences go from simple to complex. Look at Hitchcock's *The Birds* (1963) and watch the visual progressions as the birds gather and attack. Watch the visual progression in the cornfield sequence in *North by Northwest* (1959). Watch David Lean's *Lawrence of Arabia* (1962) and plot the visual progressions. Run any Fred Astaire or Busby Berkeley musical and you'll see visual progressions as the dance numbers build in their intensity. Look at the structural build at the climax of Coppola's *The Godfather* (1972). Watch how the visual progressions take you from simple to complex action sequences in Spielberg's *Raiders of the Lost Ark* (1981), or how a nervous breakdown progresses visually in Polanski's *Repulsion* (1965), or how Redford's *Ordinary People* (1980) orchestrates its visual progression in the psychiatrist's office. If you know what to look for, they're all examples of solid storytelling and visual progressions. They're about visual structure.

A point turning into a line, turning into a plane, and turning into a volume is only a mechanical illustration of a visual progression that moves from something simple to something complex. Progressions are fundamental to story or musical structure, and they're fundamental to visual structure. Once I've explained and defined the visual components, we'll tackle visual progressions and visual structure. Finally we'll discuss the important link between visual structure and story structure.

Now our job is to take this cast of characters that we call visual components and discover who they are. It's a cast that we're stuck with, but it's a great cast. In fact, these seven cast members are capable of playing any part, any mood, and any emotion, and they're great on television, a computer screen, or the big screen. This cast is so versatile that they work equally well in live-action, animation, and computer-generated media. They're the most sought after (and least understood) players around.

Space, line, shape, tone, color, movement, and rhythm. Most of Hollywood doesn't even know what the visual components are, yet they've appeared in every film ever made. The visual components have no lawyers or agents, work for free, receive no residuals, and never come to the set late. What better cast could you ask for?

It's time to meet the cast individually, but there's still one key principle we must define. It's so important that it has its own chapter—and it begins on the next page.

C H A P T E R   2

CONTRAST AND AFFINITY

THE KEY TO VISUAL STRUCTURE

Visual structure is based on an understanding of the *principle of contrast and affinity*.

What is *contrast*? Contrast means difference. Here's an example of contrast using the visual component of tone.

Remember, tone refers to the brightness of objects. We can illustrate tone with a gray scale. Contrast of tone means two shades of gray that are as different in terms of brightness as possible. On the gray scale, which two tones show maximum difference or contrast? The correct answer is the black square and the white square. So a picture illustrating maximum contrast of tone would use only black and white.

This shot, all black and white, is an example of maximum contrast of tone.

What is *affinity*? Affinity means similarity. So what is an example of affinity of tone?

Since affinity means similarity, we would pick any two grays that are next to each other on the gray scale and create a picture that only used those two grays.

This shot is an example of tonal affinity. It uses only black and very dark gray, two tones that have great similarity or affinity.

Every visual component (space, line, shape, tone, color, movement, and rhythm) can be described and used in terms of contrast and affinity, which we'll discuss in the chapters that follow.

Now that we've defined contrast and affinity, we can explain the *principle of contrast and affinity*:

> The greater the contrast in a visual component,
> the more the visual intensity or dynamic *increases*.
> The greater the affinity in a visual component,
> the more the visual intensity or dynamic *decreases*.
> More simply stated:
> **CONTRAST = GREATER VISUAL INTENSITY**
> **AFFINITY = LESS VISUAL INTENSITY**

Now, what does "visual intensity" mean? Watching a sequence of a great film, we might say: "Wow, that was really exciting!" When watching a less intense sequence we might say: "It was very low-key or quiet." These comments refer to what we're calling "intensity" or "dynamic." A computer game can be engaging or boring. A television commercial can be agitating or soothing. These emotional reactions are based on the intensity you feel when you watch them.

Intensity or dynamic relates to the emotional reaction members of an audience feel when they see a picture, read a book, or listen to music. The reaction can be emotional (they cry, laugh, or scream) or more physical (their muscles tense up, they cover their eyes, they fidget in their seats). Usually the more intense the visual stimulus, the more intense the audience reaction.

A good writer carefully structures words, sentences, and paragraphs. A good musician carefully structures notes, measures, and bars. A director, cinematographer, production designer, or editor structures visuals by applying the *principle of contrast and affinity* to the basic visual components.

Let's take an extremely simple example. We'll create two short abstract movies.

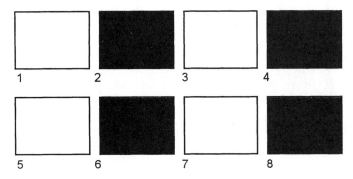

This is the storyboard for the first film. A storyboard is a set of drawings that illustrate what the final film will look like. The first shot in this film will be a white frame. One second later we'll cut to a black frame. A second later, we'll cut back to the white frame, and so on. This alternation of white and black will continue for several minutes. The audience's response will be "it's making me crazy!" The rapid contrast of black and white assaulting the audience will become too intense and impossible to watch.

Now let's switch to the second abstract film.

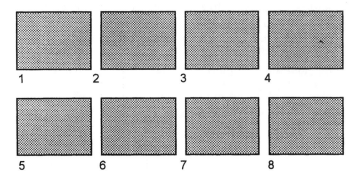

Here's the storyboard for the second film. Every frame is the same; nothing changes. We'll ask the audience to watch this movie for several minutes and, of course, they will quickly lose interest. The film is all affinity. It lacks visual dynamic.

The contrast of the black/white movie is too intense, and the affinity of the gray movie has no intensity at all.

Here's another example.

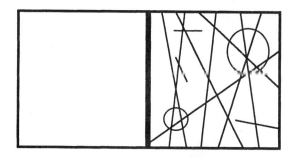

Which half of this frame is more intense? The right half or the left half? The right half of the frame is full of lines that create a visual intensity that the left half of the frame lacks.

So there is something about the black/white movie and the right half of the frame drawing that have intensity or dynamic. It is an emotional, intellectual, and muscular response an audience feels when they look at pictures. It is visual intensity.

Although the basic principle of contrast and affinity is simple, using it can get complicated. Each visual component can be broken down into many subcomponents, and all of them can be related back to contrast and affinity.

Once we understand the basic visual components and how contrast and affinity work for each one, we'll be able to devise visual structures for our productions. Visual structure will depend on how we control the contrast and affinity. Visual structure can be extremely simple (full of affinities) or extremely complex (full of contrasts) or, better yet, a combination of the two.

In the next seven chapters, I'll define each basic visual component. We'll discuss how to see them, evoke emotions by controlling them in practical production, form a visual style, and most importantly, learn how to build visual structure.

C H A P T E R   3

SPACE

Space is a complex visual component. It not only defines the screen where all of the other visual components are seen, but space itself has several complex levels or sub components that we need to understand. To simplify our discussion, this chapter on space is divided into two parts. Part One defines the four basic sub components of space and Part Two describes all of space's secondary properties.

P A R T   O N E

THE PRIMARY
SUB COMPONENTS

Let's begin by examining the space of the screen because it is upon this screen that all of the visual components will exist.

The physical nature of the screen is strictly two-dimensional. A screen is a flat surface that can be measured in height and width but practically speaking has no depth. This is true for any screen surface, from a computer or television to a movie screen.

The real world that we live in is three-dimensional, having height, width, and depth. Our challenge is to portray a three-dimensional world on a two-dimensional screen surface and have the result look believable. We'll expect a viewer to watch the two-dimensional pictures and accept the images as realistic representations of their three-dimensional world.

How can we take a two-dimensional screen surface and create pictures on it that give the illusion of three-dimensions or depth?

We're *not* talking about 3-D movies or holograms (although the latter is truly a three-dimensional picture). We're talking about normal pictures on a computer, television, or motion picture screen that look three-dimensional even though they're being shown on a flat screen surface.

The first step in understanding the visual component of space is to explore the four basic types of space: *deep space, flat space, limited space,* and *ambiguous space.*

DEEP SPACE

Deep space is the illusion of a three-dimensional world on a two-dimensional screen surface. It's possible to give an audience the experience of seeing a three-dimensional space (height, width, and depth) even though all of the depth is illusory. The depth is not actually there; it can never be there because the screen upon which the picture exists is flat.

Our ability to fool the audience into thinking there's depth on the screen when there's no depth at all comes from our knowledge and use of *depth cues.*

We could describe this picture as three people standing along a road that winds towards some distant mountains. Our description is correct, but it's also entirely wrong. In the real world we know that the road goes into the distance, because we could walk down the road and see its three-dimensional path. Here, the same road is being shown to us on a flat piece of paper (or a flat screen) and the depth isn't real; it can't be real because the page in this book is only two-dimensional, it's absolutely flat. This book page has no depth, yet we believe that the road winds into the *depth* of the picture. This means that there's something about this two-dimensional picture that convinces us we're seeing depth where there's no actual depth at all. That something is called a depth cue.

THE DEPTH CUES

Let's define and describe each of these depth cues. *Depth cues* are visual elements that make the audience feel they're seeing depth when there's no real depth at all.

Size Difference

As an object of known size gets smaller in the frame, it appears to get farther away. As an object of known size gets larger, it appears to get closer.

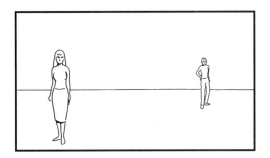

In this drawing, we believe that the larger person is closer to us and the smaller person is farther away. Their sizes are different, so one person must be closer to the camera. Of course, in reality they're both exactly the same distance away from us because they're on the same flat surface (this page).

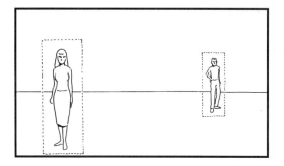

The two people have been staged on two separate planes indicated by the dotted lines. One is on the MG (midground) plane and the other is on the BG (background) plane.

This concept might seem simple and obvious, but size difference is an extremely important and basic depth cue. It's a way to create illusory depth in a picture. If you watch Orson Welles' *Citizen Kane* (1941) you'll see that the staging of actors and the illusion of depth revolves around this basic principle. In fact, this depth cue is sometimes called "staging in depth."

Perspective and Convergence

We can talk about perspective in two ways. We can discuss drawing with it and we can discuss recognizing it in the real world. *Perspective* occurs when we represent a three-dimensional world on a two-dimensional surface. *Convergence* can be defined as "parallel lines of a single plane meeting at a vanishing point," but this definition sounds meaningless. To make convergence useful, we need to understand some simple terms and look at some picture examples.

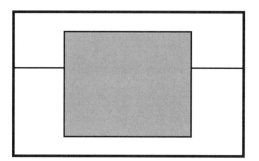

Here's the two-dimensional plane that we introduced in Chapter 1, "The Visual Components." Notice that the plane's top and bottom lines are parallel and that its left and right side lines are parallel. We call this plane a *frontal plane*. You could think of it as a large, flat wall.

For our purposes, perspective comes in three basic types: one-point, two-point, and three-point perspective. These three types of perspective form a visual progression from simple to complex. Now let's examine each one.

One-Point Perspective: Let's begin with the simplest type of perspective that may already look familiar to you.

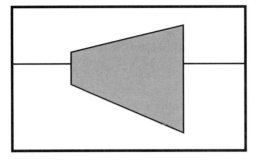

If we change our view of the frontal plane, the depth cue of perspective and convergence will appear. The top and bottom lines of the frontal plane are no longer parallel. We've created a *longitudinal plane*, an extremely important cue to illusory depth. The longitudinal plane appears to exist in depth. One side of the plane looks farther away even though it really exists on a flat paper surface.

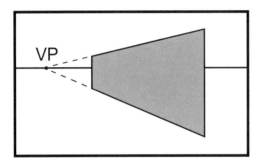

The lines along the top and bottom of the longitudinal plane appear to meet or converge at a single point on the horizon called a *vanishing point* or VP. Usually the vanishing point appears on the horizon, although it can be anywhere, as we'll see in three-point perspective.

A classic example of one-point perspective occurs when we stand in the middle of a railroad track and look down the track towards the horizon.

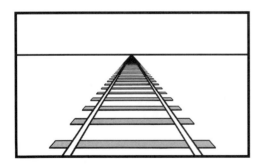

The rails of the track appear to meet or converge at a vanishing point on the horizon. The rails never actually meet; they always remain parallel, but they appear to converge towards the vanishing point. We equate this convergence with distance. The more the rails converge, the farther away they seem.

Convergence occurs in the real world and in the screen world, but in the screen world it happens on a two-dimensional surface, and therefore we call it a cue to illusory depth. The railroad tracks seem to go into the depth of the shot, but there is no depth on a flat screen.

Two-Point Perspective: If we think of one-, two-, and three-point perspective as a progression, the next most complex level is two-point perspective, which uses two vanishing points instead of one. There are several ways that two-point perspective can be produced.

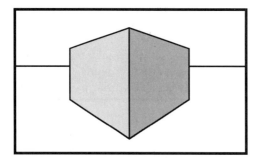

Two longitudinal surfaces can generate two vanishing points.

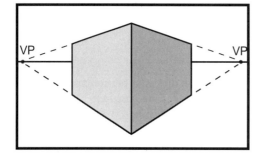

In this first example there are two longitudinal planes, each with its own vanishing point. Commonly, this occurs when we look at the corner of a building. The top and bottom lines of each longitudinal plane converge to a separate vanishing point.

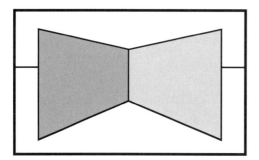

Inverting the two longitudinal planes reveals a second example of two-point perspective. This occurs when we look into the corner of a room.

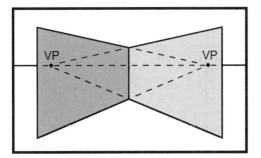

Although the vanish points are hidden behind the longitudinal planes, there are still two vanishing points here.

Two vanishing points can also appear on a single longitudinal plane. To illustrate this, let's redraw the one-point perspective longitudinal plane.

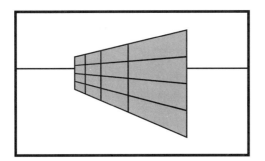

Additional lines have been added to the plane to make the convergence more obvious, but the longitudinal plane still has only one vanishing point.

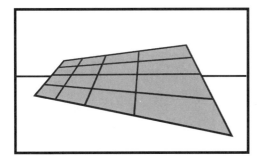

If we tip the longitudinal plane away from us, or move our view closer and lower, the plane is not only angled, it's also tilted. None of the lines on this longitudinal plane are parallel.

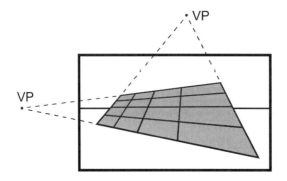

There are two vanishing points. The plane's top and bottom lines converge to one vanishing point located to the left of the frame. The left and right lines converge to a second vanishing point located above the frame.

Three-Point Perspective: Finally, we have three-point perspective, which is more complex than one- or two-point perspective.

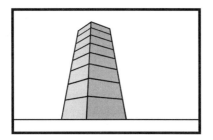

This is a view of a tall building. There are now three distinct vanishing points.

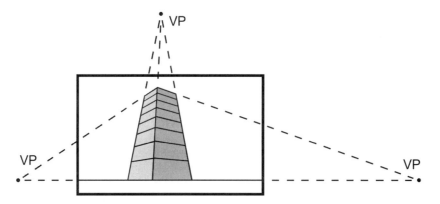

One vanishing point will appear above the building. The second and third vanishing points will appear along the horizon line to the building's left and right.

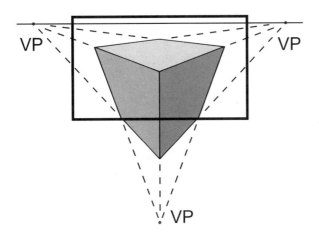

This shot also illustrates three-point perspective, but the viewing position is high above the building. This would be your view if you're in a helicopter coming in to land on the building's roof.

All things being equal, the more vanishing points the greater the illusion of depth. One vanishing point will create the illusion of depth in the screen world, but adding a second or third point will give the audience a greater sense of illusory deep space. Remember that no matter how many points you add there isn't any real depth. These drawings and every picture you've seen exist on a flat, two-dimensional surface. All of the depth is illusory.

What about adding more vanishing points? It's possible to have four, five, twenty, or more vanishing points in a shot. If this were a drawing class (and it isn't) we'd spend time discussing multiple point perspective, but we're not interested in drawing perspective, we're interested in recognizing it in our viewfinders. More importantly, an audience watching a film doesn't notice more than three vanishing points. In a drawing or painting, a viewer might become aware of multiple vanishing points because there's unlimited viewing time to notice these details. A film audience doesn't have control over viewing time and can't sense additional vanishing points beyond three. This limitation is an advantage for the filmmaker because it means there are only three levels of illusory depth possible when using perspective and convergence.

Actors can also be looked at as a longitudinal or frontal plane.

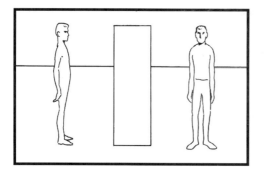

The front, back, and profile views of an actor are like planes, so creating depth cues with them is easy.

In this shot, the camera is lowered and tilted up turning the actor into a longitudinal plane. The same thing would happen if the camera was raised and tilted down to look at the actor.

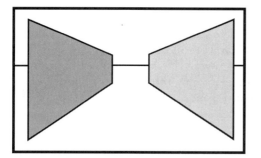

When the vanishing point is on screen or nearly on screen, the audience's attention will usually be drawn to that point. Notice how your eye is drawn to the on-screen vanishing point between the two walls.

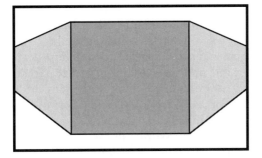

If the vanishing point is out of frame, it loses its ability to attract the audience's eye.

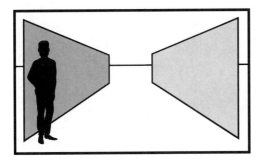

In this shot your eye is drawn to the actor, but it is also drawn to the vanishing point between the two walls. If our intent is to keep the audience's attention on the actor, we may have created a problem.

In this shot, your attention will go to the vanishing point located directly behind the actor. The vanishing point helps keep your attention in place on the actor.

Does this mean that actors must always be located on the vanishing point? Absolutely not. It's just important to know that vanishing points will usually attract an audience's attention.

Textural Diffusion

Every object has texture. A plain plaster wall has a smooth texture and a wool sweater has a nubbly texture. Every object will also have a color. Our ability to see depth due to differences of detail in texture and color is called *textural diffusion*.

Imagine you're attending a soccer game and the stadium is packed. You're sitting in the very last row behind the goal area. As you look at the fans in the seats nearby, you can easily distinguish the individual textures and colors of each person's face, hair style, clothing, and other aspects of appearance.

When you look across the stadium, to the fans sitting in the seats opposite yours behind the other goal, you can only see hundreds of little dots of color. Individual details of color and texture are blended together because you are too far away to see them.

This photograph illustrates textural diffusion. Objects with less detail appear farther away. We equate a loss of texture, detail, and individual color with distance.

Movement

Movement is an extraordinarily important way to create illusory depth. In this discussion of depth cues, we'll discuss two things that can move: an object in front of the camera or the camera itself. Later, in Chapter 7, "Movement," we'll expand this idea, but for now we're limited to movements of the object or the camera.

Object Movement: Object movement can give the viewer a sense of illusory depth. An object can be anything in front of the camera—an actor, a car, an animal, a crowd, it makes no difference.

There are only two ways that an object can move in relation to the camera. The object can either move *parallel* to or *perpendicular* to the picture plane. Remember that the picture plane is the two-dimensional "window frame" within which pictures exist.

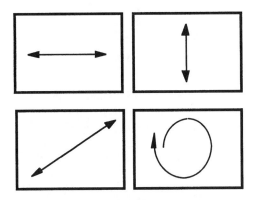

Movement parallel to the picture plane means movement up and down, left and right, diagonal or circular. A single object moving parallel to the picture plane creates flat space, which we'll discuss later in this chapter. But two or more objects moving parallel to the picture plane can produce the illusion of depth. This depth cue is called *relative movement*.

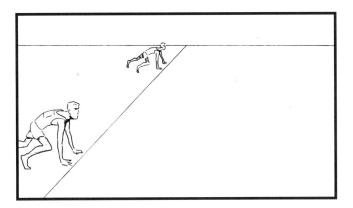

This example of relative movement shows two runners at a starting line. Both of them will run through the frame parallel to the picture plane, and both will run at exactly the same speed. Even though they begin running at the same time, the FG runner will appear to travel across the frame much faster than the BG runner.

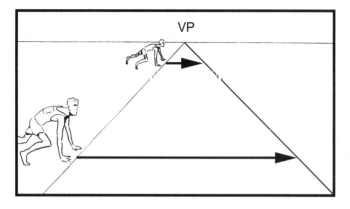

Using a vanishing point, we can accurately predict how much further the FG runner will appear to move even though both runners will actually travel the same distance. The apparent difference in speed and distance traveled produces the depth cue.

We can also create illusory depth when an object moves perpendicular to the picture plane.

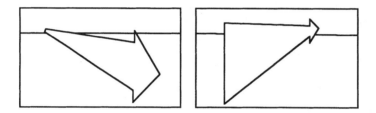

Objects that move towards or away from the camera are moving perpendicular to the picture plane. As an object moves toward or away from the camera a number of depth cues appear. Imagine a speeding train of one hundred cars moving towards you at 80 mph. As the train approaches, you'll notice a number of depth cues:

1. *Size difference.* The engine is larger than the cars behind it.
2. *Textural diffusion.* As the train approaches it gains detail.
3. *Object movement.* As the train approaches it appears to speed up.

In fact, as the train roars by at 80 mph, the engine seems to be going much faster than the caboose, which is still far away. Of course, both ends of the train must be traveling at the same speed, but the more distant train cars appear to be moving more slowly.

As an object of constant speed moves perpendicular to the picture plane towards the viewer, it will appear to speed up. Conversely, an object will seem to slow down as it moves away from the viewer. This change in apparent speed is the depth cue produced by movement perpendicular to the picture plane.

Camera Movement: There are three camera moves that will give us a greater sense of depth. It doesn't matter how the camera is being moved (by dolly, crane, hand-held, special mechanical rigs, etc.), the same basic principles apply.

A *dolly in* and *dolly out* can be described as physically moving the camera closer or farther from an object. By *dollying* the camera in and out, we'll give the viewer a greater sense of illusory depth.

Why does a dolly create depth? Let's say we're staging a shot with one actor in the foreground and two actors in the background.

CAM. POSITION #1   CAM. POSITION #2

As we dolly in, the FG actor will get larger faster than the two actors in the BG. Why? The answer lies in understanding the relative distances of the actors from the camera.

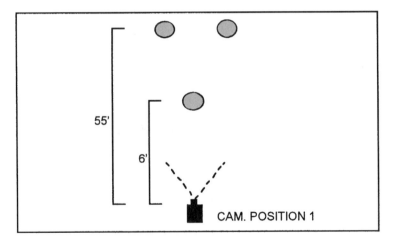

Here's an overhead view or ground plan map that will explain the answer. The camera begins 6 feet from the FG actor and 55 feet from the BG actors.

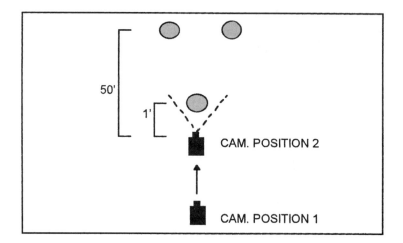

The camera dollies in 5 feet. Now we're only 1 foot from the FG actor, but we're 50 feet from the BG actors. The FG actor went from 6 feet to only 1 foot from the camera, so we'd expect to see a huge size change. The BG actors went from 55 feet to 50 feet, so their size change is minimal, because they're still so far from the camera.

This relative difference in size change (the FG object gets larger faster than the BG object) is a cue to illusory depth.

Conversely, when we dolly out (or away from the subject) the FG actor will get smaller quickly and the BG actors will barely change size at all.

We can also create illusory depth with a camera movement when we dolly left and right, often called a *tracking shot*.

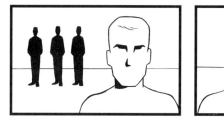

CAM. POSITION #1   CAM. POSITION #2

As the camera dollies or tracks from left to right, the FG actor passes the camera faster than the three actors in the BG.

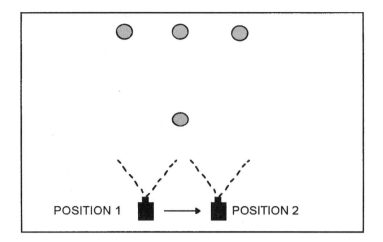

There's relative movement between the faster moving FG and the slower moving BG objects. An audience interprets the faster moving FG and the slower moving BG as a depth cue.

The third type of camera move that produces illusory depth is a *boom* or *crane* shot. It means that the camera is moved up or down. The principle is identical to the tracking shot, but instead of moving horizontally, the camera moves vertically.

CAM. POSITION #1   CAM. POSITION #2

As the camera cranes up, the actor in the FG will move quickly out the bottom of the frame and the two BG actors will move more slowly. As the camera cranes down, the FG actor will come into the frame quickly, but the BG actors will barely move.

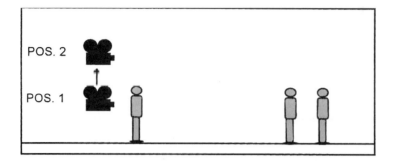

It's exactly the same kind of relative movement we saw with the tracking shot, but instead of generating horizontal relative movement, the crane shot produces vertical relative movement.

Aerial Diffusion

Aerial diffusion has visual characteristics similar to *textural diffusion*, but it occurs for different reasons. Aerial diffusion depends on particles in the air. These particles can be dust, fog, rain, smog, smoke, or anything suspended in the air that obscures our view of the distance.

Aerial diffusion will cause three things to happen visually. First, the aerial diffusion will cause a loss in detail and texture. Second, the aerial diffusion will change the shot's contrast, and third, the aerial diffusion will change the color of objects to the color of the aerial diffusion itself.

If you imagine a long, straight street in a large city we can see how aerial diffusion works. On a clear day where there's no aerial diffusion in the air (no smog, fog, rain, mist, etc.) we might say that the city looks "sparkling" or "clear." What we're describing is the wonderful detail and the individual colors and textures that we see when there isn't any aerial diffusion present. The same visual clarity occurs in rural areas where there's no smog.

Now imagine the same street scene on a rainy day with mist and fog covering the city. Looking down the same street, the visual quality is completely different. The buildings no longer have their individual textures and colors. The aerial diffusion (mist, fog, and rain) is now diffusing our view of the city and the scene will look different. The details of the buildings will be gone. You'll also notice an overall lack of contrast. Very bright and very dark building colors will be replaced with grays. Distant buildings most effected by the aerial diffusion will appear even farther away than they really are.

Imagine another weather condition on the same street. Instead of rain, the aerial diffusion will be caused by a brown industrial smog. As we look down our city street, the detail and texture of the buildings will be obscured by the smog, but the buildings will also take on a brown color. The farther away a building is, the more it will be changed from its own color to the brown color of the aerial diffusion.

For aerial diffusion to work as a depth cue, the viewer must see an object unaffected by the aerial diffusion and another object affected by the aerial diffusion in the same shot. It's the comparison between the two that creates the depth.

The loss of detail in objects due to aerial diffusion makes them seem more distant. This is similar to textural diffusion but not the same thing. Textural diffusion relies on actual distance to produce a loss in detail. Aerial diffusion does not rely on actual distance but rather on particles in the air that obscure the detail, texture, and color of objects.

This pair of photos illustrates a scene affected and unaffected by aerial diffusion.

Shape Change
When an object changes shape, we perceive the change as a cue to illusory depth. Shape change can occur in moving objects or stationary (nonmoving) objects.

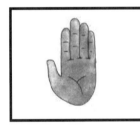 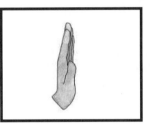

Here are two drawings of a hand.

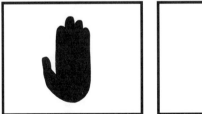 

If we reduce the hands to silhouettes, we'll see that each is a very different shape. How can the same object have more than one shape?

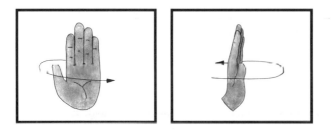

The hand can change shape by rotating or turning in space. If an object can rotate, there must be a third dimension that allows the rotation to occur. Remember, in the two-dimensional screen world the third dimension is only an illusion because the screen surface is two-dimensional and flat. As an object rotates and changes shape, we perceive illusory depth.

This picture of a building creates deep space because it shows a longitudinal surface, size difference (the windows get smaller), and because the windows change shape. We assume all of the windows are actually the same size and shape even though they appear to change.

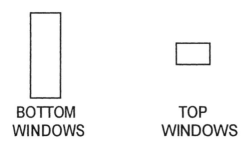

BOTTOM
WINDOWS

TOP
WINDOWS

The bottom windows appear tall and rectangular, and the top windows appear as short, squat rectangles. This change in shape is a cue to illusory depth.

Tonal Separation
Tone refers to black & white and the gray scale.

The gray scale contains no color. It's a series of steps from black to white. This depth cue deals with our perception of lighter and darker objects. Usually lighter objects appear closer and darker objects appear further away.

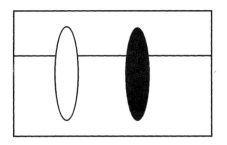

Even with two objects of identical size, a viewer will usually feel the brighter object is closer or larger and the darker object is farther away or smaller.

Color Separation
Color can be a depth cue. For now we'll use color terminology in a very simple way. We can divide colors into two basic groups: warm and cool. The warm colors are red, orange, and yellow, and the cool colors are blue and green. Chapter 6, "Color," will explain the complexities of color more fully.

Color separation means that warm colors appear closer to the viewer and cool colors appear further away.

See Color Plate 1.

The red square will seem closer and the blue square will appear further away even though both squares are the same distance from the viewer.

There are many theories about why this happens. Researchers believe it's linked to our physiological and psychological responses to different wavelengths of light. Whatever the reason, the perceptual fact exists, and we can use it when creating illusory deep space on a flat screen.

Overlap

When one object overlaps another, it creates illusory depth.

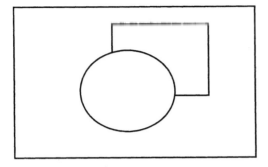

In this drawing, the square appears behind the circle because the circle covers or overlaps part of the square. If one object overlaps another there must be enough depth for an object to get behind another. The overlapping creates depth.

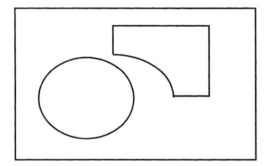

We would be surprised if we pulled these two shapes apart and the square had a piece missing. It would mean that the square was never behind the circle but was laying next to it on a flat surface. But that is a visual trick. Real overlap produces illusory depth.

Up/Down Position

Generally speaking, we perceive objects higher in the frame as farther away and objects lower in the frame as closer.

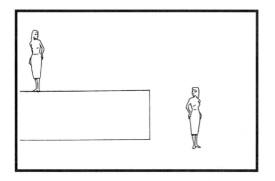

Even though these two figures are the same size, a viewer will perceive the higher figure to be farther away and the lower one as closer.

If there is a horizon line in the frame the up/down position depth cue becomes more complex.

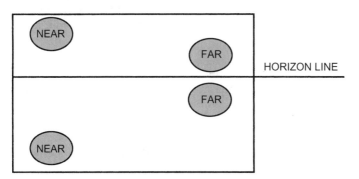

Objects closer to the horizon will appear more distant, and objects farther from the horizon will seem closer.

Below the horizon, objects higher in the frame appear farther away. The opposite is true when objects appear above the horizon where objects lower seem farther away and objects high in the frame appear closer.

Focus

Focus refers to the sharpness of anything in the picture. Focus is not an object we manipulate in front of the camera but the result of optics and lenses. We can photograph objects in sharp focus or blurred. A depth cue is only useable when it is in focus. Once an object goes out-of-focus, it looses its deep space characteristics and becomes flat. The more out-of-focus it gets the more we ignore its depth cues.

DEEP SPACE AND TELEVISION

American NTSC television is somewhat limited in its ability to reproduce deep space. Many of the depth cues needed for the creation of illusory depth fall outside the technical limits of the television system.

1. Conventional television ignores the depth cue of *textural diffusion*. Television has a limited resolution and cannot adequately reproduce objects with

great amounts of detail. Most objects when reproduced on television have about an equal amount of resolution or detail whether they're in the foreground or the background. A high-definition television system can remedy some of this problem because it doubles the resolution of the picture. Internet video can have a similar problem depending on the resolution of the downloaded image.

2. The television or computer screen's ability to show *size difference* is inadequate because the average screen is only nineteen inches wide. This physical dimension severely limits the size of large objects and makes small objects difficult to see. These screens are simply too small to adequately display size change.

3. The depth cue of *tonal separation* is difficult for television to reproduce accurately because television has a limited tonal range. Bright whites and dark blacks can't be reproduced because their contrast range falls outside television's technical capabilities. The television system itself can't reproduce black at all. Television reproduces the middle of the gray scale best.

4. Television cannot distinguish between subtle changes of color and tends to reproduce similar, but different, colors as identical. This phenomena is called *color localization* and occurs in any color reproductive medium. It reduces the depth that can be produced using *color separation* and *textural diffusion*.

Television can reproduce animated cartoons with great accuracy because most cartoons don't have details or subtle color variation. Whether the cartoon has been generated using conventional methods or a computer, most cartoons made for television lack detail. Any knowledgeable art director (from animation or live action) knows that details that are necessary in a theatrical film aren't necessary on television because it can't reproduce the details. High-definition broadcasts and Internet transmission will change the resolution capabilities of those media.

FLAT SPACE

The opposite of deep space is *flat space*. Deep space gives the illusion of a three-dimensional picture on a two-dimensional screen surface, but flat space does the opposite: it emphasizes the actual two-dimensional quality of the screen surface itself.

FLAT SPACE CUES

Just as deep space had specific cues to create illusory depth, flat space has its cues. Flat space can also be produced by eliminating the depth cues and in some cases reversing them.

Size Constancy

To emphasize the flatness or two-dimensionality of the screen we want to keep all similarly-sized objects the same size on the screen. In deep space we found that smaller objects appear farther away. Now we want to remove that depth so all of the objects in a shot should be staged on the same frontal plane.

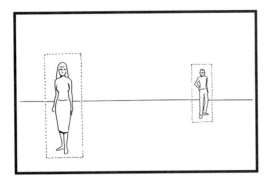

These objects have been staged on two separate planes. Each plane is indicated by the dotted lines. The two separate planes add unwanted depth.

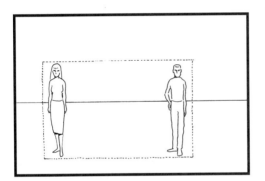

These objects have been staged on the same plane. The single frontal plane created by the staging helps keep the space two-dimensional or flat. Flat space requires us to stage objects on a single plane that is parallel to the picture plane. Television situation comedies and talk shows are excellent examples of flat staging.

Perspective and Convergence

We want to remove all converging lines and all hints of perspective. Planes should be frontal, not longitudinal, so there can be no converging lines or vanishing points.

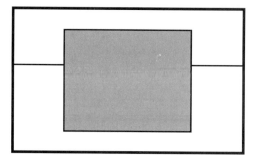

FRONTAL

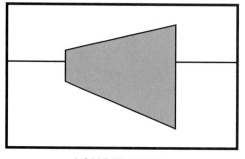

LONGITUDINAL

These two drawings show the same plane, but the frontal drawing is flat space and the longitudinal drawing is deep space. The *frontal plane* emphasizes the two-dimensionality of the screen surface. Creating flat space means excluding longitudinal planes.

Textural Diffusion

Objects with very little texture will look farther away and objects with lots of texture will look closer. To achieve flat space we want to avoid these differences because they will create depth. To emphasize flat space we want all objects to have the same amount of textural detail. We can produce a flatter space when there's a homogenization or similarity of texture throughout the shot.

Movement

As we mentioned with deep space, the two things that can move are an object in front of the camera and the camera itself.

Object Movement: To maintain flat space, objects should only move parallel to the picture plane, that is, side to side, up and down, diagonally, or in a circle (in either direction).

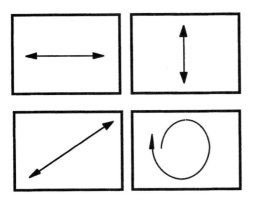

Movement towards or away from the camera will produce deep space cues like size change, textural diffusion, speed change, and so on.

An actor walking parallel to the picture plane creates flat space.

Camera Movement: The camera *pan* will create flat space.

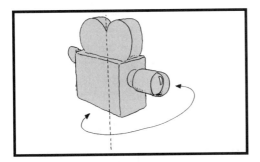

When we pan, all of the objects in the frame keep their relative positions to one another. Panning means turning the camera to the left or right on its vertical axis.

Try closing one eye and slowly rotate or "pan" your head around a room past an open doorway. Notice how everything in your room and the next room moves at the same rate of speed. Now try it again, but this time instead of "panning" your head, lean from side to side as you look out the open doorway. You'll notice that the doorway moves faster than objects in the next room. This illustrates the difference between the flat space pan and the deep space dolly.

The *tilt* is the second flat space camera move.

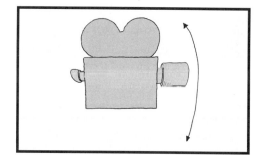

Tilting is camera movement up or down along the vertical axis. Again, close one eye and stand back six feet inside an open doorway. Look down at the ground in front of you and slowly "tilt" your head up to look out the doorway. You'll notice again that everything in view moves at the same rate. This means there's no relative movement. Now look out the doorway and slowly bend your knees into a low crouching position. As you lower yourself you'll notice that the foreground doorway is moving faster than the background. This illustrates the visual difference between a flat space tilt and a deep space crane shot.

True panning and tilting occurs when you use the nodal point of the camera, which is explained in Part A of the Appendix.

Finally, there's the *zoom*. A zoom creates flat space. Cinematographers and directors have unusually strong negative opinions about the zoom. Typically they feel that the zoom is a quick, unattractive way to achieve a dolly shot. It's true that a dolly shot will take longer to set up than a zoom, but the difference is not just economical or practical. The difference is also in the type of visual space that the zoom or the dolly produces.

A zoom creates flat space for a number of reasons. Most importantly, the camera is not physically moving, so there will be no relative size changes, no textural changes, and no relative speed changes. A zoom-in makes everything in the frame enlarge at exactly the same rate. The FG, MG, and BG grow larger in unison. This has the effect of flattening the picture because there is no relative movement.

Something else also happens when we zoom. When we zoom in, we're actually altering the focal length of the lens; we're changing from a wider angle to a telephoto lens. As the focal length of the lens increases, the depth of field decreases so areas of the frame will blur or go out-of-focus. As an object blurs, it becomes flat.

Zooms have always been considered unattractive by photographers and directors, but a zoom isn't necessarily bad. If you've designed a flat space movie (something we'll discuss in Chapter 9, "Story and Visual Structure") you should not dolly the camera, you should zoom. A zoom is what you need to maintain flat space.

There is one exception to the "no dolly" rule when you're creating flat space. You can maintain flat, frontal space by using a side-to-side tracking shot.

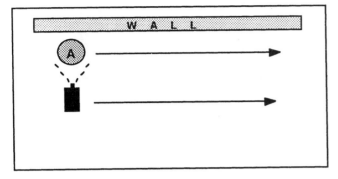

In this illustration, an actor (A) will walk along a wall and the camera will dolly along with the actor. The camera is moving parallel to the frontal plane of the wall, which will keep its surface frontal and flat.

Aerial Diffusion
Aerial diffusion can create flat space if the diffusion has the same visual effect on all areas of the shot. When all objects have the same loss of detail, contrast, and color they tend to blend together and flatten out.

DEEP   FLAT

Both of these shots contain aerial diffusion, but one is deep and the other is flat.

Tonal Separation
Tone refers to the gray scale. Keeping a space flat requires a reduction of the gray scale range within the shot. Remember, brighter objects usually appear closer and darker objects seem farther away.

Reducing the tonal range in a shot to only one third of the gray scale will reduce the tonal depth cues and keep the picture flat.

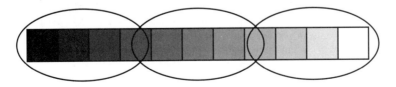

Practically speaking, flat space can be produced when all of the tones in a shot are confined to only one third of the gray scale.

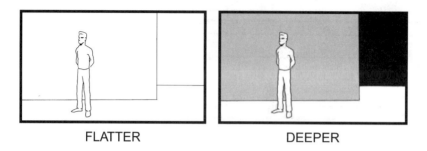

FLATTER   DEEPER

The shot with the lack of tonal contrast is flatter.

Color Separation

Just as the tonal range should be reduced, the warm/cool color range must be limited to help create flat space. Knowing that cool colors (green and blue) recede and warm colors (red, orange, and yellow) advance, we can emphasize flatness by reducing color in our production to all warm or all cool colors. The concept of warm and cool will be expanded in Chapter 6, "Color."

Overlap

Ideally, in flat space there should be no overlap at all because overlap suggests depth.

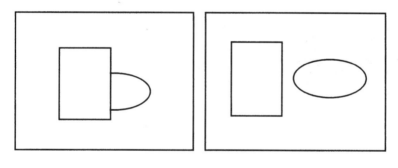

SHOT #1   SHOT #2

Shot #2 is flatter because the overlap has been reduced. Overlap can be minimized by staging actors and objects next to each other instead of behind or in front of each other.

Completely removing overlap in the creation of flat space is impossible, because every shot has a background and any object appearing in front of that background will produce overlap. We can reduce overlap in the careful arrangement and staging of objects in the frame but its elimination is impossible.

Up/Down Position

The position of objects relative to the frame line can help create flat space.

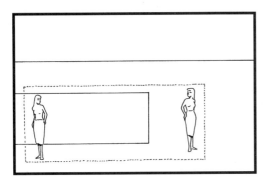

Keeping all the objects on the same horizontal plane will help flatten the picture.

Focus

Once any object is out-of-focus, it becomes flat. It doesn't matter if the object is in the FG, MG, or BG, it flattens when it becomes blurry. In fact, FG, MG, and BG objects will often blend into one flat plane when they are out of focus. Blurred objects will usually read as flat space no matter what depth cues the objects actually contain.

Reversing the Depth Cues

By reversing certain depth cues we can make them work in an opposite manner and produce flat space.

1. *Tonal Separation.* The depth cue of tonal separation suggests that brighter objects appear closer and darker ones appear farther away. By reversing this rule and putting brighter objects in the BG and darker ones in the FG, the space will flatten. The brighter BG objects will visually advance and the darker FG objects will recede. When the FG recedes and the BG advances, we are flattening the space.

2. *Color Separation.* The same rule applies to color separation. If we put warmer colors in the BG and cooler colors in the FG, the space will flatten. The warmer colors in the BG will advance and the cooler FG colors will recede, creating a flatter space.

3. *Textural Diffusion.* By having more textural detail on objects in the background and less detail on objects in the foreground, it's possible to help flatten the space.

4. *Size Difference.* Since we feel that large objects appear closer and smaller ones seem farther away, we can reverse the depth cue and produce flat space. If larger objects are placed in the BG and smaller ones in the FG, it will tend to flatten the picture.

LIMITED SPACE

Limited space is a specific combination of flat and deep space. Limited space uses all of the depth cues except two:

1. *No longitudinal planes.* In creating limited space the deep space longitudinal planes are replaced with flat space frontal planes.
2. *No object movement perpendicular to the picture plane.* Movement towards or away from the camera must be reduced or eliminated. Objects should only move parallel to the picture plane.

Limited space is a challenging spatial plan to follow. Alfred Hitchcock and Ingmar Bergman used it for many of their films.

SHOT #1

Shot #1 contains many depth cues. There's size difference in the actors. The FG actor and wall will have more textural detail than the BG actor and wall. There's overlap between the actors and the walls. The depth cue of up/down position is also used because BG objects are higher in the frame. There's also tonal separation: the FG is brighter and the BG is darker. But Shot #1 has no longitudinal planes that are normally associated with deep space. They have been replaced with frontal planes.

SHOT #1A

Shot #1A labels the three frontal planes (FG, MG, BG). In limited space, the shot can include as few as two and as many as three separate frontal planes. When there's more than three frontal planes, there isn't enough space to visually separate them. If the shot contains only one frontal plane it produces flat space. Notice how the frontal planes are visually well separated from one another. In order for limited space to work properly there must be as much visual separation between the frontal planes as possible.

The visual quality of limited space is similar to looking through a series of well separated sheets of glass.

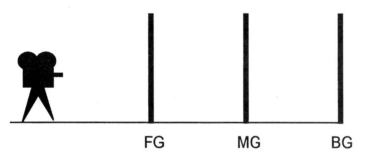

If the glass sheets appear too close together, it produces flat space. If the glass sheets are visually well separated, limited space is produced.

There's a great difference between physical separation and visual separation. Limited space requires both. Two objects may be extremely far apart physically but when the camera looks at them, they may appear to be close together.

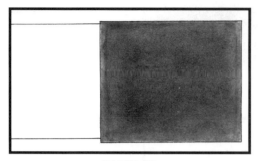
SHOT #2

Shot #2 shows us two walls. The gray wall is only 10 feet from the camera and the white wall is 100 feet from the camera. The two walls have great physical separation, but from the camera's point of view the two walls look very close together. They have no visual separation. The two walls appear to be next to each other. Shot #2 is flat space.

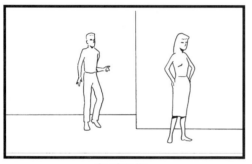
SHOT #3

Shot #3 is not limited, it's flat. Although there is minor size change and frontal planes are emphasized, the visual distance between the two walls is too small.

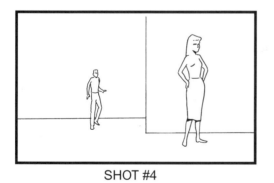
SHOT #4

In Shot #4 the frontal planes are visually separated. The different sizes of the two people tell us that there's one wall in the foreground and another wall, visually well separated, in the background. Shot #4 is a good example of limited space. It uses many depth cues, but the longitudinal planes have been replaced by frontal planes.

AMBIGUOUS SPACE

Ambiguous space is produced when the viewer is unable to understand the actual size of objects in the frame or when the viewer finds the space of the shot unrecognizable.

Most of the time our shots are not ambiguous. Most pictures contain enough visual information that tells us what we're looking at, the actual size of the objects in the frame, and where the camera is in relation to them. We'll call this kind of picture *recognizable space*. But sometimes the cues to size and space are unreliable and ambiguous space is created.

Ambiguous space can use any combination of flat and deep space cues. We can produce ambiguous flat, deep, or limited space.

The ambiguity can be created using:

1. Lack of movement.
2. Unfamiliar shapes.
3. Tonal and texture patterns (camouflage).
4. Mirrors and reflections.
5. Objects of unknown size.
6. Disorienting camera angles.

Imagine a horror film where a camera moves down a staircase into a dark basement. On the way down the steps, the space becomes ambiguous. The shadows and light patterns become too abstract to tell where you are, how big the basement is, or what you're actually looking at. The space has become ambiguous because the size and spatial relationships have been made unreliable through tonal pattern and unfamiliar shapes.

Ambiguous space is difficult to maintain. As soon as a person or object of known size enters the frame, it usually gives the audience enough information about the space, and the ambiguous nature of the shot vanishes leaving us with recognizable space.

Of course, we don't have to be in a dark basement to produce ambiguous space. Looking up or down an elevator shaft could create ambiguous space. The shot may contain many depth cues (one-point perspective, shape constancy) but the location might be unfamiliar to the viewer and not contain anything that reveals the actual size of the shaft or the camera orientation.

Imagine a flat, white plaster wall with strange shadows moving across it. It may be ambiguous space. It will appear flat, but there's no definitive information about the actual size of the wall or our relationship to it. Are we looking down at a white floor, up at a white ceiling or across at a white wall? Until something familiar moves into the shot, we may have ambiguous space.

Ambiguous space can also be created by purposefully confusing the physical relationship of objects. The true relationship of objects in the shot may not be revealed until something in the shot or the camera itself changes position.

These two shots illustrate ambiguous space.

Interestingly, we find there are certain emotional values already attached to ambiguous space, something we can't say about deep, flat, or limited space. Ambiguous space is often used in horror and mystery films. It usually generates anxiety, tension, or confusion in an audience.

COMPARING THE FOUR SPACE TYPES

We've now discussed four ways to arrange the space of a shot: *deep, flat, limited,* and *ambiguous*. If we're going to stage a scene of two people standing in a hallway, we now have four distinctly different ways to produce the space for that shot.

FLAT SPACE

The first version is the flat space rendition of the shot. The walls are frontal and there are no longitudinal planes or converging lines. The actors are staged on the same horizontal plane, and they're the same size. They also have the same amount of textural detail, and any movement will be parallel to the picture plane. The camera will zoom or dolly parallel to the frontal wall plane.

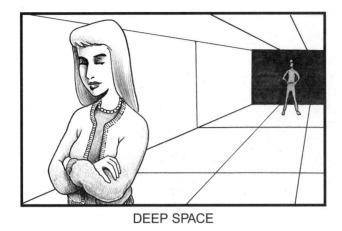

DEEP SPACE

In the second version, we've produced deep space. The shot still exists on a two-dimensional surface, but it has illusory depth. There are several longitudinal planes, one-point perspective, shape change, size difference, textural diffusion, tonal separation, up/down position, and the camera will crane down and dolly in as the foreground actor walks perpendicular to the picture plane.

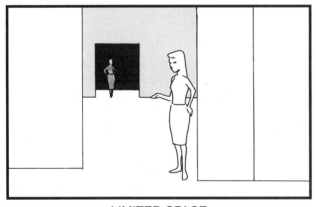

LIMITED SPACE

The third version produces limited space. The depth cues in this shot include size difference, textural diffusion, up/down position, and tonal separation, but there are no longitudinal planes and the actor's movement will remain parallel to the picture plane.

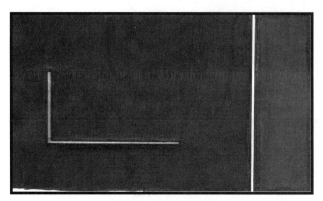

AMBIGUOUS SPACE

In the fourth version, we have the same shot of two people in the hallway but now the space is ambiguous. The lights are off in the hall, some stray light from a doorway illuminates part of a wall, the camera is low to the floor, and our two actors are somewhere in the dark. It's ambiguous because it's impossible to tell the actual size and spatial relationships in the shot. Where are we in the hallway? How close is the door? Is there a door? Are we upside-down? The ambiguous space has made things unreliable, creating a unique sense of the location.

Each of these four versions of the hallway shot brings the script to life, but each version has visual characteristics that are unique. The best spatial choice for your production will be based on your analysis of the script. You may feel that deep space best visualizes the ideas in your story. Perhaps you think flat space would tell the story best. You might discover that a combination of flat and deep space is necessary to visualize the difference between the characters. You might decide that ambiguous space is best for parts of your production because of its specific effect on the audience. Whatever your choice, you should understand that there are four basic types of visual space and that each has its own visual characteristics. We'll learn how to apply these spatial ideas to visual structure in Chapter 9, "Story and Visual Structure."

CONTROLLING SPACE DURING PRODUCTION

Let's stop defining space and look at a practical situation. Tomorrow you're going to direct a scene and you've decided to use deep space. How can you create deep space on the set?

1. *Emphasize longitudinal planes.* Any wall, floor, or ceiling can generate a longitudinal plane if the camera is in the correct position. You'll want these planes to be as longitudinal as possible, which dictates where you'll put the camera. Keep frontal planes out of the shot because they're too flat. By recognizing the longitudinal planes on your location or set you'll be able to find the vanishing points and include them in the shot if you want. The creation of longitudinal planes and vanishing points is probably the most important way to create deep space.

2. *Stage movement perpendicular to the picture plane (towards or away from the camera).* Some directors call this "staging in depth." This staging will help emphasize size difference and produce illusory depth.

3. *Take advantage of the tonal separation depth cue.* Ask the cinematographer to light the scene in a contrasty manner and make objects in the foreground brighter than objects in the background.

4. *Move the camera.* Get a dolly, lots of dolly track, and a crane. To create deep space, you'll want to keep the camera moving as much as possible. Dollying in and out, tracking left and right, and craning up and down will help produce deep space. You can move the camera without a dolly. Hand-hold the camera or use special rigs and harnesses to help you move the camera smoothly.

5. *Consider using a wide-angle lens.* A wide-angle lens has a wider field of view and a greater ability to include more depth cues in the shot. Wide-angle lenses also have a greater depth of field than other lenses. Depth of field refers to the area in front of the lens that is in acceptably sharp focus. Objects must be in focus if they're going to read as depth cues.

Now let's assume that you're going to shoot a scene using flat space. You can create the space by taking advantage of the flat space cues.

1. Eliminate the perspective of longitudinal planes and emphasize frontal planes.

2. Stage the actors parallel to the picture plane. Keep movement parallel to the picture plane. This is sometimes called "flat staging."

3. Ask your cinematographer to light the scene more flatly and condense the gray scale. It will be important to reduce tonal contrast. The production designer should have condensed the brightness level of the sets and reduced the general tonal range to any third of the gray scale. The color range should be limited to all warm or all cool colors. Reversing the depth cue of color and tonal separation will further enhance the flat space. Remember, warm colors and brighter backgrounds appear to advance, and cool colors and darker foregrounds tend to recede.

4. You won't use a dolly or crane for camera movement unless the dolly moves parallel to frontal planes. A tripod and a zoom lens will be fine because you only need to tilt and pan to maintain flat space. Your crew will appreciate the convenience a dolly provides, but it isn't needed for production. Zooming will keep the space flat, but if you hate the zoom lens then don't zoom.

5. Consider using telephoto lenses that will exclude depth cues because of the lens's narrow field of view. The longer lens will force you to stage objects further away from the camera, eliminating the depth cues of size difference and textural diffusion. When objects are the same size, the picture looks flatter. Don't be fooled into thinking that a telephoto lens flattens the image. See Part B in the Appendix for a complete explanation of lenses and space.

6. A shallow depth of field will allow the backgrounds to go out-of-focus. Blurred objects create flat space.

Part One of this chapter has outlined the basic types of visual space. But space is a complex visual component. In Part Two we'll discuss some secondary properties of space.

P A R T   T W O

SECONDARY PROPERTIES

Part Two explains various secondary spatial considerations we must understand when creating our pictures. This includes defining the shape of the screen or frame's space which is called aspect ratio, controlling and changing that space, creating space outside of the actual screen, and finally an overview relating space to the Principle of Contrast and Affinity.

ASPECT RATIO

Aspect ratio is a pair of numbers indicating the size relationship between the width and height of a frame. For example, 1.5:1 is an aspect ratio. The first number, 1.5, is the width of the frame. The second number is always a 1 and it stands for the height of the frame. The two numbers are always separated by a colon (:). The aspect ratio numbers tell us the width and height proportion, not the actual size, of the frame.

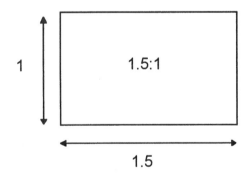

This frame has an aspect ratio of 1.5:1, which was determined by measuring the height (always given the dimension of 1) and then comparing the height to the width. Because the width is 1 $^1/_2$ times greater than the height, the aspect ratio is 1.5:1.

The aspect ratio of any frame or screen can be determined by dividing the height into the width. For example, a screen 20 feet high and 60 feet wide has an aspect ratio of 3.0:1. The math for this calculation is simple: 60 ÷ 20 = 3. The screen is three times wider than it is high.

The term aspect ratio can be applied to any kind of frame. We're concerned with the aspect ratio of the film frame and the screen frame (television, computer, or movie screen). Let's examine the film frame's aspect ratio first.

THE FILM FRAME

Standard 35mm motion picture film is made up of a series of frames. Each 35mm frame of film is four perforations high. The largest possible frame size (called Full Aperture) is approximately 1.33:1, or a frame which is 1 $^1/_3$ wider than it is high.

Super 35 and Full Aperture cameras photograph an image in this entire 1.33 area.

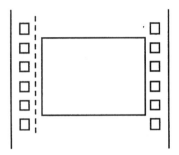

Most 35mm film cameras photograph on a smaller 1.33 area of the frame called Academy Aperture. These cameras don't photograph an image on the left side of the frame because that area is used for the film's sound track (indicated by the dotted line).

SCREEN ASPECT RATIO

Aspect ratio can also refer to the shape of the screen or picture plane. Remember that the picture plane is the "window" within which the pictures will exist. Understanding the different screen aspect ratios is important because you must know the frame proportion that you will use in production. The visual planning for a television movie will be completely different from a feature film. If you produce visuals for the Internet, you have the opportunity to create a new or changing aspect ratio.

There are many standard aspect ratios in use. First, let's look at the aspect ratios for theatrical feature films.

The most common screen aspect ratio for theatrical films in the United States is 1.85:1. This means that the screen is approximately 1 $^7/_8$ times wider than it is high.

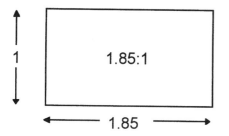

Measuring the 1.85:1 frame or screen, we'll find that the width is approximately 1 $^7/_8$ times greater than the height.

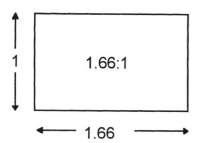

The motion picture screen aspect ratio standard in Europe is 1.66:1. This means the screen is 1 $^2/_3$ wider than it is high.

We also use a much wider theatrical screen aspect ratio.

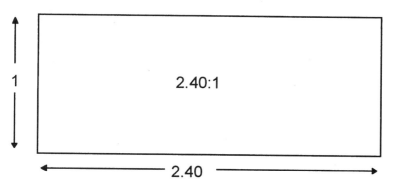

This aspect ratio is 2.40:1 or almost 2 $^1/_2$ times wider than it is high. This system uses anamorphic lenses to produce this unusually wide aspect ratio. A complete discussion of this system is included in Part C of the Appendix.

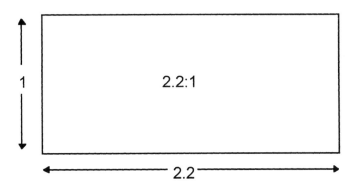

Films can also be photographed and/or released in 70mm, which has an aspect ratio of 2.2:1. More details about 70mm are outlined in Part C of the Appendix.

Today, there's a wide range of unusual formats and aspect ratios that have grown out of developments for World's Fairs and museums. Imax and Omnimax, which were developed in the late 1960s, are two giant-screen formats that both use special 65mm cameras and unique 70mm projectors. Each frame is 15 perforations wide giving a screen aspect ratio of approximately 1.3:1. Imax uses flat, spherical lenses and is projected on a huge, flat screen. Omnimax uses fisheye lenses and is projected on an large, tilted, dome-shaped screen.

Now let's look at the aspect ratios for television and computer screens. Standard NTSC television and most consumer computer screens are approximately 1.33:1.

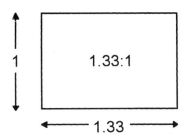

Measuring the 1.33:1 frame or screen, the width is only 1 $\frac{1}{3}$ times greater than the height.

Television aspect ratio is often referred to as "3x4" meaning it is three "units" high and four "units" wide. The 3x4 (height and width) is the same proportion as 1.33:1 (width and height).

A longstanding aspect ratio problem occurs when we present 1.85 movies on a 1.33 television screen. There are two methods available for showing a standard 1.85 movie on a conventional 1.33 television screen.

1.33:1 TELEVISION

One option is called letterboxing. It means that the top and bottom of the TV screen will not be used, allowing the film's proper aspect ratio to appear in the middle of the TV screen. In a letterboxed version, a 1.85 feature film has almost no picture loss from side to side. The narrow black bands on the top and bottom of the television screen alter the screen's apparent aspect ratio to 1.85:1.

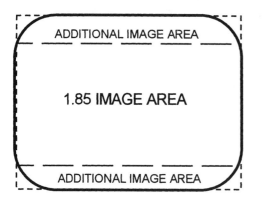

1.33:1 TELEVISION SCREEN

A 1.85 movie can also be viewed full screen on a 1.33 television. There is almost no picture cut off from side to side and the image area at the top and bottom of the 1.85 picture is revealed to accommodate the 1.33 screen. A television viewer actually sees the area above and below the 1.85 frame that was not projected in theaters.

The problem becomes worse when presenting a 2.40:1 movie on a 1.33:1 television screen. There are two solutions.

The first solution is letterboxing. A 2.40:1 aspect ratio will not fit onto a 1.33:1 screen unless large bands at the top and bottom of the TV screen remain unused. General audiences won't accept letterboxing because so much of the television screen remains blank.

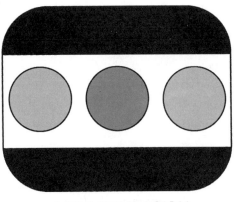

1.33:1 TELEVISION

The other solution is to "pan and scan," which means that only a portion of the 2.40:1 frame will appear on the TV screen.

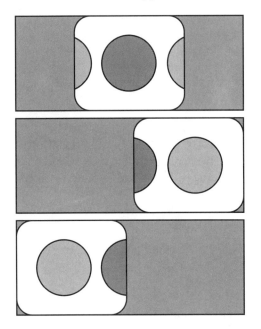

These diagrams show the three composition choices available when a 2.40:1 film is panned and scanned for 1.33 television. The television can only show a portion of the much wider 2.40 image. In "panning and scanning" the center, left, or right areas of the original 2.40 picture can be selected for 1.33 broadcast. Panning and scanning radically changes the 2.40:1 film's visual composition and may force the "pan and scan" version to appear reedited in comparison to the original film.

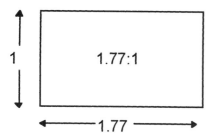

High-definition television has an aspect ratio of 16x9 or sixteen "units" wide and nine "units" high. This produces an aspect ratio of approximately 1.77:1. This aspect ratio is far more compatible with standard 1.85:1 and 1.66.1 feature films, but it doesn't solve the aspect ratio problem when a 2.40:1 movie must be presented.

The most flexible medium for aspect ratios is the Internet. Although most computer screens are 1.33:1, there are no rules for the aspect ratio of original programs that are sent out over the World Wide Web. On the Internet you can define a new aspect ratio within the confines of the standard computer screen's 1.33:1 shape. The aspect ratio can even change during a program. This means that any aspect ratio can be created for still and moving picture images.

In the next section of this chapter we'll discuss the advantages to changing an already existing aspect ratio.

SURFACE DIVISIONS

We use the term "surface division" because the screen is a flat surface and we're going to divide it up into smaller areas. Dividing the frame will give us a new tool for telling our stories visually.

DIVIDING THE FRAME

Before we get specific about what's dividing the frame, let's look at the ways it can be divided.

Halves

The simplest way to divide the frame is in the middle. There are three ways to do this:

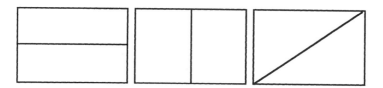

The division of the middle can be either horizontal, vertical, or diagonal (the diagonal can be left to right or right to left).

Thirds

Next, we can divide the frame into thirds.

Most often, the divisions are vertical, but they can also be horizontal. In paintings, the vertical division is called a triptych.

Grids

Then, obviously, we can divide the frame into fourths, fifths, sixths, or more. We can also divide the screen into irregular portions. We call all of these divisions a grid.

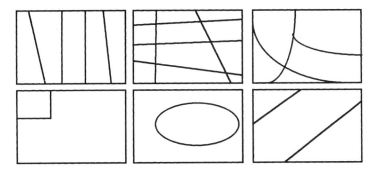

A grid can have any number of variations and divisions.

Square on a Rectangle

This is a unique surface division that occurs within any rectangular frame.

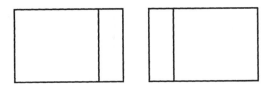

This division generates a square within the frame. The height of the square is the same as the height of the screen. The square can occur on the left or right side of the overall frame.

The Golden Section
The division system of the Golden Section is more complicated to create.

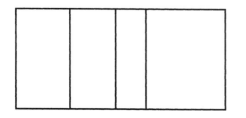

This frame has been divided using the Golden Section proportion. Most popular in painting during the Renaissance, this surface division creates a complex, yet stable frame. No two divisions will ever be the same size, yet they will always relate back to the overall frame. A detailed explanation of the Golden Section is included in Part D of the Appendix.

THE SURFACE DIVIDER

A surface division is generated by anything that divides the frame into two or more smaller areas. The division appears because of tonal or color contrasts created in the shot.

The divider can be a mechanical split screen (as in Ross Hunter's *Pillow Talk* [1959] or Brian DePalma's *Dressed to Kill* [1980]), but the divider is usually a real object that's actually in the shot.

A division of the middle may be a telephone pole between two people.

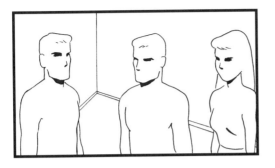

A square-on-the-rectangle division can be the corner of two walls.

A division of three can be windows on either side of a person.

A grid division can be patterns of light and dark cast on a wall.

THE PURPOSE OF SURFACE DIVISIONS

What are the directorial values of surface divisions? Here are several reasons why surface divisions can help tell your story.

1. Surface divisions can help show similarities and differences between objects Let's say we have a shot of two people and we want to show how different or how similar they are.

Without a surface division, we get this shot.

With a surface division, we get something different. Here are the same two people, but now we want to compare them. The surface division has changed one large screen into two small screens. Again, the actual surface division can be anything: a pole or post, the corner of a building, a shadow on a wall, or anything else. By creating the division, we're asking the audience to compare and contrast the two halves of the divided frame.

2. Surface divisions can help direct the eye to specific areas of the frame for directorial emphasis. Let's say we're shooting a film in a 2.40:1 aspect ratio.

The full 2.40:1 frame allows the viewer's eye to wander.

Adding a surface division not only places the actor in a new, smaller area of the frame but also helps confine the audience's attention to one portion of the overall frame. The surface division controls and limits the audience's ability to visually roam around the screen. The surface division acts like a visual fence.

Here, the grid surface division tends to block off most of the space of the frame. It causes us to concentrate more on the figure in the doorway and ignore the rest of the frame. The surface division is directing our eye to part of the frame and keeping it there.

3. Surface divisions can change the aspect ratio. A movie or television show is limited to one aspect ratio. (Some exceptions to this rule change aspect ratio during the film, such as Able Gance's *Napoleon* [1927] and Douglas Trumbull's *Brainstorm* [1983]). We can use surface divisions to alter a film's fixed aspect ratio. Why would we want to change the aspect ratio?

a. A fixed aspect ratio may get boring.

b. A fixed aspect ratio might not always be appropriate for telling the story.

A viewer is first confronted with the 1.33, 1.85, or 2.40 screen when they enter the theater or sit down in front of the television or computer. This aspect ratio (the height and width of the screen) doesn't change and that might be inappropriate for your production.

Imagine an art museum where all the paintings are exactly the same size, the same shape, and all in identical frames. How can one frame be right for every picture? Wouldn't it be dull?

The same thing is true for our aspect ratio. Why should we be limited to one fixed size? Depending on the story, we may need some visual variety in the screen proportions. Even in a film with rigid spatial controls, a certain amount of variety in the aspect ratio can help tell the story better. By dividing the frame into halves, thirds, grids, or squares, we can explore and use changes in the size and shape of the frame to tell the story better.

Here's a division of the middle. The action will take place only in the right half of the frame. We have created a new aspect ratio because the wall has left us a 1:1 square for our action. We've created a new aspect ratio that may be more appropriate for the scene. We've also achieved some visual variety.

4. Surface divisions are produced by lines, and these lines add visual rhythm to a shot.

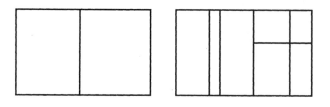

The visual rhythms produced by the surface divisions in each of these shots is completely different. One shot has a slow rhythm, the other a fast rhythm. Visual rhythms are explained in Chapter 8, "Rhythm."

CLOSED AND OPEN SPACE

There is a type of space that exists outside the frame lines of our screens. It is called open space and it's difficult to create, but when it does occur, it pops open the normally fixed, rigid frame lines that surround all of our pictures and gives the audience a sense of space beyond the frame.

First, let's define the opposite of open space, which is closed space. Almost all the pictures we see are excellent examples of closed space.

This frame is the reason that most of the pictures we produce are closed space. Perhaps a better term is "enclosed space," because that's what happens when we put a frame around a picture. The space inside the frame becomes enclosed by the frame lines. These four frame lines are so visually strong, so omnipresent, and so fixed that almost all the pictures we place within their borders are visually locked in, stopped, or closed by the frame lines. The frame lines make us aware of where the picture stops. There is no picture beyond the borders of the frame.

In a magazine or book, the frame lines are the edges of the picture itself or the page. Museums display pictures in frames that create a closed border around the picture. Televisions and computer monitors have screens that are set in frames, and of course movie screens are surrounded by dark fabric that clearly shows the limits of the screen. Closed space is easy to produce because it always happens automatically.

Not only do the frame lines around the picture enclose it, but some of the visual components in the picture itself tend to help lock the picture into the frame. Although we haven't discussed line (that's in Chapter 4, "Line and Shape"), let's take a picture and look at it in terms of line:

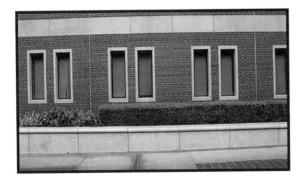

Here's a shot that is a good example of closed space. Not only are you aware of the edges of the picture, but the picture itself is full of horizontal and vertical lines that visually parallel the frame lines.

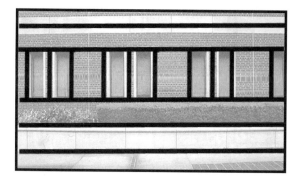

Here's the same photo, but now all the verticals and horizontals have been exaggerated. See how much of the picture relies on vertical and horizontal lines that link up with the frame? This is closed space. Vertical and horizontal lines are usually present in most pictures, in fact it's difficult to make a picture without them. After you've read Chapter 4, "Line and Shape," you'll see how horizontal and vertical lines exist everywhere and that removing them from shots is practically impossible. This means that 99.9% of pictures are closed space.

So what about open space? What's so special about the remaining 0.1% of the pictures? Does open space occur when we photograph open desert or outer space where there are millions of miles between stars? No. Creating open space has nothing to do with the actual location. In fact, creating open space in a desert or in outer space is very difficult.

Open space occurs when we feel that the picture extends beyond the frame lines. Of course, the picture never can really extend past the frame (and 3-D movies aren't open space). Open space is produced when something in the frame is visually powerful enough to remove the frame and create space beyond it.

How can open space occur? There are several factors needed to generate open space:

1. A relatively large screen.
2. Movement that is visually stronger than the frame.
3. Elimination of objects that can close the space.

LARGE SCREENS

Open space needs a large screen. The giant screens used for Imax or Omnimax movies can easily generate open space; so can large conventional movie screens in big theaters.

Television and computer screens cannot create open space because they're too small and have overwhelming frame lines. In most television viewing situations the room is full of common household objects, creating additional verticals and horizontals that enhance the already strong frame lines of the television itself. There's not a chance that the images on a television screen will become more visually powerful than the surrounding room. The space of a television picture will always remain closed. Even consumer big-screen TVs can't produce open space. There's simply too much visual competition and too strong a frame to overcome.

In a movie theater, we have a better chance of creating open space because of the large screen and a darkened theater with no visual distractions.

STRONG VISUAL MOVEMENT

How can we produce movement that is stronger than the mighty frame line? It's difficult. The frame lines are solid, locked-down visual anchors that want to enclose the picture. If we could create a movement or group of movements that were very dynamic, it would be possible to overwhelm the frame line and give the audience the sense that the movement was occurring both within and beyond the frame.

There are two kinds of movement that can open the frame. One is a very random, multidirectional movement, the other is a large, unidirectional movement.

When we generate a random, multidirectional movement that fills the frame, it is possible to push the frame open and create open space.

This pattern of movement will usually have enough visual intensity or strength to push open the frame lines and create space beyond the actual frame. This kind of random movement can be created by a swarming mob of people, a cattle stampede, moving white-water, birds in flight, fireworks, or other intense actions that move in and out of frame in random patterns.

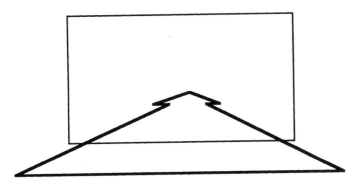

Perpendicular movement in or out of the frame can produce open space. The movement must be very large in relation to the frame itself and must be slow enough that the movement can be felt by the audience yet fast enough to generate intensity to overpower the frame line.

The most familiar example of this type of open space is the beginning of George Lucas's *Star Wars* (1977). When the large spaceship enters the top of the frame, the audience feels that it is not only on screen, but also over their heads beyond the screen. The ship's movement perpendicular to the picture plane is creating open space. Open space is also created when the spaceships in *Star Wars* travel at "light speed." The sudden stretching of the stars creates movement that is more visually powerful than the frame lines.

Shots of a car or truck driving past the lens will not create open space. A moving car is usually too small in relation to the frame and moving too slowly to produce open space. If the car moves quickly, it usually moves too quickly and never gets a chance to open the space.

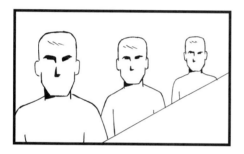

Here, the pattern of actors and the longitudinal surface tend to push our eye beyond the sides of the frame. This gives the impression of more screen space outside the frame but its effect is weak.

A better way to produce open space is using the movement of the camera. Although the movements won't be as multidirectional or severe, random camera movement, including rotations on the axis of the lens, can help to open the visual space.

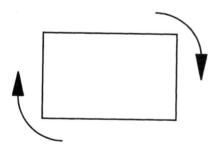

When we move the camera, its motion is transferred to the objects in the frame. If we rotate the camera on the axis of the lens, all of the objects in frame will move in the opposite direction of the camera rotation. This will give the stationary lines movement. This increased dynamic may be enough to overpower the frame lines and create open space.

ELIMINATION OF VISUAL ELEMENTS

In creating open space, you must remove the visual components that keep it closed. Open space is so delicate that minor closed space components, like stationary lines, will easily overwhelm the open space and keep it closed.

This shot of a large truck roaring past a wide-angle lens will probably remain closed because of all the stationary horizontal, vertical, and even diagonal lines in the background of the shot. This includes horizon lines, lines created by telephone poles, buildings, and so on. Open space can only be created when all of the closed-space components, like stationary lines, are removed from the shot.

What's the visual or dramatic purpose of open space? Because it's so difficult to produce, it rarely appears in our pictures. Open space creates an unusual spatial contrast and generates tremendous excitement or intensity for the viewer. Deep, flat, and limited space have no guaranteed emotional meanings for an audience, but open space is an exception. It will always generate a bolt of excitement in an audience. We'll see how important that can be in Chapter 9, "Story and Visual Structure."

You should now begin to understand what a visual component is all about. Space can be deep, flat, limited, ambiguous, open, or closed. Later, in this chapter, we'll discuss how to create other variations of space's basic subcomponents but the fundamentals of space as an important visual component should be clear to you now.

CONTRAST AND AFFINITY

Now that space has been defined, we can relate it to the *principle of contrast and affinity*. Remember, contrast and affinity can occur in three ways: within the shot, from shot to shot, and from sequence to sequence.

Let's create examples of various kinds of contrasts and affinities of space.

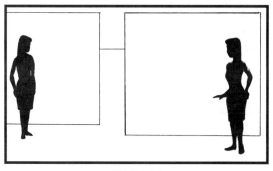

SHOT #1

Shot #1 is an example of affinity of space within the shot. Note the surface division of the middle and that both halves of the frame are flat space. This gives unity to the shot. Because there's affinity of space, the overall visual dynamic or intensity of the shot is low.

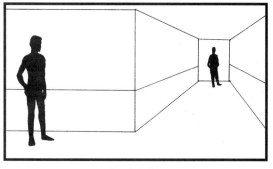

SHOT #2

Shot #2 is an example of contrast of space within the shot. One half of the shot is deep and the other half is flat. As the contrast between the two spaces increases, the shot's intensity will also increase.

SHOT #3   SHOT #4

Shots #3 and #4 are examples of affinity of space from shot to shot because both are flat. These shots are low in visual intensity because of their affinity of space.

SHOT #5   SHOT #6

Shot #5 is flat space and Shot #6 is deep space. Together they illustrate contrast of space from shot to shot.

Contrast of space can also occur from sequence to sequence, where one group of scenes is all flat and the next group is all deep. Affinity from sequence to sequence occurs when all shots in a number of sequences use the same type of space.

There are other ways to produce contrast or affinity of space. There is contrast or affinity of ambiguous and recognizable space, and there's contrast and affinity of open and closed space. Contrast and affinity can also occur with surface divisions.

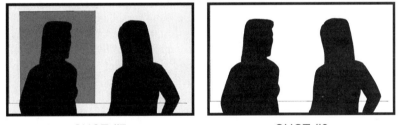

SHOT #7   SHOT #8

Shot #7 has a surface division of the middle, and shot #8 has no division at all. Shots #7 and #8 show contrast of surface divisions from shot to shot.

Deep space is usually considered more intense than flat space because deep space is produced through contrasts and flat space is created using affinities. Producing deep space requires large and small objects, light and dark tones, warm and cool colors, and textured and untextured surfaces all of which create contrasts. Contrast creates more intensity so the deeper the space the greater the visual intensity.

Flat space, on the other hand, usually relies on affinities or similarities. If everything is staged on a single plane, there is no size difference in most objects. In flat space we try to give objects a similar tone and texture. It is possible to produce flat space using contrasts, but it's usually created with affinities that lack intensity.

People will often comment that deep space looks interesting or exciting and flat space looks dull. That's a generalization that is easy to disprove but you can understand how this happens. The viewer is simply responding to the contrasts or affinities that have produced the space.

Space is a large, complex visual component. When you browse through a magazine, view pictures in a museum, or watch television or a film, you should try to notice the visual space in the pictures. Try to define the space you see. Is it flat, deep, limited, or perhaps a combination? A lot of pictures will show little or no control over the space, and you might realize that a different kind of space would have been better. Learn to recognize the space in other work, and then train yourself to see it when you look through the viewfinder of your camera.

Are there only four types of space? No. There are as many as you want. A scale with flat space at one end and deep space at the other suggests the variations available.

Flat and deep are at the extreme ends of the scale, and limited space would appear closer to deep space. But what would you call the types of space between them? Since you have a vocabulary that allows you to describe and control space, you can mix and match the subcomponents of a space and create any type of space that you prefer. You can use the classic flat, deep, limited, or ambiguous space or you can invent a combination of your own.

As you'll see later in this book, each visual component has subcomponents that you can mix and match in hundreds of combinations to create your visual structure. So far we've only discussed space, so there are still six basic visual components left to explore. Once you understand them, you'll be ready to discover the extraordinary link between visual structure and story structure.

FILMS TO WATCH

It helps to see space in use. There are brilliant examples in television commercials, music videos, television programs, and short films. Unfortunately, most of these examples are inaccessible. Fortunately, we also have feature films that are readily available and are excellent examples of visual structure.

If you've never seen the films listed below, you should watch them on video immediately. The visual aspects of a film are best revealed when you view the film with the sound off (although your first viewing of any film should always be with sound on). The more times you watch a film silently, the more you'll learn about its visual structure.

One of the wonderful aspects of studying the visual aspects of film is that it has no secrets. The ingredients in food, for example, can be hidden. You eat a delicious meal but can't guess the secret recipe. Film's visual structure can't hide because everything is visible on the screen. The more times you watch a film, the more the visual ingredients will reveal themselves.

These films are excellent examples of well-controlled space:

1. DEEP SPACE
   Citizen Kane (1941)
   > Directed by Orson Welles
   > Written by Welles and Herman Mankiewicz
   > Photographed by Greg Toland
   > Art Direction by Van Nest Polglase

   Touch of Evil (1958)
   > Directed by Orson Welles
   > Written by Orson Welles
   > Photographed by Russell Metty
   > Art Direction by Robert Clatworthy

2. FLAT SPACE AND SURFACE DIVISIONS
   Klute (1971)
   > Directed by Alan Pakula
   > Written by Andy and Dave Lewis
   > Photographed by Gordon Willis
   > Art Direction by George Jenkins

   Manhattan (1979)
   > Directed by Woody Allen
   > Written by Allen and Marshall Brickman
   > Photographed by Gordon Willis
   > Production Design by Mel Bourne

   Witness (1985)
   > Directed by Peter Weir
   > Written by Earle Wallace and William Kelley
   > Photographed by John Seale
   > Production Design by Stan Jolley

   American Beauty (1999)
   > Directed by Sam Mendes
   > Written by Alan Ball
   > Photographed by Conrad Hall
   > Production Design by Naomi Shohan

   Ordinary People (1980)
   > Directed by Robert Redford
   > Written by Alvin Sargent
   > Photographed by John Bailey
   > Art Direction by Phillip Bennett

3. LIMITED SPACE
   Fanny and Alexander (1982)
   > Directed by Ingmar Bergman
   > Written by Ingmar Bergman
   > Photographed by Sven Nykvist
   > Production Design by Anna Asp

Suspicion (1941)
> Directed by Alfred Hitchcock
> Written by Hitchcock and Samson Raphaleson
> Photographed by Harry Stradling
> Art Direction by Van Nest Polglase

4.   AMBIGUOUS SPACE AND SURFACE DIVISIONS

Don't Look Now (1973)
> Directed by Nicolas Roeg
> Written by Allan Scott and Chris Bryant
> Photographed by Anthony Richmond
> Art Direction by Giovanni Soccol

Brazil (1985)
> Directed by Terry Gilliam
> Written by Gilliam, Tom Stoppard, and Charles McKeowen
> Photographed by Roger Pratt
> Production Design by Norman Garwood

C H A P T E R   4

LINE AND SHAPE

We see lines in almost every object we encounter. For example, doorways have vertical lines and sidewalks have horizontal lines. The real world is also full of shapes. A door is rectangular and a ball is circular. Since it appears that lines create shapes, we should discuss them together.

LINE

Line differs from the other visual components because it really doesn't exist: it's a perceptual fact. Line only exists because of tone or color contrasts. Since lines don't exist, how do we perceive these things we call lines? There are seven ways to create what we perceive as a line.

EDGE

All two-dimensional objects have height and width, but practically speaking, no depth.

This is a drawing of a piece of paper. Obviously a piece of paper is not truly two-dimensional, it has some thickness, but for our purposes the paper can be considered two-dimensional. When you look at this drawing and see four lines you imagine a piece of paper. Examine a real piece of paper like this book page. There aren't any lines around it at all. We call the imaginary lines we see around the boundaries of any two-dimensional object *edge*.

A shadow cast onto a wall is also an example of edge. The shadow is a two-dimensional object, and we see a line around the shadow even though there's no actual line there at all.

Color and tonal changes on two-dimensional surfaces like walls and fabric are also examples of edge because these surfaces are essentially two-dimensional.

CONTOUR

Most objects in the real world are three-dimensional. They have height, width, and depth. A basketball (a three-dimensional object) looks like this:

We accept the curved line in this drawing as the boundary of the ball itself, but a real ball doesn't have a line around it. Any three-dimensional object has a boundary, and the imaginary line we see there is called *contour*.

CLOSURE

We have a natural tendency to connect primary points of interest in a scene with imaginary lines.

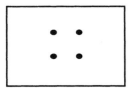

This is a drawing of four dots but we see a square.

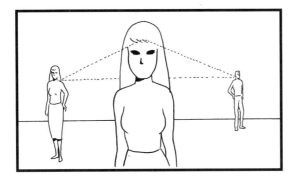

In our minds we've connected the dots or the primary points of the shot to produce a square. The primary points can be important objects, colors, tones, or anything that attracts the viewer's attention. We unconsciously connect the dots to form curved or straight lines, triangles, squares, or other shapes.

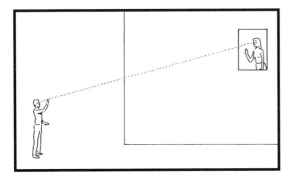

Here, the primary points are people's heads. The closure creates a triangle.

Closure can also generate a diagonal line.

INTERSECTION OF PLANES

When two planes meet or intersect, they create a line.

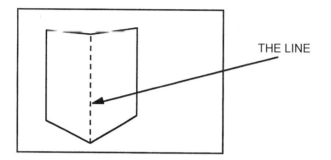

Every corner of every room creates a line, although there isn't an actual line there at all. The corners of furniture, boxes, and buildings all have lines wherever two planes intersect.

IMITATION THROUGH DISTANCE

Imitation through distance occurs when an object reduces itself to a line or lines because it's so far away.

We know the girders of this tower are not lines, they're large steel beams. Yet at a distance, they look like lines. The same is true for the telephone pole and the tree. We know that the pole is not a line but a large diameter post, and that the tree limbs and trunk are not lines. When we get far enough away from them, however, the girders, telephone pole, and tree appear thin enough to imitate a line.

AXIS

Many objects have an invisible axis that runs through them, and we often see this as a line. People, animals, and trees are examples of objects that have an axis.

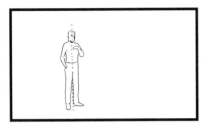 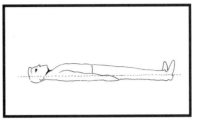

A standing person has a vertical axis. A reclining person has as horizontal axis.

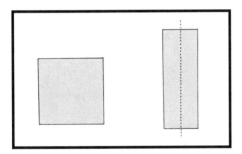

Not all objects have an axis. A square has no definite, single axis, but a rectangle does.

TRACK

Track is the path of a moving object. As any object moves it will leave a track or line in its path. There are two types of tracks, *actual* and *virtual*.

Actual Tracks

When certain objects move, they actually leave a track or line behind them. A skier moving down a snowy hillside will produce a line in the snow from the skis, and a skywriting airplane leaves a line of smoke behind it as it flies. The indentation in the snow and the smoke aren't actually lines, of course, they're either imitation through distance or contour, but we still perceive them as lines.

Virtual Tracks

Most objects don't leave an actual line when they move, but they do generate a virtual or invisible line. A virtual line is a line we must imagine. Here are drawings of some virtual tracks.

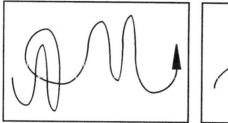 

A butterfly in flight and a baseball being thrown are virtual tracks. The line that the butterfly or baseball leave behind is only in our imagination. Since track deals with moving objects, we'll return to line and track in Chapter 7, "Movement."

LINEAR MOTIF

Now that we understand how we perceive lines, we can look at any shot and break it down into its basic lines. We call these basic lines the shot's *linear motif*. Any shot can be reduced to a line or group of lines that represents the linear motif.

A picture's linear motif can be circular or straight lines, vertical, horizontal, or diagonal lines, or a combination.

Here's a photograph and a drawing of the photograph's linear motif. The linear motif appears when you squint at the photograph, because squinting increases the shot's contrast and makes the primary lines visible. You can get the same visual effect by looking at the photograph with a contrast viewing glass. A contrast viewing glass is used like a monocle but its glass is extremely dark (usually a deep brown or blue-gray color). When you look through the glass it increases the scene's contrast and reveals the linear motif.

Line requires tonal or color contrast to be seen. Lines disappear if there is too much affinity of tone or color. When the tonal contrast is lowered in this photograph, the linear motif is gone.

CONTRAST AND AFFINITY

Now that we understand how we see line, we can discuss it in terms of contrast and affinity. There are three ways that line can be used to produce contrast or affinity: quality, direction, and orientation. Remember that contrast and affinity can occur within the shot, from shot to shot, and from sequence to sequence.

QUALITY

Quality of line refers to the linear (straight) or curvilinear (curved) nature of a line.

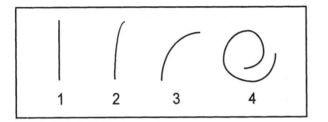

Lines 1 and 2 have great affinity of quality of line because they're both nearly straight. Lines 1 and 4 have great contrast because one is very straight and the other very curved.

Certain adjectives and emotional moods are often associated with straight and curved lines. Most of the other basic visual components don't have preexisting emotional characteristics associated with them, but straight and curved lines do.

Generally speaking, a straight line is associated with these qualities: direct, aggressive, bland, honest, industrial, ordered, strong, unnatural, adult, and rigid. A curved line is often associated with these qualities: indirect, passive, pertaining to nature, childlike, romantic, soft, organic, safe, and flexible.

This is hardly a complete list, and your own feelings about straight and curved lines will effect how you use them. Later in this chapter you'll see how these terms also relate to shape.

AFFINITY   **CONTRAST**

Each shot in this pair illustrates contrast or affinity of quality of line within the shot. The affinity of the straight lines keeps the visual intensity low. The contrast of the straight and curved lines increases the overall visual intensity.

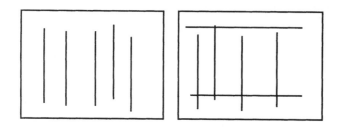

This pair of shots illustrates affinity of line quality. All of the lines in both shots are straight.

DIRECTION

Direction refers to the angle of the line created by the track of a moving object. We're going to discuss motion in more detail in Chapter 7, "Movement," but we have to mention it here because it's an important aspect of line.

In the following drawings, the arrows indicate the direction of the moving object or the line created by the path of a moving object.

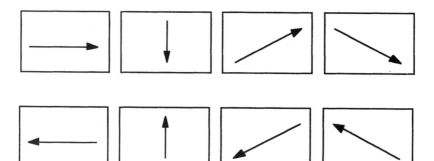

There are only eight directions that an object can move on the screen.

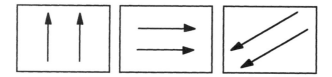

Maximum affinity of direction within the shot is created when two objects in the same shot move in the same direction. Here are three examples of affinity of direction of line within the shot. They illustrate affinity because both objects in the frame are moving in the same direction.

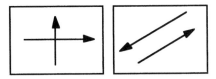

Here are two examples of maximum contrast of direction of line within the shot. They illustrate contrast because the two objects are moving in different directions. The horizontal/vertical contrast is greater than the contrast of the two diagonals because the lines are perpendicular rather than parallel.

This pair of shots illustrates affinity of direction of line from shot to shot. In both shots, an object is moving vertically from top to bottom.

These shots illustrate contrast of direction of line from shot to shot.

ORIENTATION

Orientation means the inherent intensity of the line itself. Whereas direction refers to lines created by moving objects, orientation of line relates to nonmoving or stationary lines. Where do we find stationary lines? Everywhere. Most lines created by edge, imitation through distance, and the intersection of two planes are stationary lines. This includes the corners of rooms, doors, windows, furniture, sidewalks, curbs, trees, and buildings.

As with direction of line, horizontal, vertical, and diagonal are the three types of line orientation.

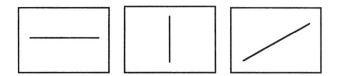

The diagonal line is the most dynamic or intense, and the horizontal is the least dynamic or intense. The vertical line's intensity falls between the other two.

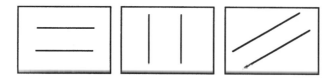

These three drawings each illustrate affinity of orientation within the shot. The horizontal pair of lines are least intense, the vertical lines are next most intense, and the diagonal lines are most intense.

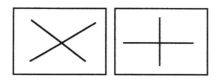

Each of these two drawings illustrate contrast of orientation of line within the shot. The opposing diagonal lines are more intense than the horizontal and vertical combination.

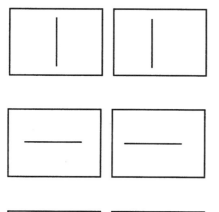

Each of these pairs of drawings illustrates affinity of orientation from shot to shot because the angle of the stationary line remains the same.

This pair of drawings illustrates maximum contrast of orientation of line from shot to shot.

SHAPE

Just as there are basic types of space and line, there are basic shapes. What qualifies as a basic shape? A basic shape is an object that will reveal its basic shape properties no matter how it is viewed. Let's define the basic shapes.

There are two- and three-dimensional basic shapes.

The two-dimensional basic shapes are the circle, square, and equilateral triangle.

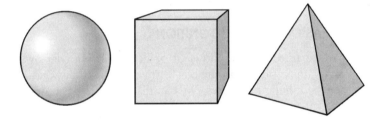

The three-dimensional basic shapes are the sphere, cube, and the three-sided pyramid. A shape can only be basic when it always reveals its basic shape properties regardless of viewing angle. A three-sided pyramid gives the viewer all the information needed about the size and shape of its hidden sides. The cube does the same, and of course a sphere remains identical no matter how it's turned. The unseen sides of a basic shape can always be correctly imagined based on the sides that are visible. Other three-dimensional shapes are often thought to be basic but are not.

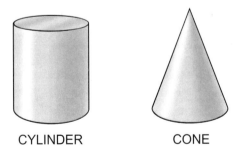

CYLINDER   CONE

The cylinder or cone are sometimes incorrectly classified as basic shapes.

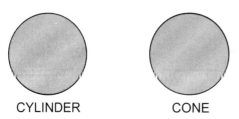

CYLINDER   CONE

When viewed from below, the cylinder and cone appear identical and give no clue that one is pointed. This disqualifies them as basic shapes, because they hide their true shape identities.

Another reason why many shapes don't qualify as basic shapes is because it gets too complicated. Can an audience sense the difference between a three-sided pyramid and a four-sided pyramid? Probably not. Visually speaking, an audience reaches a point where it can't see differences in the shapes of objects. The six basic shapes are visually different, useful, and within the perceptual reach of an audience. If we keep the list of basic shapes simple, the audience will notice the differences and respond to them. Don't overcomplicate the concept.

BASIC SHAPE RECOGNITION

The real world seems to be filled with millions of objects each with its own unique shape. But if you examine objects in the real world, you'll see how easily they fall into one of the basic shape categories. We can discover the basic shape of any object by reducing it to a silhouette. The silhouette of any object is made up of straight or curved lines so, like line, we can assign general emotional values to the basic shapes.

The same emotional adjectives we associated with curved and straight lines can be linked to rounded, square, and triangular shapes. Rounded shapes are often described as indirect, passive, romantic, pertaining to nature, soft, organic, childlike, safe, and flexible. Square shapes are direct, industrial, ordered, linear, unnatural, adult, and rigid, and triangles (because of their diagonal lines) are often described as aggressive and dynamic. Remember, these emotional associations are not rules.

When you examine the silhouettes of objects in the real world, you'll see how easily they fall into one of the three basic shape categories.

Let's examine the basic silhouettes of three cars.

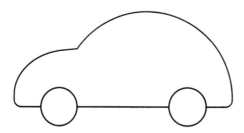

This car is essentially a circle. Many people see this car as a VW "Bug" or Volkswagen. The car is made up of circles. Most people describe cars with a circular shape as friendly or cute. The circle is the most benign of the basic shapes. It has no up or down, no left or right. A circle has no direction or natural dynamic.

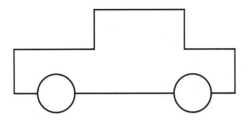

Here's another car, obviously based on a square shape. It's certainly less friendly than the circular car, but it seems to posses a visual stability and solid quality that the circular car lacks.

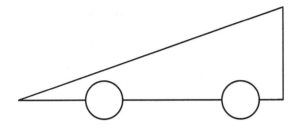

Clearly, this is the fastest of the three cars. Its a triangle. It may look like a high-performance race car, but it's really a triangle, and that's what makes it look so fast. We know the triangle is the most dynamic of the three basic shapes because it's the only one that contains at least one diagonal line. A triangle is an arrow. It points in a particular direction, which is something the square and circle can't do.

Faces can be categorized as basic shapes.

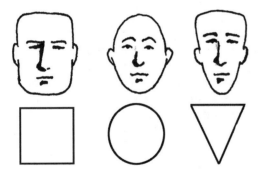

Trees come in the three usual basic shapes, too.

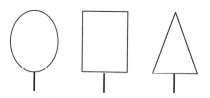

Finding the silhouette is the key. We can always find the basic shapes of any object: furniture (from a chair to a four-poster bed); architecture (from windows and doorways to entire buildings); vehicles (from a child's wagon to an airplane); and people (from their faces to their entire bodies).

Basic shapes can also be produced by light patterns. A shadow can have any shape. A highlight on a wall can be round, square, or triangular depending on the mood you're trying to create.

CONTRAST AND AFFINITY

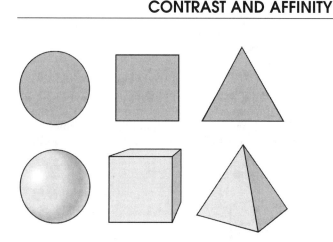

An examination of the two-dimensional shapes alone reveals that the circle and triangle have maximum contrast. Among the three-dimensional shapes, the sphere and the three-sided pyramid have maximum contrast. If you group two- and three-dimensional shapes together, maximum contrast is best created with the sphere and the triangle or the circle and the three-sided pyramid. They create contrast in the basic shape as well as in their two- or three-dimensional differences.

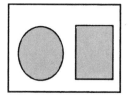

Here's an example of contrast of shape within a shot. Perhaps this is a close-up of two picture frames.

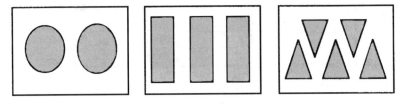

Each of these drawings illustrates affinity of shape within a shot.

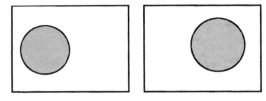

Here's affinity of shape from shot to shot

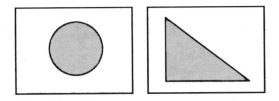

These drawings illustrate contrast of shape from shot to shot.

CONTROLLING LINE AND SHAPE

Most of the time, the lines in our shots are vertical and horizontal because trees, buildings, and most other objects in the real world are upright and usually at a 90-degree angle to the ground. A diagonal line will usually stand out in contrast to all of the more traditional horizontals and verticals. Since horizontal lines are least intense, you can use them to lower visual intensity. Where do diagonal lines exist and how can you create them to increase visual contrast in our shots?

How can you emphasize verticals, horizontals, or diagonals through art direction? How can the design of your set or choice of location incorporate specific ideas about line? If you reduce the lines in your location or set to a basic linear motif, what kind of lines are actually present? Buy a contrast viewing glass, or learn how to squint properly to recognize the lines that are present in your shots.

Since line exists because of tonal or color contrasts, we can control line through art direction and lighting. As your lighting gains contrast, more lines will appear. How can you use lighting (and darkness) to create lines or obscure the lines that are already there?

Line becomes an important factor in the planning shots. Let's look at a storyboard, which is usually a series of drawings showing the composition of shots. In this case, the storyboards will reveal the orientation of lines from shot to shot.

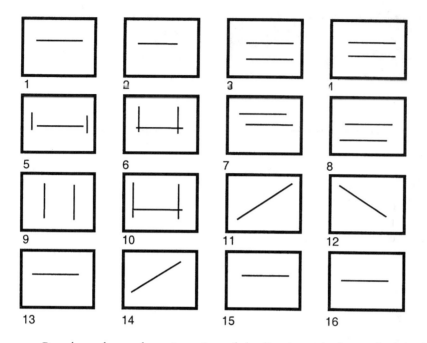

Based purely on the orientation of the line in each shot, where is the most intense part of this storyboard? The maximum contrast is found in panels 12-13-14: they have the greatest visual contrast because the orientation moves from diagonal to horizontal to diagonal. If you are staging an action sequence, a title sequence, a dance, or a conversation, the lines in the shot are going to add affinity or intensity to the sequence. You can use contrast and affinity of line to orchestrate the intensity changes of the scene.

Controlling shape involves careful examination of the basic shapes of all the objects you place in front of the camera. Look at an object's silhouette, not the object itself.

1. *The actor.* If the actors are reduced to silhouettes, what basic shape do they become?

2. *The location or set.* What shape is the space you're going to shoot in?

3. *The set dressing and props.* On the set, what is the basic shape of a chair, a couch, or a table lamp? Do the shapes communicate the correct emotional mood?

4. *Lighting.* How can lighting change the basic shapes or add additional ones?

Make rules for yourself about what shapes will be acceptable. This will give your production visual unity and visual structure, as we'll see in Chapter 9, "Story and Visual Structure."

FILMS TO WATCH

Line and shape in motion pictures are more difficult than space to notice. The linear motif of a sequence or an entire film is usually easier to study.

1. VERTICAL AND HORIZONTAL MOTIF
   Notorious (1946)
      Directed by Alfred Hitchcock
      Written by Ben Hecht
      Photographed by Ted Tetzlaff
      Art Direction by Carroll Clark

   Driving Miss Daisy (1989)
      Directed by Bruce Beresford
      Written by Alfred Uhry
      Photographed by Peter James
      Production Design by Bruno Rubeo

2. DIAGONAL LINEAR MOTIF
   Die Hard (1988)
      Directed by John McTiernan
      Written by Jeb Stuart and Steven deSouza
      Photographed by Jan De Bont
      Production Design by Jackson DeGovia

   The Third Man (1949)
      Directed by Carol Reed
      Written by Graham Green
      Photographed by Robert Krasker

3. SHAPES OF SPACES
   The Conformist (1969)
      Directed by Bernardo Bertolucci
      Written by Bernardo Bertolucci
      Photographed by Vittorio Storaro
      Production Design by Fernando Scarfiotti

   Star Wars (1977)
      Directed by George Lucas
      Written by George Lucas
      Photographed by Gilbert Taylor
      Production Design by John Barry

   The Shining (1980)
      Directed by Stanley Kubrick
      Written by Kubrick and Diane Johnson
      Photographed by John Alcott
      Production Design by Roy Walker

   Contempt (1963)
      Directed by Jean-Luc Godard
      Written by Jean-Luc Godard
      Photographed by Raoul Coutard

C H A P T E R   5

TONE

Tone is the easiest visual component to explain and understand. Tone does not refer to the tone of a script (angry, happy) or sound qualities (bass and treble). Tone refers to the brightness range of the objects in the shot.

We can illustrate the limits of the brightness range with a gray scale. Whether we're shooting in black & white or color, we must understand how to control the brightness of the objects in the frame.

The audience will usually look at the brightest area of the frame first, especially if there isn't any movement. The brightness of objects also has a large effect on the mood of a scene. Generally, an audience associates darkness with drama or tragedy and brightness with happiness or comedy. These emotional values are stereotypes, and we'll discover in Chapter 9, "Story and Visual Structure," how to make other choices. We can begin our discussion of tone by understanding the ways we can control it.

CONTROLLING THE GRAY SCALE

There are three ways to control the tone or brightness of objects in a shot: reflective control (art direction), incident control (lighting), and exposure.

REFLECTIVE CONTROL (ART DIRECTION)

One method of controlling the brightness range of objects is by controlling the actual reflectance values of the objects. If we want our production to have a dark look, then we'll only put dark objects in front of the camera. If we want a bright look, we'll use only brighter objects. To give our production a contrasty look, we'll only put very dark and very bright objects in our shots.

If you're making a dark movie, keep bright objects out of the shot. An actor can't wear a white shirt; it should be dyed dark gray or black. The darkness of the movie will be determined by how dark the objects actually are on the set. The production will look dark because everything photographed was dark.

If we were going to be very strict and use only reflective control for an entire production, all the lighting would be shadowless and flat. There would be the same amount of light everywhere because we've chosen to control the gray scale through the actual brightness value of the objects, not by lighting. This puts the tonal control in the hands of the art director and costume designer.

Television situation comedies, talk shows, and news programs have tonal ranges using reflective control. This is done to solve technical problems. Since these shows use multiple cameras, the entire set is lighted evenly to give the actors freedom of movement and to accommodate any possible camera angle. Since the lighting is even, the tone or brightness of the production will be controlled by the art director and costume designer. If the art director creates a dark set, it will appear that way on screen. Lighter costumes will appear light and darker costumes will appear dark. The lighting will not influence the actual brightness range of the objects in the shot.

INCIDENT CONTROL (LIGHTING)

The second method of controlling the tonal range or brightness of a scene is through lighting. In this case the gray scale is controlled by the amount of light falling on objects in the shot.

We may have an actor standing in front of a white wall, but the wall can be shadowed so it will appear dark. The gray scale is now being controlled by the amount of light falling on the wall rather than by the actual brightness of the wall. Bright objects can be made to look dark and dark objects can be made to look bright.

Imagine an actor standing in a jail cell with shadows from the bars creating black and white stripes across the floor and walls. This tonal pattern is being produced by the lighting, which we call incident control of the tonal scale.

Excellent examples of tonal control using light can be seen in films we call *film noir*. The term, coined by the French, means "dark film" and was first used to describe Hollywood movies of the 1940s and early 1950s. The tradition has continued today in films like Roman Polanski's *Chinatown* and Stephen Frears' *The Grifters*. Film noir, horror, and suspense stories often emphasize incident control of the gray scale.

The terms "reflective" and "incident" used here should not be confused with incident or reflective light meters. In regards to tonal control, reflective refers to the reflectivity of an object's surface and incident refers to light falling on an object. A reflective light or spot meter only reads the brightness of an object's surface and can't calculate the object's actual surface reflectivity. An incident light meter ignores object surfaces and is used to measure light which is falling onto the objects.

Of course there was plenty of incident control of lighting before *film noir*. Silent films depended on expressive and complex lighting schemes to communicate the moods and emotions of the story. The silent film cinematographers who later blossomed in the Golden Age of Hollywood (1935–1945) were masters of using light and shadow for expressive purposes. Incident control of tone was their most important tool.

CONTROL BY
ART DIRECTION

CONTROL BY
LIGHTING

Here are two shots of the same scene: one uses reflective control, and the other uses incident control.

EXPOSURE

The third way to control the tonal range of a shot is changing the amount of light that exposes the picture in film or video. This type of control is less selective than reflective or incident. As we adjust the camera lens' f-stops or shutter, the entire scene will get brighter or darker. We can't selectively make someone's shirt lighter or a wall darker without affecting everything else in the shot.

COINCIDENCE AND NONCOINCIDENCE

Coincidence and noncoincidence of tone refer to the relationship between the subject of the shot and the tonal organization of the shot. The subject can be a face, an entire person, a group of people, a prop, or any object that contains visual information pertinent to the story or a subject that the audience wants to see. Like any other visual component, we can think of this aspect of tone as having two extremes:

1. Coincidence of tone occurs when the tonal range reveals the subject.
2. Noncoincidence of tone occurs when the tonal range obscures the subject.

To understand if a shot has coincidence or noncoincidence of tone, you must first determine the subject of the shot.

In this case, the shot is a close-up of a person and the subject of a close-up is the face.

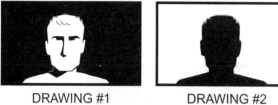

DRAWING #1   DRAWING #2
COINCIDENCE   NONCOINCIDENCE

In drawing #1 the subject is clearly revealed by the tonal organization. The tonal scheme allows the audience to see the face. The subject and the tonal organization coincide, so Drawing #1 is *coincidence* of tone.

In Drawing #2, the subject (the face) is not revealed. There's no light on the face and the subject is obscured. Drawing #2 is *noncoincidence* of tone. The tonal organization of the shot hides the subject (the face) from the audience. The audience cannot see the object that interests them most.

DRAWING #3
COINCIDENCE

Drawing #3 is coincidence of tone. The subject is "a person." The lighting scheme coincides with the subject because the person is revealed.

But Drawings #2 and #3 are both silhouettes, so how can one silhouette be coincidence and the another silhouette be noncoincidence? The actor standing in the doorway of Drawing #3 may be in silhouette like drawing #2 but what is the subject of the shot? The subject is not a face; the subject is "a person standing in the doorway." Even if the person were well lighted, the audience couldn't see the actor's face because the actor is so far away.

DRAWING #4
NONCOINCIDENCE

Drawing #4 is another version of the person in the doorway. It's noncoincidence of tone because the person who is still standing in the doorway is not revealed. This shot is noncoincidence of tone.

Coincidence and noncoincidence of tone can be confusing unless you have clearly identified the subject of your shot. When an object is physically hidden behind another object, you have not produced noncoincidence of tone. The obscuring must be accomplished through the control of tone. Noncoincidence of tone can be created using patterns of light or the absence of light that obscures the shot's subject.

Most films use coincidence of tone. The general tonal rule for comedy is to light scenes brightly so the actors can be seen. Does a comedy have to be bright? Of course not, but we probably don't want the actors to be so dark that the audience can't see what's going on. They might miss the joke.

On the other hand, horror, mystery, and suspense films capitalize on noncoincidence of tone. Often, the key ingredient to their visual structure is the audience's inability to see things because of the noncoincidence of tone. The subject of the shot (the attacker, victim, witness, etc.) is hidden, which makes the audience anxious. The subject is there but you can't see it. That's all noncoincidence of tone.

CONTRAST AND AFFINITY

The gray scale organizes tone, making contrast and affinity easy to understand. Remember that contrast and affinity can occur within the shot, from shot to shot, and from sequence to sequence.

Maximum contrast of tone is black and white. Maximum affinity is any two grays next to one another on the gray scale.

Tonal control must be overt if it's going to be noticed. A shot designed for maximum contrast of tone (black and white only) must truly eliminate the other shades of gray.

This drawing illustrates contrast of tone within the shot. The tones in the shot emphasize black and white with no middle grays at all.

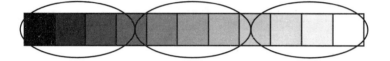

Affinity of tone is difficult to achieve and maintain. Dividing the gray scale into thirds makes it easier to control tonal affinity. By limiting the tonal range of a shot or sequence to only one third of the gray scale, tonal affinity can be achieved. Restricting the tonal range to only the upper or lower half of the gray scale will not work as well because a middle gray and a white may appear to have too much contrast.

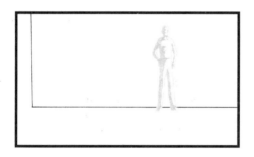

This shot illustrates affinity of tone. All of the grays here are in the upper third of the tonal scale.

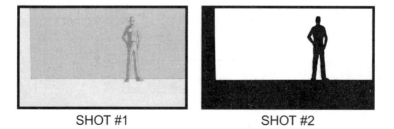

SHOT #1   SHOT #2

These two shots illustrate tonal contrast from shot to shot. Shot #1 is all middle grays, and Shot #2 is black and white with no middle grays.

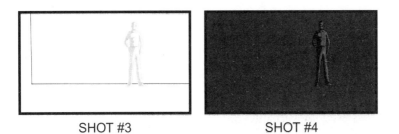

SHOT #3   SHOT #4

These two shots also illustrate contrast of tone from shot to shot. Shot #3
uses all lighter tones and shot #4 uses all darker tones.

FILMS TO WATCH

1. CONTRAST OF TONE
   Sunset Boulevard (1950)
   > Directed by Billy Wilder
   > Written by Wilder, Charles Brackett, and D. Marshman
   > Photographed by John Seitz
   > Art Direction by Hans Dreier and John Meehan

   T-Men (1947) and *Raw Deal* (1948)
   > Directed by Anthony Mann
   > Written by John Higgins
   > Photographed by John Alton
   > Art Direction by Edward Jewell

   In Cold Blood (1967)
   > Directed by Richard Brooks
   > Written by Richard Brooks
   > Photographed by Conrad Hall
   > Art Direction by Robert F. Boyle

   Cat People (1942)
   > Directed by Jacques Tourneur
   > Written by De Witt Bodeen
   > Photographed by Nicholas Musuraca
   > Art Direction by Albert S. D'Agostino

2. CONTRAST AND AFFINITY OF TONE
   Bonnie and Clyde (1967)
   > Directed by Arthur Penn
   > Written by David Newman and Robert Benton
   > Photographed by Burnett Guffey
   > Art Direction by Dean Tavoularis

3. TONAL CONTROL DUE TO REFLECTANCE OR INCIDENCE
   A Night at the Opera (1935)
   > Directed by Sam Wood
   > Written by George S. Kaufman and Morrie Ryskind

Photographed by Merritt Gerstad
Art Direction by Ben Carre and Edwin Willis

The Conformist (1969)
Directed by Bernardo Bertolucci
Written by Bernardo Bertolucci
Photographed by Vittorio Storaro
Production Design by Fernando Scarfiotti

Repulsion (1965)
Directed by Roman Polanski
Written by Roman Polanski
Photographed by Gilbert Taylor
Art Direction by Seamus Flannery

Manhattan (1979)
Directed by Woody Allen
Written by Allen and Marshall Brickman
Photographed by Gordon Willis
Production Design by Mel Bourne

Who's Afraid of Virginia Wolff? (1966)
Directed by Mike Nichols
Written by Ernest Lehman
Photographed by Haskell Wexler
Art Direction by Richard Sylbert

Apocalypse Now (1979)
Directed by Francis Ford Coppola
Written by Coppola and John Milius
Photographed by Vittorio Storaro
Production Design by Dean Tavoularis

Yojimbo (1961)
Directed by Akira Kurosawa
Written by Kurosawa and R. Kikushima
Photographed by Kazuo Miyagawa

C H A P T E R   6

COLOR

Color, without a doubt, is the most misunderstood visual component. Probably due to the misguided color education we received as children, our knowledge of color and how it works is almost unusable.

LIGHT

Before we can discuss color directly, we need to learn something about light. Let's begin with an experiment you may remember from science class.

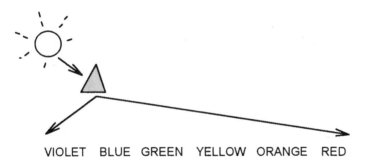

VIOLET   BLUE   GREEN   YELLOW   ORANGE   RED

Take a glass prism and shine a beam of sunlight through it. Out the other side of the prism you'll see a rainbow, or the visible spectrum: red, orange, yellow, green, blue, and violet. The prism experiment shows that sunlight contains all the colors of the visible spectrum.

Naively, we might say that sunlight is natural or normal light. Since sunlight doesn't seem to change the color of objects, we think that the light from the sun is not reddish, greenish, or bluish, but normal or natural "white" light.

By contrast, when we're in a dark room illuminated with only deep blue light, colors appear changed and unnatural. Everything looks blue. We know the blue light is not "normal."

But the light from the sun is not normal or white either. In fact, true, normal white light doesn't really exist. Understanding the actual color of light is critical to understanding color. See Color Plate 2.

Again, by refracting sunlight through a prism we get a rainbow or the visible spectrum. Now let's perform the same experiment with a 60-watt household lightbulb instead of the sun. See Color Plate 3.

The 60-watt light bulb also produces a rainbow, but the amount of each color is different. Sunlight contains far more blue light than the 60-watt bulb, which is more red-orange.

Let's examine a group of light sources to see what color light they actually produce. We'll look at a candle, a 60-watt lightbulb, a light used on movie sets, a sunset, and daylight. See Color Plate 4.

Here are five rainbows, each produced by a different light source. A candle produces a reddish light, a 60-watt light bulb an orangish light, and daylight is very blue by comparison. Although none of these light sources produce white light, our human vision system has the ability to adjust for their deficiencies and make the sources appear as "normal" or white light. For a detailed explanation of light sources and their relationship to film and color temperature, see Part E of the Appendix.

COLOR SYSTEMS

There are two basic systems that simplify color organization. These two systems share terms and certain characteristics but each must be considered separately.

THE ADDITIVE SYSTEM

The additive system of color involves the mixing of colored light. What do we mean when we say mixing of lights? Simply that a light of one color and a light of another color are beamed onto a common surface, and where the two colors overlap or mix, we get a third color.

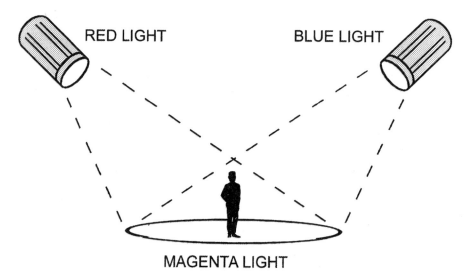

RED LIGHT   BLUE LIGHT

MAGENTA LIGHT

Imagine you're attending a concert in a large indoor arena. The stage is dark except for a red spotlight and a blue spotlight that are aimed at a singer. Where the red and blue light overlap, you'll see a magenta color.

This is additive color mixing. The red light is adding its wavelengths to the blue light, and a third color, magenta, is the result.

We use the additive system most often in theatrical lighting (plays, rock concerts, musical events, ice shows, night clubs, etc.). Lights of different colors are aimed at a common area and where the lights overlap, a new color is produced.

There are other technical areas involved in video and film that use the additive system, but we don't encounter them during normal production. We'll discuss color in postproduction later in this chapter.

Television and computer screens do not mix color using the additive system. See Part F of the Appendix for an explanation of color mixing on color monitors.

THE ADDITIVE SYSTEM COLOR WHEEL

A color wheel organizes colors and shows their relationship to each other.

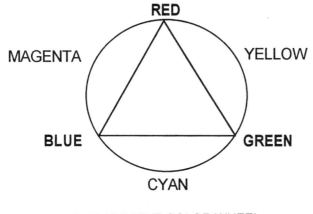

THE ADDITIVE COLOR WHEEL
MIXING LIGHT

The primary colors in the additive system are red, green, and blue. Combining two primary colors will produce the other colors needed to complete the color wheel. Remember, the additive system is the mixing of light.

RED + BLUE = MAGENTA
GREEN + BLUE = CYAN
RED + GREEN = YELLOW

Magenta is similar to violet or purple but more reddish. Cyan is like turquoise but more greenish.

When we mix the additive primaries together equally we get white light (or what appears to us as white light).

Colors opposite one another on the color wheel are called complementary colors. In the additive system, cyan and red are complementary, green and magenta are complementary, and blue and yellow are complementary.

THE SUBTRACTIVE SYSTEM

The subtractive color system is completely separate from the additive system even though they share terms and certain definitions. The subtractive system is used in the mixing of pigments, which includes paint and dyes.

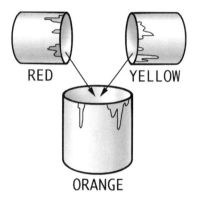

RED   YELLOW

ORANGE

When we mix red and yellow paint together we'll get orange paint. The red and yellow paints subtract their wavelengths from each other and create a new color.

Almost everything in our real world has been painted, dyed, or pigmented in some way and all of those colors were mixed using the subtractive system. When we select colors at a paint store, our choice is mixed using the subtractive system. The dyes used in fabrics, printing inks for magazines, books and newspapers, paint for walls, cars, furniture, the naturally occurring pigments in grass, leaves, trees, and the color in everything made from plastic was mixed using the subtractive system. In photography, all lighting and camera filters also use the subtractive system. This list of uses for the subtractive system is really endless.

THE SUBTRACTIVE SYSTEM COLOR WHEEL

The subtractive color wheel looks similar to the additive wheel but the primary colors are different.

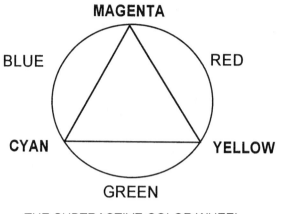

THE SUBTRACTIVE COLOR WHEEL
MIXING PIGMENT

The primary colors on the subtractive color wheel are magenta, yellow, and cyan. Mixing primary color pairs will give us the other colors needed to complete the color wheel.

MAGENTA + YELLOW = RED
YELLOW + CYAN = GREEN
CYAN + MAGENTA = BLUE

When we mix magenta, yellow, and cyan pigments together equally, we'll get black.

Colors opposite one another on the subtractive color wheel are called complementary colors. For example, on the subtractive wheel, magenta and green are complements.

If magenta, yellow, and cyan are the subtractive primary colors, why didn't we learn this in grade school? Why do most people think that the primary colors are red, green, yellow, or blue? The additive and subtractive systems are often mistakenly combined, which leads to color theory confusion. Many elementary school teachers feel that red, blue, and yellow "look" more primary than magenta or cyan. For whatever reason, the colors magenta and cyan aren't usually taught in children's art classes. Sometimes cyan doesn't show up until college.

Another problem with teaching color is that color identification is subjective. How can we know what color we really mean when we say red, yellow, green, or blue? The variety of colors we accept as red covers a huge range. Manufacturing the proper color of paint to create a primary color is also nearly impossible, so we tend to accept a very wide range of colors as primary.

Ask anyone in the business of printing magazines or picture books and they'll tell you that the subtractive primary colors have always been magenta, yellow, and cyan (and black to compensate for certain inadequacies in the inks). The range of printed colors in magazines, books, and newspapers using these colors produces an adequate range of colors.

Camera and lighting filters also use the subtractive system, but instead of mixing paint we mix colored glass or sheets of colored acetate called gels. If we overlap magenta, yellow, and cyan gels, we can get the same subtractive mixtures produced by mixing paint. Overlapping a cyan filter and a magenta filter creates a blue color, for example. How camera filters can affect the color of light is briefly explained in the Appendix, Part G.

THE BASIC COMPONENTS OF COLOR

This is not an instruction book about mixing watercolors and oils for artists. The theories and rules for mixing artist's colors varies greatly. We're trying to identify, organize, and control color in our film and video productions.

Talking about color is difficult because words cannot accurately describe a color. Paint stores give names to describe their colors of paint. Here are some color names you'll find in any paint store:

1. King's Ransom
2. Liberty
3. Sorrento

Do you have any idea what colors they're talking about? What color is Liberty? Interior designers use words like "mushroom" or "peach," which may generally describe a color but still aren't very specific. Sometimes colors are given names like "seacalm" or "romance," which tell more about the emotion the color hopes to evoke rather than a description of the color itself. What color is "romance"? Blue? Red? Green?

Ultimately, it's impossible to talk about colors accurately. When we want to describe a specific color, we must have an actual sample of the color in hand. Two commercially available systems, the Pantone Color System and the Munsell Color System, provide color swatches that are accepted worldwide. These systems allow you to specify a color based on numbered charts or swatches of color rather than a verbal description.

But what if you're not carrying color swatches and you have to describe a color? We need some terms that will help us. They are hue, brightness, and saturation.

HUE

Hue tells us the position of a color on the color wheel: red, orange, yellow, green, cyan, blue, violet (or purple), and magenta. That's it. There are only eight hues. Pink, brown, turquoise, and beige are not hues. Using the hue name, we can begin to describe a color. Most fire engines are red, a lemon is yellow, and grass is green. Although this lacks subtly, we are describing color using words and it hasn't gotten confusing or misleading.

BRIGHTNESS

Brightness (sometimes called value) is the addition of white or black to the hue. Adding white to a red hue creates a bright red (which we'd call pink). Adding black to a red hue produces dark red (which we'd call maroon). Brightness is the position of a color on the gray scale.

At noon, the sky is bright or light blue. At twilight, the sky is dark blue. We're still not being very specific but words can only describe a color in a general way.

SATURATION

The third component of color is saturation (sometimes called chroma or intensity). Saturation and its opposite, desaturation, are more difficult to understand.

What does saturation mean? Saturation refers to the purity of a hue. For example, a fully saturated red is as red as a red color can be. It's a red that hasn't been contaminated by any other hue. It's 100% red. Saturation means the hue is very vivid.

Desaturation involves a saturated hue and its complementary color. Let's look at the subtractive color wheel again.

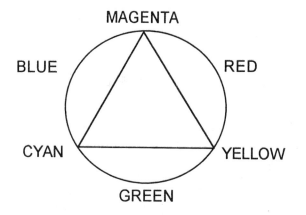

Colors opposite one another are complementary. On the subtractive color wheel, cyan and red are complementary, magenta and green are complementary, and yellow and blue are complementary.

Let's take the hue of red as it appears on the color wheel. Like all the colors on the wheel, this red is the purest, most vivid, saturated color possible. If we add a small amount of cyan (red's complement) to the red hue, it begins to change. The saturated red becomes less vivid. The saturated red begins to turn gray. This is called desaturation. The more cyan we add, the grayer the red will become. When we mix equal amounts of red and cyan together, we'll end up without a trace of either hue. We will be left with gray. We can make any color desaturate (or turn gray) by adding its complementary color. When a hue is extremely pure or vivid we call it saturated. The grayer the color becomes the more desaturated it appears. Color Plate 5 shows a saturated red and cyan that desaturate when mixed together.

Hue, brightness, and saturation are the only terms we need to describe a color. Are these three terms exact? Not really. But using them is better than words like "seacalm" or "liberty." To precisely describe a color you must show a sample of the color, but you can describe a color verbally using hue, brightness, and saturation.

There are a few other color terms that we frequently hear. "Tint" and "pastel" mean adding white to a hue. "Shade" usually means adding the complementary color, but sometimes it means adding black. To avoid confusion, don't use these terms at all.

Look around you and try to describe the color of objects in terms of hue, brightness, and saturation. Most objects contain color even if they appear gray. They're just desaturated.

Color Plate 6 shows a variety of colors available when starting with a saturated red. The red rectangle on the right is the most saturated. The red colors desaturate as they move to the left. The colors become brighter as they move up and darker as they move down the diagram. Any one of the colors can be described in terms of hue, brightness, and saturation.

BRIGHTNESS VERSUS SATURATION

The color wheel displays the basic hues in their fully saturated (most pure or vivid) state. Although the colors are all equally saturated, the brightness of each hue is different.

Let's take swatches of saturated yellow, orange, red, green, cyan, blue, and violet and photograph them in black and white. It will reveal the wide brightness range inherent in fully saturated colors.

Color Plate 7 is a color wheel and beside it, the same wheel reproduced in black & white. Yellow is the brightest saturated color. Orange is almost as bright. A saturated red, green, and cyan appear near the middle of the gray scale. Blue and violet are the darkest saturated colors.

Knowing the inherent brightness levels of different saturated hues is important. A saturated yellow will always attract the viewer's eye first not only because it is saturated but because it is also very bright. A saturated blue will always appear much darker than a saturated yellow. If we raise the brightness level of a blue to match the yellow, the blue can't retain its saturation because it contains so much white.

CONTRAST AND AFFINITY

There are many ways to produce contrast or affinity of color. Remember contrast and affinity can occur within the shot, from shot to shot and from sequence to sequence.

HUE

We can create contrast or affinity of hue. See Color Plate 8.

An actor standing in a green room wearing a red shirt and blue jeans and holding a yellow box illustrates contrast of hue within the shot.

Affinity of hue means that all colors use the same hue. An actor wearing a red shirt, dark red pants, and holding a desaturated red box enters a red room. Every color in the shot is the same hue even though the brightness and saturation can vary. Kubrick's *The Shining* and Bergman's *Cries and Whispers* are examples of affinity of hue.

Color Plate 1

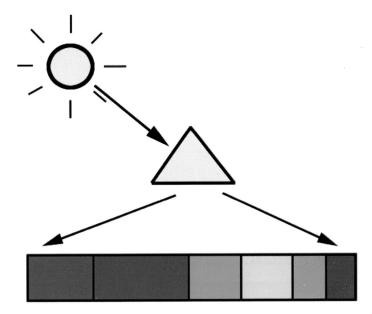

Color Plate 2

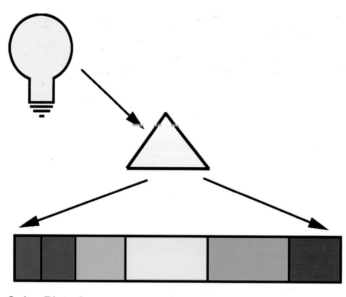

Color Plate 3

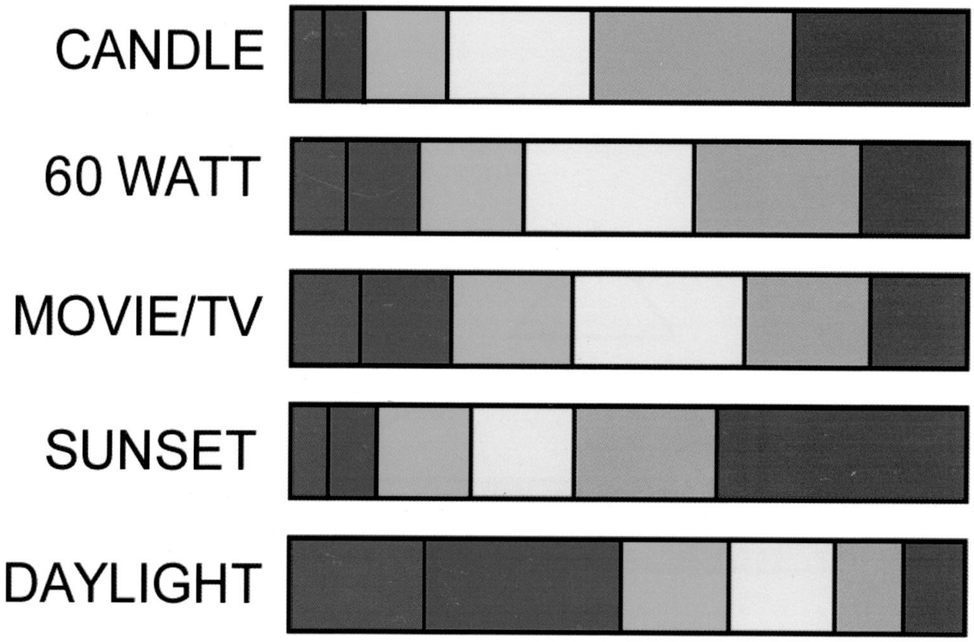

CANDLE

60 WATT

MOVIE/TV

SUNSET

DAYLIGHT

Color Plate 4

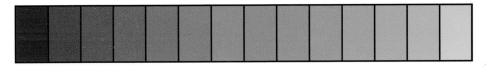

Color Plate 5

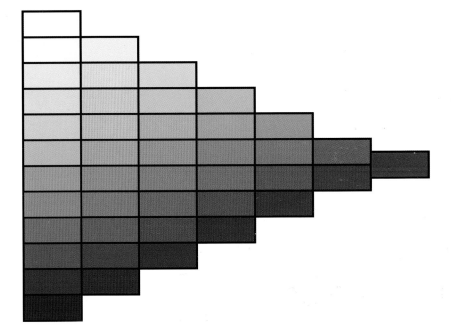

Color Plate 6

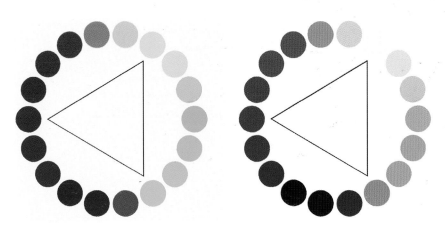

Color Plate 7

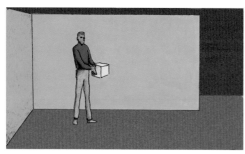

Color Plate 8A

Color Plate 8B

Color Plate 9A

Color Plate 9B

Color Plate 10A   **Color Plate 10B**

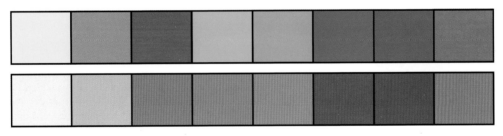

Color Plate 11

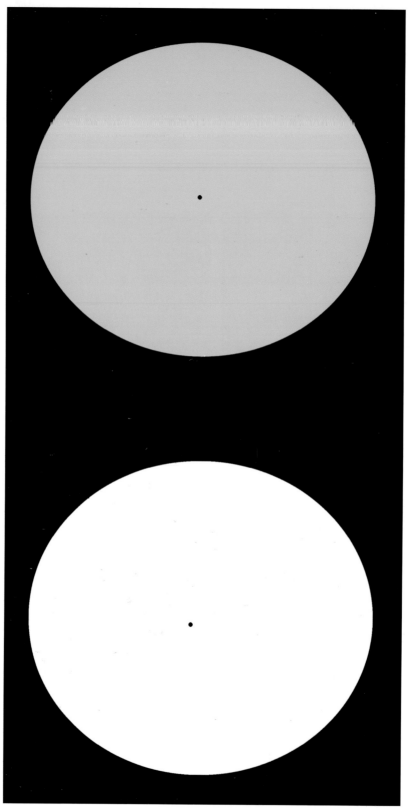

Color Plate 12

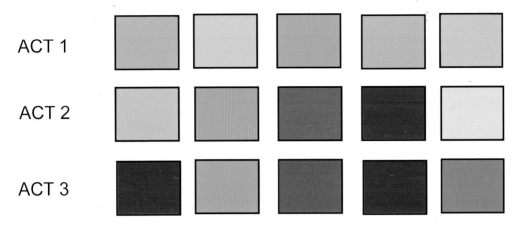

ACT 1

ACT 2

ACT 3

Color Plate 13

Color Plate 14

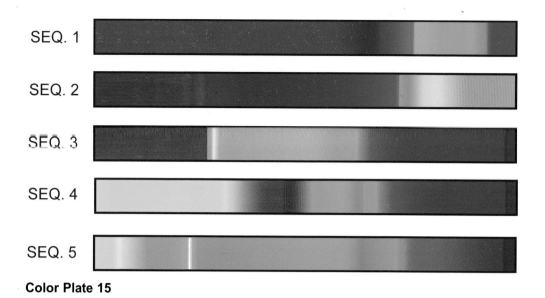

SEQ. 1

SEQ. 2

SEQ. 3

SEQ. 4

SEQ. 5

Color Plate 15

BRIGHTNESS

We can create contrast or affinity of brightness of color. Brightness refers to the tonal range of the colors in the shot.

A scene that uses only very bright and very dark colors illustrates contrast of brightness. A scene that uses only bright colors will show affinity of brightness. See Color Plate 9. Color Plate 9A illustrates affinity of brightness within the shot and Color Plate 9B illustrates contrast of brightness.

SATURATION

An entire production might use only saturated colors, which will create affinity of saturation. This will help to give the production overall color unity. Each sequence in a film may alternate between saturated and desaturated colors giving the production a contrast of saturation from sequence to sequence. See Color Plate 10. Color Plate 10A shows contrast of saturation and Color Plate 10B illustrates affinity of saturation.

WARM/COOL

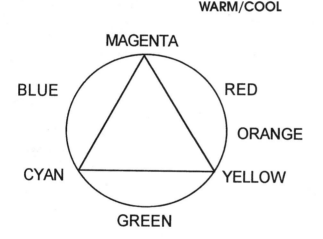

The warm colors are red-magenta, red, orange, and yellow. The cool colors are blue-magenta, blue, green, cyan, and yellow-green. Because magenta is made up of warm red and cool blue, magenta can appear warm or cool. We therefore divide magenta into red-magenta (warm) and blue-magenta (cool). Yellow is clearly a warm color, but as soon as it's mixed with a little green, it usually appears to lose its warmth and becomes cool.

Contrast of warm/cool could be a single shot that uses both warm and cool colors for dramatic contrast, or a pair of shots, one warm and one cool. Sequence-to-sequence contrast would suggest that one sequence is all warm and the next sequence all cool.

You can assign the warm/cool color contrast to any aspect of the production's color. The actors could use warm colors and the backgrounds cool, or certain actors could be dressed in warm colors and other actors in cool colors, or the front light is cool and the backlight is warm.

You can also have affinity of warm/cool, meaning you'll choose only warm or only cool colors for a shot, group of shots, a sequence, or an entire production.

COMPLEMENTARY

Audiences don't know which hues are complementary, but they will respond emotionally to them. Although we can't create affinity of complementary colors because the term complementary means opposites, we can have contrast of complementary colors.

Based on the subtractive color wheel, the complementary pairs are magenta/green, red/cyan, and yellow/blue. This means that the complementary hue contrast for a shot, shots, or a sequence would be limited to one of these pairs of colors.

We could use complementary pairs for a color scheme in a film that took place in two basic locations (a city and a desert, for example). The city could use cyan colors, and the desert could use red colors. We might use a complementary scheme for the general lighting of a film where the daylight is yellowish and the nighttime is bluish.

EXTENSION

Contrast and affinity of extension deals with the brightness and size of the area a color occupies in relation to other colors.

It's easiest to explain extension by using hues in their most saturated state. Remember, fully saturated hues vary in their brightness or tonal value. See Color Plate 11.

Here are the saturated hues in color and black & white. A saturated yellow is very bright. Red and green have a brightness level near middle gray, and a saturated blue and magenta are darkest.

Contrast and affinity of extension occurs with any number of colors, but the principle can be demonstrated most easily using the complementary pair yellow and blue.

Here's our shot. A saturated yellow wall in front of a saturated blue background. Since both are saturated, the yellow color is much brighter and the blue is naturally darker. Both colors occupy a similar sized area of the frame.

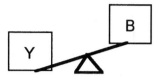

If these equal areas of yellow and blue are placed on a scale that measured the color's ability to attract the audience's attention, the yellow would have more weight (more ability to attract the viewer's eye) because the yellow is brighter. Both colors occupy the same amount of area in the shot, but the yellow, being lighter, will attract the audience's attention first. This creates contrast of extension so the scale is out of balance.

In order to balance the scale, the area that the yellow color occupies in the frame must be reduced.

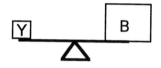

This is affinity of extension. By reducing the area of yellow, the large area of blue can balance it. The audience's attention will be drawn to both colors equally.

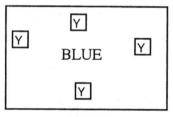

AFFINITY

The yellow color occupies small areas and is distributed evenly around the frame. This produces an affinity of extension because the proportions of the area covered by the blue and yellow have been changed. The audience's attention will be drawn to both colors equally.

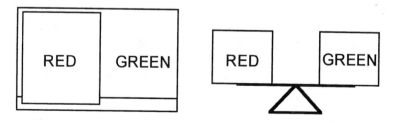

Since a saturated red and a saturated green share a similar brightness, equal sized areas have affinity of extension. The scale is balanced.

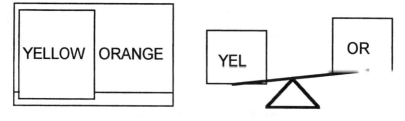

Saturated yellow and orange are nearly equal, but the yellow is a little brighter so it has more ability to attract the audience's eye. This saturated yellow and orange illustrate a minor contrast of extension.

Extension doesn't apply only to complementary pairs of colors. Contrast and affinity of extension can involve any number of colors from anywhere on the hue, brightness, or saturation scale.

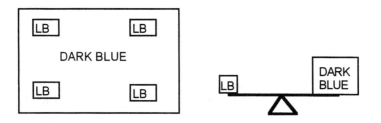

This time we're comparing a light blue (LB) and a dark blue color. In this proportion, they show affinity of extension, because it will take very little light blue to equal a large amount of dark blue.

The key to understanding extension is to examine the color's brightness in relation to the size of the area that the color occupies. The brighter the color, the less area it needs to attract the viewer's attention or balance other darker colors.

Contrast of extension can be used to draw the viewer's attention to a particular area of the screen or give a scene balance. Once you know where you want the audience to look, you can adjust extension to help direct attention. By creating affinity of extension, a scene will have low visual intensity. As the contrast of extension increases, so will the overall dynamic intensity of the shot or group of shots.

Because extension with a large group of colors is complex to control, it's best to analyze it in black & white. This removes the hue and let's you see the true brightness of areas of the shot. Taking a black-&-white Polaroid photograph of a scene will give you a quick reference for extension. A look through a contrast viewing glass will do the same. If you have video assist or if you're shooting on video, turning off the color in the monitors will also give you a general idea of the brightness range and the area that each gray covers. Then you can adjust the brightness of objects or change the size of the area to create contrast or affinity.

INTERACTION OF COLOR

The artist Josef Albers, in his famous color studies at Yale University, demonstrated and defined what has come to be called color interaction.

Albers' studies clarified old theories about how colors appear to change their hue, brightness, or saturation when placed next to other colors. His writings, based on his own work and the work of his students, has given us a set of rules that accurately predict how colors will interact.

The apparent visual change of a color requires two ingredients:

1. An appropriate color that will change, called a "susceptible color."
2. A proper neighboring color to activate the change in the susceptible color.

Let's look at three rules of color interaction.

HUE + BLACK OR WHITE

Color interaction occurs when white or black is placed next to a color, but the results vary depending on the proportion of the black or white area to the color. We'll use cyan as the susceptible color and see how it changes as it interacts with its background.

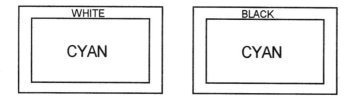

When a cyan color is surrounded by a small amount of white, the cyan will look lighter. Surrounding the same cyan with a small amount black will make the cyan look darker. The susceptible color shifts towards the brightness of the surrounding tone.

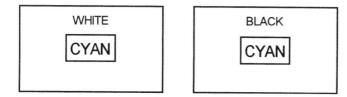

If we shrink the size of the susceptible hue, the opposite result occurs. A large area of white surrounding the cyan makes the cyan look darker. A large area of black surrounding the cyan makes it look lighter.

As the proportion of white or black background grows in relation to the susceptible hue, the hue's tone appears to shift farther away from the background tone. As the area of the susceptible hue grows, its brightness will appear more similar to the surrounding background tone. Because this color interaction occurs within the shot, we call this simultaneous contrast.

COMPLEMENTARY COLORS

The second type of color interaction involves complementary colors that increase in apparent saturation when placed next to each other.

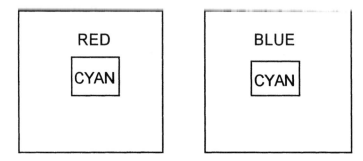

This becomes clear when we place a swatch of cyan on a red background and a swatch of the same cyan on a blue background. Even though the two cyan swatches are identical, the cyan swatch on the red background will appear more saturated than the cyan swatch on the blue background.

In this case, the susceptible color is cyan. It appears to gain saturation when placed next to its complementary color. This is simultaneous contrast, because both colors are in the shot at the same time.

We can create the same interaction from shot to shot.

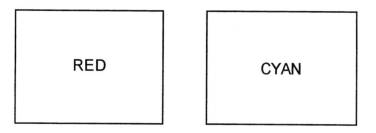

If one shot is primarily red and we cut to a shot that is primarily cyan we will perceive the cyan as more saturated due to the color interaction from shot to shot. We call this successive contrast.

ANALOGOUS COLORS

Analogous colors are colors that are next to each other on the color wheel.

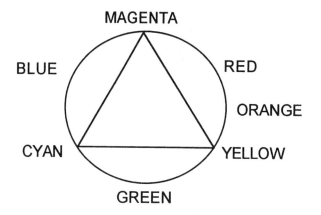

For example, red, and orange are analogous, as are green and cyan. When analogous colors are placed next to one another, they appear to push apart or separate in their position on the color wheel.

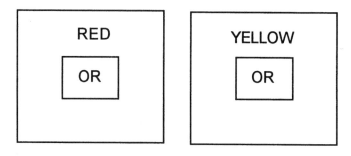

In this illustration, orange is the susceptible color. An orange swatch on a red background will seem more yellow, and an orange swatch on a yellow background will appear more red.

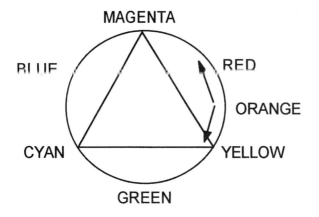

If we look at a color wheel we can explain this interaction. The red background makes the orange swatch seem more yellow. The orange color is being "pushed away" from the red towards the yellow. The yellow background makes the orange appear more red. The yellow background "pushes" the orange away from the yellow towards the red hue on the color wheel.

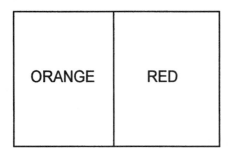

Here, the red will make the orange appear more yellow and the orange will make the red appear more magenta. The two colors are pushing apart.

How can we use color interaction? Suppose the end of a story takes place in a burning house. You've spent the entire film building up to this crucial sequence, so when the fire finally arrives, you want it to have a particularly strong visual impact. The Special Effects Crew will produce a fire that's unusually red in color and the cinematographer has conducted exposure tests that will render the fire as red as possible. Unfortunately, the red is still not saturated enough.

Using interaction of color, it's possible to create a situation on screen that will help the fire appear more red. The solution involves simultaneous and successive contrast.

If you include a cyan-colored background behind the red flames, the red fire will look more saturated because complementary colors will increase apparent saturation. This is simultaneous contrast (just like contrast within the shot). The red flames will appear more red because the viewer is simultaneously looking at complementary colors.

Another solution to the problem involves preceding the fire sequence with a series of cyan shots. We call this successive contrast because the cyan color is seen first and the complementary red color follows (just like contrast from shot to shot).

The exact physiological reasons why successive and simultaneous contrast works is not completely understood, however we can provide a simple experiment that demonstrates the phenomena. See Color Plate 12.

Position this book in a strong light source about twelve inches from your eyes. Get comfortable. Stare at the dot in the cyan circle for about a minute, then shift your eyes to the dot in the white circle. You should see a red colored circle appear briefly in the white circle.

This is called an afterimage. The afterimage appears for a number of reasons. The eye will always produce the complementary color to what it sees. As you stared at the cyan circle you might have sensed that the cyan was getting less saturated or less vivid. This was partly due to the color receptors in your eyes beginning to fatigue. At the same time, your brain, being bombarded by a cyan color, adjusted to find a normal "white" color. Remember that our brains are always looking for white light. Since red is the complement of cyan and mixing the two equally will give us neutral gray (a satisfying equivalent for white), your brain began to add the red color trying to make the cyan neutral. When you shifted your attention to the white circle, you got a glimpse of the red color your vision system had added to the cyan in an attempt to make it appear neutral or white.

If we apply this principle to the problem of the red fire, we can see how preceding or surrounding the red with a cyan color will force the audience to generate a more saturated red color for the fire.

COLOR SCHEMES

A color scheme is a color plan. What is the plan for the color in your production? Saturated, desaturated, bright, dark, warm, cool? It's all part of the color plan or scheme. Since color has so many variables, it would be difficult to review all of the possibilities, but let's discuss some of the basic schemes.

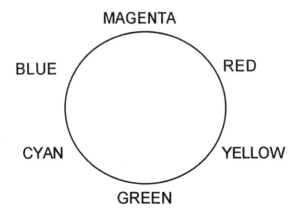

The color wheel is a good place to begin looking for a color scheme, because it has already organized all of the hues in a simple circle. You can include (or exclude) as many hues as you think necessary to tell your story. Here are some possible color schemes.

1. *One Hue.* Sometimes called a monochromatic color scheme, it involves finding a single hue for your entire production. Warren Beatty's *Reds* and Ingmar Bergman's *Cries and Whispers* use only the hue of red.

2. *Complementary Hues.* A very common color scheme is complementary pairs, the most common being an orangish/bluish scheme. Remember that complementary colors are opposite each other on the color wheel. The pair of hues can be assigned in different ways: one group of characters are blue, the others are orange; one location is blue, the other is orange; foregrounds are blue, and backgrounds are orange. Any complementary pair can be used.

3. *Split Complementary Hues.* Instead of taking a pair of colors opposite one another, you take one hue and split off from its complementary color getting a pair of nearly complementary hues.

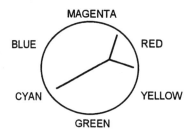

This gives you three hues to work with. An example would be cyan and its split complementary orange and red-magenta.

4. *Three-Way Split.* This color scheme uses any three hues usually equidistant around the color wheel. Like the complementary scheme, you can assign whatever story values you want to the three color choices.

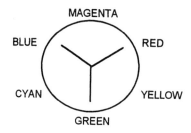

For example, you could pick red, blue, and green as your three hues. Maybe your production is a rural adventure, so there'll be the blue sky, green grass, and your actors will be dressed in various red hues. Or you might assign blue to your heroes, red to their enemies, and green to the location. Perhaps nighttime scenes are blue and green and daytime scenes are red. Remember, we're only picking the hue. The hue can vary in saturation and brightness to produce a wide range of subtle colors.

5. *Four-Way Split.* Obviously, this involves four hues usually equidistant around the color wheel. A four-way split is an extremely complex scheme.

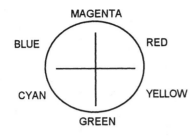

An excellent example of this scheme is Disney's animated feature *Sleeping Beauty* (1959). Magenta and green are assigned to the evil characters, and orange and blue-cyan are assigned to the good characters.

Next, you'll need to decide the brightness and saturation of the colors in your production. This is where color can get complicated and difficult to discuss and control. At a certain point, discussing a color becomes impossible because words can't accurately describe it. A solution to the problem is a color script.

A color script outlines the basic story and then indicates with actual swatches the colors you have in mind.

These swatches of color can be displayed like storyboards, but instead of illustrating each shot, the colors will reveal the overall color of a scene, sequence, or the entire production. See Color Plate 13.

Color Script #1 illustrates the general color of each act of the story. Notice the contrast of warm and cool colors between acts. See Color Plate 13.

Color Script #2 simply displays the colors for the entire production. The color scheme is all cool, desaturated colors. See Color Plate 14.

Color Script #3 is the most complex of the color scripts. Here, each sequence in the film is given a single color panel that illustrates all the colors for that sequence in their correct proportion. This method allows you to study complex changes in color as a story unfolds. See Color Plate 15.

Having actual color samples eliminates the problem of discussing color. Animated films rely heavily on color scripts, since all of the color must be created. In a live-action film we often take color for granted since it's already there. Don't underestimate color's value as a visual component. In Chapter 9, "Story and Visual Structure," we'll look at an even easier way to create and control color schemes.

CONTROL OF COLOR

Let's take what we've learned and apply it directly to the production problem of controlling color. How can we control color?

THE COLOR PALETTE

The best way to control color is to control the color palette itself. The palette means the actual color of the objects (sets, props, wardrobe) in the shot. If you want your finished production to be blue and desaturated, then only put desaturated blue objects in front of the camera. Give yourself strict rules about the color of your production and remove colors that are wrong.

A great production designer knows how to control color. It's not just wardrobe and wall colors. Art departments can paint grass with vegetable dye to make it yellow-green or green-blue or brown. In *Peggy Sue Got Married* (1986) the visual look of 1950 Kodachrome film was achieved by spraying grass an unusually saturated green and painting sidewalks purple. In Michelangelo Antonioni's *The Red Desert* (1964), everything in a street scene, including fruits and vegetables on a cart, was painted gray. You'd be surprised how much manipulation of natural color can occur without the audience noticing.

An audience has a very poor color memory. If we show a viewer a blue swatch of color and then remove it from sight, they will be unable to select that blue from a group of similar but different blue colors. We can use this deficiency to our advantage in the control of color. We can actually manipulate the hue, brightness, and saturation of an object's color from scene to scene or from sequence to sequence and the audience will be unaware of the color change. We can essentially change the color of objects with paint in the same way that we change the brightness of objects with light.

Color is a complex visual component. Limiting your color choices will allow the colors you use to have visual meaning to the audience. Keep your color palette simple.

FILTERS

We can control color by using filters on the camera lens and our light sources.

Camera Filters

Whenever we put a colored filter over our camera lens we're using the subtractive system. A filter cannot add any color, it can only subtract color. A filter will always subtract its complementary color and transmit its own color. Adding a blue filter to the camera lens makes objects in the shot appear more blue but the filter isn't adding blue. Actually, the yellow (complement of blue) is being removed and the remaining blue color appears more dominant.

Adding colored filters to the camera lens can be tricky. Standard color filters are extremely reliable and change colors in specific ways. Working with non-standard colored filters presents a problem because the results aren't predictable. The color you see with your eye may not be the color you get on film or video. A filter that looks blue to the eye might appear magenta on film. Certain yellow gels photograph yellow-green. Experience or tests are the only method of properly predicting how a film stock will react to a nonstandard filter. Using filters in video is more predictable because accurate results are visible on the monitors.

Lighting Filters

We can also use filters on our lights. Several manufactures provide a wide range of colored plastic sheets, called gels, that are available in any imaginable color.

Placing gels on lights uses the subtractive process. Whenever a gel is placed over a light, the output of the light decreases, proving gels use the subtractive system. A gel or filter absorbs its complementary color and transmits its own color.

Again, it's important to test nonstandard colored filters because the color we see may not be the color that's photographed.

Time/Location

We have control over the color of daylight when we're shooting outdoors, but it requires waiting for a particular time of day, or weather condition, or carefully choosing the outdoor environment.

We know that a sunrise appears more lavender, noon daylight is more blue, and a sunset is more red. Filming during the "magic hour" (periods of daylight when the sun is below the horizon) produces an unusual quality of daylight that has no shadows.

On an overcast day, the skylight is more blue because the direct rays from the sun (which are more red than the skylight) are held back by the clouds.

The color of outdoor light will also change depending on the surrounding environment.

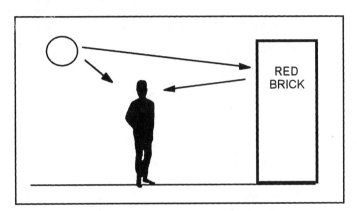

When we're photographing around red brick walls, the overall color of the light reflected from the environment will be more red than the light coming directly from the sky. In a forest, the light that filters through the tree's leaves is more green than the light coming directly from the sky.

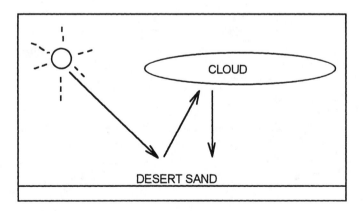

Clouds are also big reflectors. If we're shooting in a desert location the ambient color of the light will be yellow-orange. Daylight will be reflected off the desert sand and appear more yellow-orange. This light will also bounce off the underside of white clouds and send more yellow-orange light onto the location.

FILM

We can also control color by the choice of the film stock and the method by which we expose it. Generally speaking, the lower the film's ASA (sensitivity to light) the more saturated the colors will appear.

There are more film stocks available today than ever before. Different film stocks have different visual characteristics depending on the manufacturer and ASA. Some stocks look warmer or cooler, more or less saturated, have better shadow detail or appear more contrasty. The only way to determine which film stock will be best for your project is to test it.

You can also alter the color through exposure of the film or video signal. The variables here are great. The film can be under- or overexposed, and then brightened or darkened at various stages of postproduction to control saturation and brightness. A video signal can be under- or overexposed in a similar manner to produce different color qualities. This book will not go into the complexities of exposure. Again, experience and actual testing are necessary.

LABORATORY

The lab itself can provide a number of services that can help control the color on the film.

Flashing

One service is flashing the film. Flashing means the film is exposed to light twice. Once when you photograph the scene and again at the lab either before (pre-flashing) or after (postflashing) principal photography. The lab's flashing exposes the film to a precisely measured amount of light (colored or white) that will tend to desaturate the color and lower the scene's contrast. One camera manufacturer has added a special light inside the camera body so the flashing can occur as the scene is being photographed.

Pushing

The lab can also alter the length of time the film is developed in the chemical baths. Usually this involves leaving the film in the developer for a longer period of time, which is called "pushing" or "force developing" the film. The original scene is usually underexposed during photography and developed longer to compensate for this underexposure. Pushing the film will desaturate the color.

Chemical Development

Today, labs are willing to experiment by removing or adding steps in the chemical development process to alter the film's color saturation, contrast, or brightness. Some labs have special chemicals or processing steps already in place that change the look of the film's color. Check with your lab and see what they can offer you.

Timing

The lab can also "time" or color correct the film. The term timing refers to early 1900s lab technicians who, using stopwatches, would control the brightness or darkness of the black-&-white film by the length of time it was left in the chemical baths.

What exactly is modern timing? It's a way to correct each shot of a film or video so that there's a smooth visual continuity of brightness and color from shot to shot. Video timing can also change the contrast, brightness, and saturation of individual hues in shots. Timing can add general warming or cooling color shifts to sequences or your entire production.

Digital

Digital technology allows for extraordinary color flexibility. The digital world can manipulate hue, brightness, saturation, and contrast in an entire shot or a single object within a shot. In the digital world any type of color change can be made in any frame. Whether you're working in film or video, digital technology allows unlimited color flexibility in postproduction but it shouldn't be used as an excuse to ignore color control during production.

FILMS TO WATCH

1. SATURATED HUE
    Cries and Whispers (1972)
    > Directed by Ingmar Bergman
    > Written by Ingmar Bergman
    > Photographed by Sven Nykvist
    > Production Design by Marik Vos-Lundh

    Ran (1985)
    > Directed by Akira Kurosawa
    > Written by Kurosawa and Masato Ide
    > Photographed by Takao Saito

2. COMPLEMENTARY COLORS (BLUE AND YELLOW)
    Man in the Moon (1991)
    > Directed by Robert Mulligan
    > Written by Jenny Wingfield
    > Photographed by Freddie Francis
    > Production Design by Gene Callahan

    The English Patient (1996)
    > Directed by Anthony Mingella
    > Written by Anthony Mingella
    > Photographed by John Seale
    > Production Design by Stuart Craig

3. WARM/COOL COLORS
    The Shining (1980)
    > Directed by Stanley Kubrick
    > Written by Kubrick and Diane Johnson
    > Photographed by John Alcott
    > Production Design by Roy Walker

    Wings of the Dove (1997)
    > Directed by Iain Softley
    > Written by Hossein Amini

Photographed by Eduardo Serra
Production Design by John Beard

The Last Emperor (1987)
Directed by Bernardo Bertolucci
Written by Mark Peplow and Bernardo Bertolucci
Photographed by Vittorio Storaro
Production Design by Fernando Scarfiotti

4. WARM COLORS
The Godfather (1972)
Directed by Francis Ford Coppola
Written by Coppola and Mario Puzo
Photographed by Gordon Willis
Production Design by Dean Tavoularis

5. CONTRAST OF SATURATED/DESATURATED COLORS
Pennies from Heaven (1981)
Directed by Herbert Ross
Written by Dennis Potter
Photographed by Gordon Willis
Production Design by Ken Adam

6. LIMITED COLOR PALETTE
Shawshank Redemption (1994)
Directed by Frank Darabont
Written by Frank Darabont
Photographed by Roger Deakins
Production Design by Terrence Marsh

Chinatown (1974)
Directed by Roman Polanski
Written by Robert Towne
Photographed by John A. Alonso
Production Design by Richard Sylbert

A Little Princess (1995)
Directed by Alfonso Cuaron
Written by Richard LeGravenese and Elizabeth Chandler
Photographed by Emanuelle Lubezki
Production Design by Bo Welch

Days of Heaven (1978)
Directed by Terrence Malick
Written by Terrence Malick
Photographed by Nestor Almendros
Art Direction by Jack Fisk

Three Kings (1999)
Directed by David O. Russel
Written by David O. Russel
Photographed by Tom Sigel
Production Design by Catherine Hardwicke

C H A P T E R   7

MOVEMENT

Although there have been many films made without movement (Chris Marker's 1964 film *La Jette* uses still photos, for example, as do most historical documentaries), an audience expects things on screen to move. Shouldn't movies always move? Yes. They always move. Even when we look at a still picture there's always movement. There are four ways to create movement.

ACTUAL MOVEMENT

Actual movement only occurs in the real world. Almost everything in our three-dimensional world that moves is classified in this category. Walking people, flying birds, and moving cars are examples of the constant actual movement we see everyday.

APPARENT MOVEMENT

When one stationary object is replaced by another stationary object the change between objects may be perceived as the movement of a single object. This creates *apparent movement*.

Film and video rely on this principle. Once we photograph movement from the real world onto film or video, it's transformed into a series of still pictures. Film and video can play back these still pictures at 24 or 30 fps (frames per second), and the pictures appear to move. But the movement is apparent, not actual. To prove it, we can "freeze frame" or "step" through the film/video frames and see each still picture individually. Animation is made up of a series of individual drawings which, when shown at 24 or 30 fps, appear to move.

Apparent movement also occurs in the real world. Rows of light bulbs on outdoor signs are sometimes wired to blink in a specific sequence. When the rate of blinking is fast enough, the lights seems to "chase" or move along the row of bulbs.

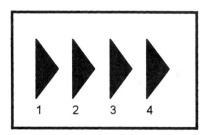

A series of stationary arrows on lighted signs can give the appearance of a single moving arrow. If each arrow is lit for a short time in rapid succession (indicated by the numbers 1 to 4) the arrows appear to move.

All of these examples are apparent movement because there's not really any movement at all.

INDUCED MOVEMENT

Induced movement occurs when a moving object transfers its movement to a nearby stationary object. The stationary object then appears to move and the moving object appears to be stationary.

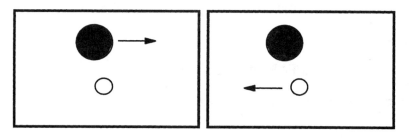

REAL MOVEMENT   INDUCED MOVEMENT

The black circle is moving to the right but, under certain conditions, we will perceive the white circle moving to the left. Usually the movement will transfer to the smaller and brighter object.

Moving clouds over a stationary moon is a good example of induced movement. If the cloud speed is correct, the moon will appear to move and the clouds will appear stationary. The induced movement of the moon will be in the opposite direction of the cloud's actual movement.

Induced movement sometimes occurs at a traffic intersection. Imagine you are in a car stopped next to a large bus. If the bus slowly moves forward, you may feel as if your car is drifting backwards. You're not really moving, but the forward movement of the bus induces the sense of movement in your car and you feel that you are moving in the opposite direction from the bus.

RELATIVE MOVEMENT

Relative movement occurs when the movement of one object can be gauged by its changing position relative to a second, stationary object.

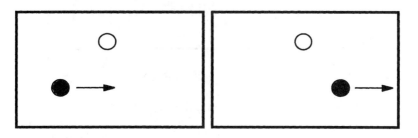

The black circle appears to move because its position changes relative to the stationary white circle and the frame.

Visual movement on a screen can only be produced when an object moves in relation to the frame line. When objects do not move in relation to the frame line, there's no on-screen movement. Here's an example.

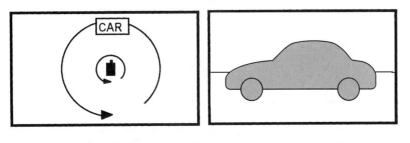

MAP   CAMERA VIEW

We will photograph a moving car in the open desert. The map shows that the car will drive in circles around the camera and the camera will pan with the car keeping it centered in the frame. The result will be that the car appears stationary in the frame and there is no relative movement.

Let's move to a new location. We'll leave the desert and find an open area in a forest.

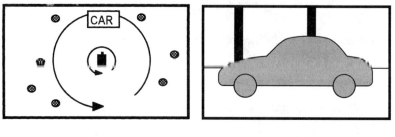

MAP   CAMERA VIEW

Again, we'll drive our car in a circle around the camera. As we pan the camera to follow the car, trees in the background will move in the opposite direction of the camera pan. The tree movement will show us the car is moving, but the car is still not moving in relation to the frame. Any movement within the frame will be generated by the moving trees.

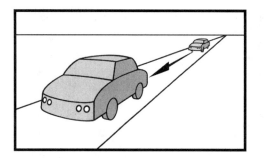

Let's move to a third location on an open road. This time, the car will drive through the shot and the camera will remain stationary. There will be no camera movement. Now the car creates useful movement because it's moving in relation to the frame. The car will move through the frame from upper right to lower left.

SIMPLE AND COMPLEX MOVEMENT

In the real world actual movement occurs in two or three dimensions. But the surface of the screen is only two-dimensional, so objects in the screen world can only move in two dimensions. There can be no movement in depth because the screen is flat.

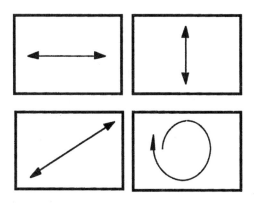

There are only a few ways an object can move in the screen world: horizontal, vertical, diagonal, or circular. These are called the *simple* moves.

What about objects in the real world that moved perpendicular to the picture plane advancing or receding from the camera when they were photographed? On the screen, these objects can't move in depth because the screen is flat. How do we define the movement of objects that create the illusion of depth on the screen? We call their movement *complex* because they're actually groups of simple moves combined onto a single moving object.

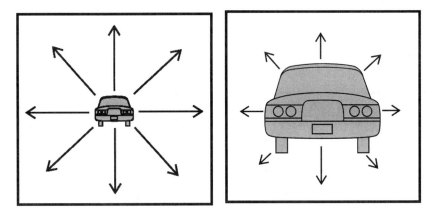

In the real world, a car can actually move in three dimensions and drive towards the camera. In the screen world it can't move towards us because the screen is flat. The car's movement, which appears deep, is a group of simple moves. The top of the car is moving up, the bottom is moving down, the left side is moving left, and the right side is moving right. It's a complex move because it combines many simple moves onto a single object. The more simple moves we combine on a single object, the more complex the movement will appear on screen.

We've defined various types of movement that exist in the real world and the screen world, but what is moving? In the screen world, there are three things that can move:

1. An object in front of the camera.
2. The camera.
3. The audience's point of attention as they watch the screen.

OBJECT MOVEMENT

A moving object generates a track. Track is defined as the path of a moving object. Track was discussed in detail in Chapter 4, "Line and Shape." Since all moving objects generate a track or line, our knowledge of line's subcomponents will help us understand the subcomponents of object movement. Object movement has four subcomponents.

DIRECTION

An object can move in a limited number of directions on a screen because the screen is only two-dimensional. Even when an object on the screen appears to move in three dimensions, all of the movement is only on the screen surface.

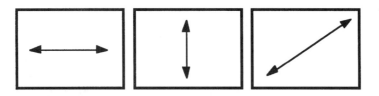

An object can make a horizontal, vertical, or diagonal move. Remember, object movement can only be seen when the object moves in relation to the frame line.

QUALITY

The movement of an object can be straight or curved.

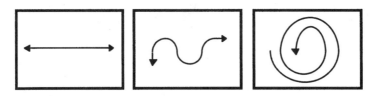

As the movement becomes more curved, it's complexity increases. Since moving objects generate a line, we can associate the same adjectives and emotional responses to straight and curved movement that we assigned to straight and curved lines.

Generally, a straight movement is associated with these terms: direct, aggressive, conservative, ordered, linear, unnatural, and rigid. A curved movement can be associated with these terms: indirect, passive, pertaining to nature, nonlinear, and flexible. This list is not complete or exact. You will elaborate and change this list according to your own personal feelings and the needs of your production.

SCALE

Scale refers to the distance an object moves on screen.

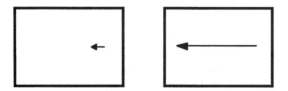

An object can travel a short distance or a longer distance in relation to the frame.

SPEED

A moving object will have a rate of speed: fast, medium, or slow, for example. A viewer will judge the object's speed relative to the frame.

CAMERA MOVEMENT

Camera movement has subcomponents, too. Some are similar to object movement, but some are not.

DIRECTION

A camera can move in two or three dimensions. The two-dimensional camera moves are the pan, tilt, and zoom. The three-dimensional camera moves are the dolly, track, and crane.

The audience perceives camera movement through the movement of objects in frame. Camera movement is transferred to the objects in frame that move in the opposite direction of the camera move. When the camera pans right, all objects will move to the left. A tilt up causes objects in frame to move down.

The same thing happens with three-dimensional camera moves. A track to the left will make objects in frame move to the right, and a crane up will make objects move down.

SCALE

Scale refers to a camera move's length of travel. A moving camera that dollies for hundreds of feet is not a reference to scale. Scale refers to the distance an object travels within the frame due to camera movement.

Creating well-motivated camera moves relies on linking the camera's movement with the movement of actors or other objects in the frame. Many photographers and directors dislike unmotivated camera movement.

SPEED

A camera movement can occur at different speeds, such as slow, medium, and fast. A distinct difference occurs in the speed of objects when we compare two- and three-dimensional camera moves. Remember that camera movement transfers its movement to objects in front of the camera.

If the camera pans, tilts, or zooms (two-dimensional moves) all objects in the frame will move at the same rate of speed. There is no relative movement. When the camera pans to the right, FG, MG, and BG objects will move in unison to the left. Tilting down will cause all objects in frame to move upwards at the same speed. A zoom in or out will create identical complex moves on all objects in the frame.

Three-dimensional camera moves can add relative movement. In a tracking shot, FG objects will move faster than BG objects. The same is true for a crane shot or a dolly in/out. A complete description of relative movement can be found in Part One of Chapter 3, "Space."

POINT OF ATTENTION

The third type of movement is called *point of attention* which refers to where the audience is looking. Human vision can only look at one small area at a time. Although we have peripheral vision, which allows us to see a wide field of view, we can only concentrate our attention on a small area. When you look at a crowd of people, you can only examine individuals one at a time. You may shift your attention from person to person to get a sense of the group, but you can only look at one person at a time.

The same thing happens when the audience looks at a screen. Although they're aware of the entire frame, they can only look at one small area of the screen at a time. This is fortunate, because it means we can predict and control what area of the frame the audience will be watching at any time.

But what does the audience want to look at? What attracts the audience's eye? Movement is first. The viewer's attention will always be drawn to a moving object. Brightness is second. If there is no movement, the viewer's point of attention will be drawn to the brightest area in the frame. If the moving objects also happen to be the brightest area of the frame, the viewer will notice that area even faster. When the audience is looking at an actor's face, their point of attention will always be drawn to the eyes.

The subcomponents for point of attention are similar to the subcomponents for object and camera movement.

DIRECTION

As the audience moves their point of attention around the frame, their eye movement creates a track. Remember, track is the path of a moving object, and here the moving object is the audience's point of attention.

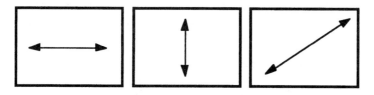

Since the screen is flat, there are only three directions point of attention can move. As usual, the choices are horizontal, vertical, and diagonal.

QUALITY

If the audience is watching a moving object that generates a curved line, their eye movement will also be curvilinear. If the movement they're watching is linear, their point of attention will generate straight lines. As the audience moves their point of attention between stationary objects, they will take the shortest path to get there. So their eye movement will always create straight lines.

SCALE

Scale refers to the distance the audience's point of attention travels in relation to the frame line.

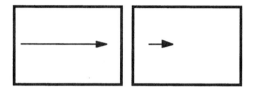

Later in this chapter we'll discuss continuum of movement where the scale of the audience's eye movement is critical.

CONTRAST AND AFFINITY

Since movement can be produced by an object, the camera, or the audience's point of attention, there are many ways to create contrast and affinity. Remember, contrast and affinity can occur within a shot, from shot to shot, and from sequence to sequence.

MOVEMENT OF A SINGLE OBJECT

A moving object generates a track, which is an actual or virtual line.

Direction

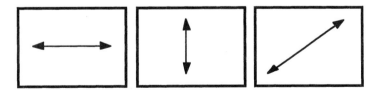

A horizontal movement appears to be the least intense. A vertical movement will have more intensity, and a diagonal movement (in any direction) will be the most intense.

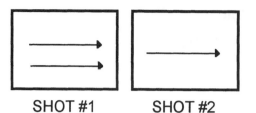

SHOT #1   SHOT #2

Shot #1 is an example of affinity of direction of movement within the shot. There are two separate objects and they're both moving in the same direction. Shots #1 and #2 illustrate affinity of direction of movement from shot to shot. Since Shots #1 and #2 have affinity, their visual intensity or dynamic is low.

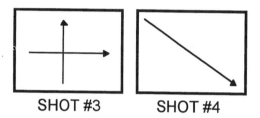

SHOT #3   SHOT #4

Shot #3 is an example of contrast of direction of movement within the shot. Shots #3 and #4 illustrate contrast of direction of movement from shot to shot, so their visual intensity or dynamic is high.

Quality
Object movement can generate straight or curved tracks.

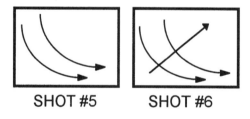

SHOT #5   SHOT #6

Shot #5 illustrates affinity of quality of movement within the shot, and Shot #6 illustrates contrast within the shot. Shot #5 is less intense than Shot #6.

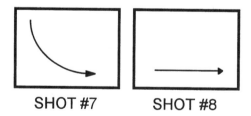

SHOT #7   SHOT #8

Shots #7 and #8 illustrate contrast of quality of movement from shot to shot. One movement is curved and the other is straight. This contrast of quality of line produces visual contrast.

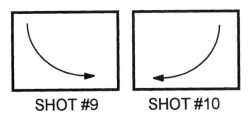

SHOT #9   SHOT #10

Shots #9 and #10 illustrate affinity of quality of object movement. The visual intensity is low because the movement in both shots generates a curved line or track.

Scale

Another factor to consider is the size of the object's movement relative to the frame.

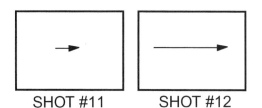

SHOT #11   SHOT #12

A larger move will have greater visual intensity than a small move. These two shots illustrate contrast of movement scale from shot to shot.

Speed

A moving object will have a speed: slow, medium, or fast, for example. If all objects move slowly, affinity of speed is produced and the intensity will be low. If one object moves faster in a group of slow-moving objects, contrast is created, which will generate more visual intensity.

MOVEMENT OF AN OBJECT WITH A BACKGROUND

We can also examine the contrast and affinity that can be created between the line generated by a single moving object and the linear motif of a background. Remember, linear motif is the shot reduced to its primary or basic lines.

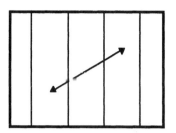

The arrow represents the moving object, and the lines are the linear motif of the background. When a moving object and the linear motif of a background are combined, a relationship is immediately created. This pairing of object and background is the basis for another visual progression.

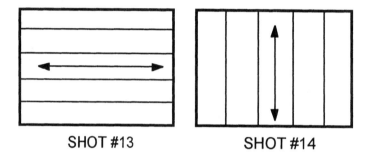

SHOT #13   **SHOT #14**

The least visually intense pairing of object movement and background linear motif is illustrated in Shot #13. It shows a horizontal background and an object moving horizontally. We know that horizontals are inherently the least intense or dynamic line, therefore parallel horizontals are the least dynamic combination of background linear motif and object movement. More dynamic, but still quite low in intensity, is Shot #14 where the object is moving parallel to the vertical linear motif of the background.

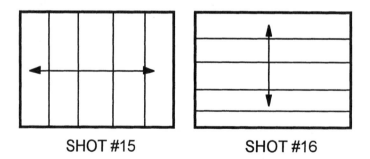

SHOT #15   **SHOT #16**

Shots #15 and #16 have more overall intensity. The lines created by the background are in opposite direction to the moving object. This contrast in direction of line creates more visual contrast and greater overall intensity.

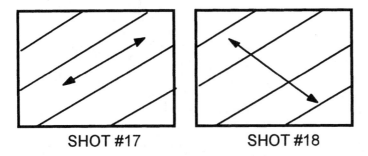

SHOT #17   SHOT #18

These combinations produce the most intensity in our visual progression. Shot #17 creates intensity because it uses diagonals. We learned in Chapter 4, "Line and Shape," that the diagonal line is most intense. When the object movement is parallel to the diagonal linear motif of the background, the intensity will be high because there are so many diagonals. Shot #18 is the most intense because it uses opposing diagonal lines. This gives us contrast of direction and a shot comprised of diagonals, which have the greatest amount of inherent visual intensity.

This progression of moving object and background is not exact because you must always look at the specifics of your visual situation. The speed, size, tonal range, and, of course, the actual subject against the complexity of the background, can alter the affinity or contrast of the visual relationships. These diagrams are only a general guide.

CAMERA MOVEMENT

Affinity will keep the camera movement consistent within a shot, from shot to shot, from sequence to sequence, or for an entire production. You might decide to only use two-dimensional camera moves (pan, tilt, and zoom), or you might limit yourself even further and use only pans. On the other hand, you might decide to use one or more of the three-dimensional camera moves (dolly, track, and crane). Whenever you limit your choice of subcomponents, you will create visual unity in your production.

Contrast of camera movement is more complex because there are so many ways to achieve it. Consider these pairs of contrasting camera movements:

1. *Movement/No Movement.* The greatest contrast to camera movement is no movement at all. If an entire production is photographed with a stationary camera, a camera move will produce visual contrast and intensity. On the other hand, if the camera is constantly moving and stops, visual contrast will also be created.

2. *2-D/3-D Moves.* You can limit your choices of camera movement to two-dimensional (pan, tilt, zoom) or three-dimensional (dolly, track, crane) moves. The visual difference between them is large. Two-dimensional moves will prevent relative moment from occurring, and three-dimensional moves will generate relative movement. The relative movement can be increased by placing FG as close to the camera as possible and BG objects very far away.

2a. *Pan/Track*. A pan will create more visual affinity than a tracking move. This is due to the three-dimensional relative movement created by the tracking of the camera. Relative movement is discussed in detail in Part One of Chapter 3, "Space."

2b. *Tilt/Crane*. The tilt is usually less intense. The crane shot, depending on the FG and BG object placement, will be more intense.

2c. *Zoom/Dolly*. A zoom lens will enlarge or shrink all objects in frame at exactly the same rate. There will be no relative size or speed changes between any objects in a zoom shot. A dolly, especially with a wide lens, produces more visual intensity because it generates changes in the relative size and speed of objects.

There is one exception to this rule: a "snap zoom," which is an extremely rapid zoom in or out. A snap zoom will always add unusual visual intensity because it produces sudden contrasts in size and movement speed that cannot be achieved with a moving camera.

3. *Level/Unlevel*. A tripod- or dolly-mounted camera will have more affinity when compared to a hand-held camera move. The physical nature of a dolly is to keep the camera movement level to the horizon. A hand-held camera, being used without the aid of special harnesses or leveling devices, will create additional movement. Vertical and horizontal lines will become diagonal as the camera moves, and this will translate into an increase in visual intensity or dynamic.

The extreme version of an unlevel camera is an *axis rotation*. Most of the time, we keep our cameras level to the horizon. Vertical and horizontal lines remain upright and level. As the camera rotates, these lines shift into moving diagonals. Diagonal lines are always more intense than horizontals or verticals. Many different types of camera rigs exist that will allow the camera to rotate on the axis of the lens, giving the shot a spinning motion. The greater the degree of spin, the more intense the visual contrast when compared to a level camera.

4. *Scale of Movement*. Generally speaking, the larger the camera move the greater the visual intensity, and the smaller the camera move the less the visual intensity.

5. *Object/Camera Movement*. Object and camera movement shouldn't be separated, because object movement usually motivates camera movement. There are four fundamental combinations possible between the movement of the object and the camera:

1. Stationary object and stationary camera.
2. Moving object and stationary camera.
3. Stationary object and moving camera.
4. Moving object and moving camera.

We can look at these four combinations as a visual progression. A progression can be used to intensify a sequence or group of sequences by moving from simple to complex. The least intense is #1 (stationary object and stationary camera). The most intense is #4 (moving object and moving camera).

6. *Frames per Second Speed*. We can alter the speed of a movement by changing the speed of the camera. Classically this is called overcranking (slow motion) or undercranking (fast motion).

A film projector always runs at 24 fps (frames per second), and when the camera is run normally at 24 fps, the movement recorded by the camera will look normal when projected. An identical situation occurs with video where recorders and playback systems normally run at 30 fps (technically the speed is 29.9 fps).

If the camera's film is run at 48 fps and projected at 24 fps, the photographed action will take twice as long to view. There were 48 pictures filmed each second, but they're being projected at 24 each second, so it will take two seconds to playback what was photographed in one second. This will produce slow motion. There are cameras that run film at hundreds, even thousands of frames a second, which can make a one-second event last five minutes when projected.

If the film camera is run at only 12 fps and the projector still runs at 24 fps, the film will move twice as fast during projection so the action will speed up.

The extreme example of undercranking (the camera running at less than 24 fps) is time-lapse photography. We can photograph objects that move very slowly (a flower blooming or clouds moving) and speed them up so that their slow movement becomes visible. For example, if a building under construction is photographed with only one frame of film a day, an entire year can be condensed into 15 seconds (365 frames projected at 24 fps will run about 15 seconds).

Fast or slow motion photography can be used for various effects in storytelling. Speed changes from shot to shot or within a shot can enhance the flow of movement in a scene. An audience will become more aware of movements when they're slowed down or sped up. Certain events that may happen too quickly (like an action sequence) can be seen more clearly when the speed of the event is slowed down. Speed changes can also suggest moving from real time into a dream or mental time. A change in the movement's speed can increase the dramatic value of the story.

CONTINUUM OF MOVEMENT

Earlier in this chapter, eye movement and the audience's point of attention were defined. Let's discuss these in more detail. Contrast and affinity of continuum of movement allows us to control the visual intensity generated by the audience's eye movement as they watch the screen. This movement occurs within the shot and from shot to shot. Like any visual component, a contrast in the continuum will always create greater visual intensity. As the affinity of continuum of movement increases, the visual intensity will decrease.

The smaller the screen the less critical continuum of movement becomes. Since the average television or computer screen is only nineteen inches, the physical range available for contrast of continuum is quite small. On the other hand, theater screens and especially giant formats like Imax (with screens in the hundred-foot range) have continuum of movement possibilities that cannot be ignored.

Continuum of movement deals with two concepts:

1. How the viewer's point of attention moves within a shot.
2. How the viewer's point of attention moves from shot to shot.

Defining continuum of movement within a single shot will help us understand what continuum is all about.

CONTINUUM WITHIN THE SHOT

The eye is always attracted by movement. The audience's point of attention will always follow a moving object.

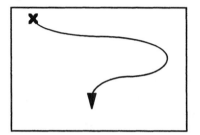

This arrow indicates movement of an object through the frame. The moving object might be a car, a falling leaf, or a person jogging along a path. Whatever the cause of the movement, the audience's point of attention (indicated by the X) will follow the object as it moves around the frame. The audience's moving point of attention will generate a curved line identical to the movement of the object.

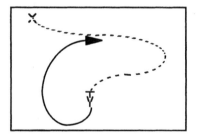

If a second object starts to move in the same shot beginning where the first object stopped, we have created affinity of continuum of movement. The audience's point of attention will be smoothly transferred from the first object to the second object because the second object started where the first object ended. This affinity of continuum moves the audience's point of attention around the screen in a choreographed pattern following the first then the second object. Ernst Lubitsch's movies of the 1930s and the long continuous takes in many Martin Scorsese films use this technique.

We can also create contrast of continuum within a shot.

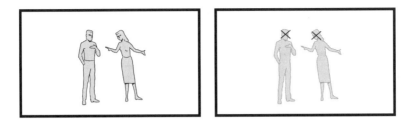

Here is a shot of two people talking. The audience's point of attention will move back and forth between the two faces depending upon who is talking. Because the audience has to move their point of attention during the shot from one face to another, and there is no on-screen movement to lead them back and forth, contrast of continuum of movement is created. The audience's point of attention is not visually guided from face to face (affinity of continuum), so they must abruptly move their point of attention each time the conversation changes speakers.

If the distance between the two people is increased, the contrast of continuum increases. Now the audience must shift their point of attention from one side of the frame to the other.

CONTINUUM FROM SHOT TO SHOT

Let's look at a pair of shots and see how continuum of movement can be used from shot to shot.

SHOT #1   SHOT #2

Shot #1 is a wide shot of an actor standing in a doorway. Shot #2 is a close-up of the same actor looking around. Our point of attention in Shot #1 will be the actor in the doorway and our point of attention in Shot #2 will be the eyes of the actor's face. When these two shots are cut together, we'll create contrast of continuum of movement because on the edit, our attention will shift from the doorway to the actor's eyes on the opposite side of the frame.

If we superimpose the two shots, we can see the two different attention points at the same time.

On the cut, the audience's point of attention jumps from screen right to screen left. This generates contrast of continuum of movement.

We could recompose these two shots to create affinity of continuum of movement.

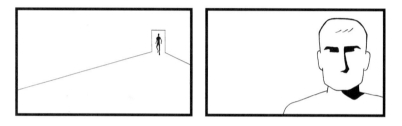

The actor in the doorway is the same, but the close-up of the actor has been composed differently. With both shots superimposed we can see how the points of attention match.

We've produced affinity of continuum of movement because the audience's point of attention is the same in both shots. The audience is looking at the same area of the screen on the last frame of the outgoing shot and the first frame of the incoming shot. The audience will not have to move their point of attention at the cut.

To help us remember what area of the frame the audience is watching, we can draw a nine-area grid and place it over our screen or frame. We call it a *Continuum Grid*.

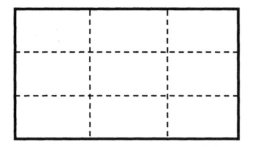

We'll need a method of labeling the areas of the Continuum Grid, and there are several ways to do this:

1	2	3
4	5	6
7	8	9

A	B	C
D	E	F
G	H	J

Use numbers or letters (leave out the I, it's often confusing).

TL	TC	TR
CL	C	CR
LL	LC	LR

UR	UC	UL
CR	C	CL
DR	DC	DL

Use camera/screen directions like top-left (TL), center-left (CL), lower left (LL). You can also use stage directions from the theater (which are the opposite of camera directions): up-right (UR), center-right (CR), and down-right (DR).

Any one of the four systems is fine, just pick one and use it consistently through your preparation, production, and postproduction.

The director, camera operator, script supervisor, or editor can indicate on the Continuum Grid where the audience's point of attention is located at any time during a shot. This area can be recorded in the continuity script, storyboard, or editing notes and referred to when the following or preceding shot is photographed. Television monitors make this process extremely easy because you can actually play back previously shot scenes and check the audience's point of attention.

Continuum of movement becomes particularly critical when intercutting shots of stationary objects. A classic example is the over-the-shoulder shot. This usually involves two stationary actors facing each other. Typically the camera photographs the scene from both sides of the conversation and the two shots are intercut as often as the nature of the scene dictates.

Individually, these two over-the-shoulder shots might appear acceptable but when they're intercut, the contrast of continuum of movement will make the editing harsh and abrupt. This may be what you had planned, but often the idea is to make the intercutting of over-the-shoulder shots as smooth as possible.

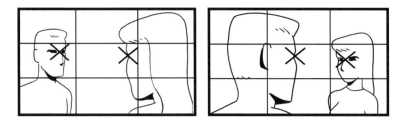

Let's place an "X" on the eyes of each person. The eyes are the places the audience is most likely to watch in each shot. The Continuum Grid helps to show us that there is contrast of continuum of movement from shot to shot. If the audience is watching the man, they will have to move their attention from the left to the center area of the frame when the editor cuts to the second angle.

When the two shots are overlapped, the contrast of continuum becomes clear. Look how far the audience must move to keep their point of attention focused on the man.

Over-the-shoulder shots are composed for the purpose of intercutting. Affinity of continuum of movement will help create a smooth cut that goes unnoticed by the audience.

Now the two shots have been recomposed to create affinity of continuum of movement from shot to shot.

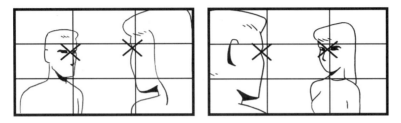

The Continuum Grid shows that the audience's points of attention are now in the same areas of the screen in both shots.

Superimposing the two shots confirms the affinity of continuum. When these recomposed over-the-shoulder shots are intercut, the affinity of continuum will help make the edit smooth and more invisible to the audience.

Continuum of movement is used by the director and cinematographer, but it ultimately comes under the control of the editor. Obviously, the editor's continuum control will be limited by the shots produced during production, but sequences shot without any attention to continuum of movement can still be manipulated by the editor who understands how continuum works.

Once in the editing room, it is easy to determine where the audience is looking in any shot. Run the shot on your editing equipment and be aware of your own point of attention. Stop the footage and mark the viewing screen with a grease pencil. You've probably found the correct point of attention based on your own natural sensibilities. If you're still not sure, watch the footage without sound in a darkened room and your natural visual intuition will usually take over and direct your eye to the same point on the screen that will attract the audience.

Continuum of movement is a nearly invisible visual component. As the screen size increases so does the chance for greater contrasts of continuum of movement. As the screen shrinks in size, the chances for contrast of continuum diminish.

How does contrast and affinity of continuum of movement effect an audience? First, it guides their point of attention as they look around the frame, and secondly it changes the affect editorial cutting has on the audience.

Affinity of continuum guides the audience's point of attention around the frame. Using affinity of continuum, the picture-maker has control over what area of the screen the audience is watching (a very important consideration in television commercials) and how the eye moves to those different areas. This smooth movement of the audience's point of attention will give great visual continuity to a series of movements within a shot.

Continuum of movement also affects the audience's awareness of cuts or edits. A film is made up of many shots that are edited together. There are some wonderful exceptions like Hitchcock's *Rope* (1948), which appears to be one long, continuous eighty-minute shot with no edits at all. But usually our films are assembled from many shots that have been edited together.

In a completed film, we don't want the audience to notice every edit. They should believe that the edited shots are taking place smoothly and continuously. We want them to feel that the various camera setups that may have taken weeks to complete actually occurred in real continuous time. Affinity of continuum of movement will improve visual continuity and is such a powerful visual tool that it will disguise edits with continuity errors or that jump the stage line. Affinity makes visual events appear continuous and smooth. The films of Ernst Lubitsch, such as *Trouble in Paradise* (1932) and *Ninotchka* (1939), owe much of their visual "Lubitsch Touch" to affinity of continuum of movement.

If affinity of continuum is such a great tool, why would we ever use contrast of continuum of movement? Often we want to create events that are visually jarring and abrupt. We may want to show that one event is over and a new event is beginning. We may want the audience to feel that a sequence is not smooth, but disjointed and intense. The visual intensity created by contrast of continuum will have an effect on the viewer. We can make the audience become agitated or excited by forcing them to quickly move their attention to different points on the screen.

The contrast or affinity of continuum of movement in a shot or series of shots can be planned in a storyboard.

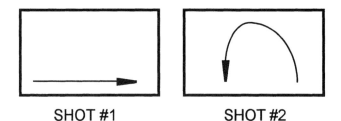

SHOT #1   SHOT #2

Shot #1 indicates that an object's movement (a moving car, a running actor, etc.) starts in the lower left and moves in a straight line to the lower right of the frame. In Shot #2 the movement begins in the same spot where the movement ended in Shot #1 and moves in a curved line around the frame.

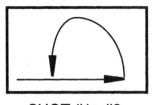

SHOT #1+ #2

When overlapped, the continuum of movement is easy to see. The audience's point of attention will move with Shot #1 and smoothly transition into Shot #2. This is an excellent example of affinity of continuum of movement from shot to shot.

SHOT #3   SHOT #4

Shots #3 and #4 illustrate contrast of continuum of movement from shot to shot. In Shot #3 the object moves from lower left to lower right, but on the cut to Shot #4, the audience's point of attention must quickly move to the upper right to find the start of the next moving object. Because the audience shifts their attention on the cut, contrast of continuum of movement is created.

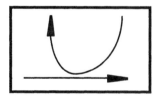
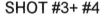

SHOT #3+ #4

When Shots #3 and #4 are combined, we can see the contrast of continuum of movement. There are two tracks or lines generated by the moving objects.

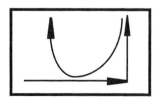

SHOT #3+ #4

But the combination of Shots #3 and #4 really has three lines. Two are created by the moving objects and a third line is generated by the audience's point of attention moving from the lower right area of the frame to the upper right to find the moving object in Shot #4.

To understand the importance of continuum of movement, let's look at a moving object's linear motif in a longer storyboard sequence. Remember, linear motif is the shot's movement reduced to its basic line.

STORYBOARD #1

Here's a storyboard showing the linear motif of a single moving object in a series of shots.

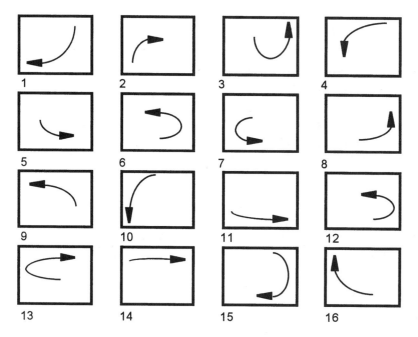

Notice the curved (curvilinear) motif and the affinity of continuum of movement. The viewer's point of attention will be left off and picked up at the same area of the frame from shot to shot.

Combining all of the Storyboard #1 panels into a single frame reveals the linear motif created by the object movement from shot to shot. It looks like this:

STORYBOARD #1   SHOTS 1-16

You can see how the eye's path of movement during Storyboard #1 will be circular and fairly smooth.

STORYBOARD #2

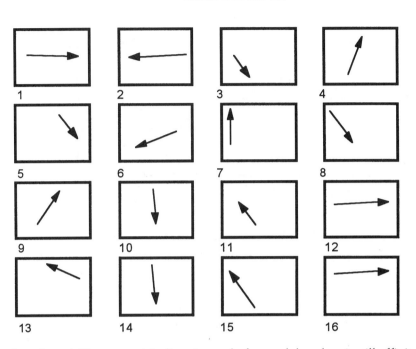

Storyboard #2 uses straight lines instead of curved, but there's still affinity of continuum of movement. The incoming frame picks up where the outgoing frame left off.

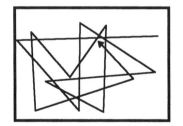

STORYBOARD #2   SHOTS 1-16

When we combine all the panels of Storyboard #2 into a single frame, the linear motif of the movement is angular but there's still a strong continuous feeling generated by the affinity of continuum of movement.

STORYBOARD #3

This linear motif is full of contrasts.

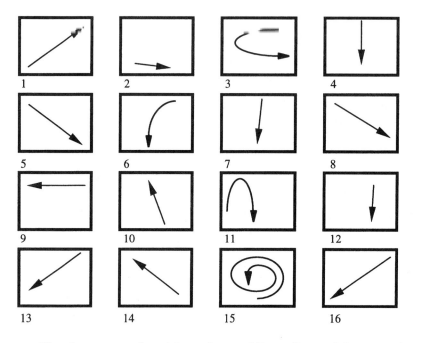

There's contrast of straight and curved lines, diagonal, horizontal, and vertical tracks, and contrast of continuum of movement. The point of attention is never the same on the last frame of the outgoing shot and the first frame of the incoming shot.

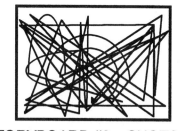

STORYBOARD #3   SHOTS 1-16

This is the linear motif of the panels in Storyboard #3, which is obviously more intense because it shows so much visual contrast.

The total number of lines has doubled. First, there are the lines generated by the tracks of the moving objects, but there are also lines produced by the track of the audience's moving point of attention.

Storyboards #1, #2, and #3 create a visual progression. Based purely on its amount of contrast and affinity, Storyboard #1 has the least intensity because there's so much visual affinity. Storyboard #3 is the most intense because of the visual contrasts of line quality, line direction, line intensity, and continuum of movement.

FILMS TO WATCH

1. CONTINUUM OF MOVEMENT
   Ninotchka (1939)
   Directed by Ernst Lubitsch
   Written by Charles Brackett, Billy Wilder, and Walter Reisch
   Photographed by William Daniels
   Art Direction by Cedric Gibbons

   Lawrence of Arabia (1962)
   Directed by David Lean
   Written by Robert Bolt
   Photographed by Frederick Francis
   Production Design by John Box

   Die Hard (1988)
   Directed by John McTiernan
   Written by Jeb Stuart and Steven deSouza
   Photographed by Jan DeBont
   Production Design by Jackson DeGovia

   Goodfellas (1990)
   Directed by Martin Scorsese
   Written by Scorsese and Nicholas Pileggi
   Photographed by Michael Ballhaus
   Production Design by Kristi Zea

   Touch of Evil (1958)
   Directed by Orson Welles
   Written by Orson Welles
   Photographed by Russel Metty
   Art Direction by Robert Clatworthy

2. CAMERA MOVEMENT
   Das Boot (1981)
   Directed by Wolfgang Peterson
   Written by Wolfgang Peterson
   Photographed by Jost Vacano
   Production Design by Klaus Doldinger

   The Verdict (1982)
   Directed by Sidney Lumet
   Written by David Mamet
   Photographed by Andrzej Bartkowiak
   Production Design by Edward Pisoni

   The Insider (1999)
   Directed by Michael Mann
   Written by Mann and Eric Roth
   Photographed by Dante Spinotti
   Production Design by Brian Morris

3. OBJECT MOVEMENT

8 1/2 (1963)
    Directed by Frederico Fellini
    Written by Fellini and Ennio Fiaiano
    Photographed by Gianni di Venanzo
    Art Direction by Piero Gherardi

Gold Diggers of 1935 (1935)
    Directed by Busby Berkeley
    Written by Manuel Seff and Peter Milne
    Photographed by George Burns

Gold Diggers of 1937 (1937)
    Directed by Lloyd Bacon
    Choreographed by Busby Berkeley
    Written by Warren Duff
    Photographed by Arthur Edeson

C H A P T E R 8

RHYTHM

Rhythm is easy to experience but difficult to describe. We perceive rhythm in three different ways. There's rhythm we can hear, rhythm we can see, and rhythm we can feel. Any rhythm is made up of three subcomponents: alternation, repetition, and tempo. Since we're most familiar with rhythm we can hear, let's define rhythm's subcomponents using the sound from a musician's metronome. A metronome's ticking sound creates beats that we recognize as rhythm.

ALTERNATION

We understand a metronome's rhythm because there's a beat followed by a moment of silence and then another beat. We hear the rhythm because of the alternation between sound and silence. Without alternation there can't be any rhythm.

The type of alternation can vary. There is alternation between sound and silence, strong sounds and weak sounds, or groups of sounds and single sounds.

The sounds of a ticking clock, walking feet, and a bouncing ball reveal their rhythms because of the alternation. The sound of a constantly humming motor doesn't have rhythm because it lacks the ingredient of alternation. White sound has no rhythm because it's continuous and without alternation.

REPETITION

We recognize the rhythm of a metronome because the alternation repeats. The alternation must repeat. A single beat from a metronome doesn't produce a rhythm.

We can't recognize the rhythm of walking feet if the walker only takes one step. If a ball only bounces once, it won't create a rhythm. In order for a rhythm to be recognized, the alternation must repeat so that a rhythm can be established.

TEMPO

A metronome has a speed control to change the time between beats. Any rhythm has a rate of alternation and repetition that is called *tempo*. The rhythmic difference between walking and running is tempo. If the interval of time between beats is short, a faster tempo is created. If the interval of time between beats is long, it's a slower tempo.

A metronome produces a rhythm we can hear, but now we must define rhythm we can see and learn how to use it. The same subcomponents of alternation, repetition, and tempo apply to visual rhythm. Visual rhythm can be created by stationary objects, moving objects, and editorial cutting.

RHYTHM OF STATIONARY OBJECTS

We create visual rhythm by placing stationary objects in the frame. This is called composition. Composition is the arrangement of objects within the frame. First, let's look at a frame that doesn't contain any objects.

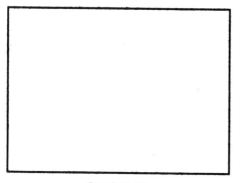

SHOT #1

Shot #1 is an empty frame. It is the visual equivalent of white sound. This shot has no visual rhythm because there isn't any alternation, repetition, or tempo.

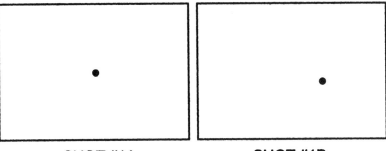

SHOT #1A   **SHOT #1B**

Now, an object, a dot, has been added and the empty frame suddenly takes on a rhythmic personality.

Shots #1A and #1B both have rhythm, but why does Shot 1B appear more intense than Shot 1A?

A clue to the answer is revealed when we draw lines through the dot.

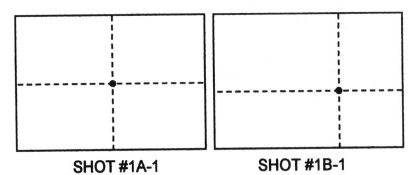

SHOT #1A-1   **SHOT #1B-1**

Shot #1A-1 divides the frame into four equal areas, and Shot #1B-1 divides the frame into four unequal areas. The Principle of Contrast and Affinity tells us that affinity (four *equal* areas) reduces visual intensity and contrast (four *unequal* areas) increases visual intensity. How the frame is divided and how we look at the divisions is the key to understanding visual rhythm in stationary objects.

With this basic concept in mind, let's place a more complex object in our frame and discuss the results in greater detail.

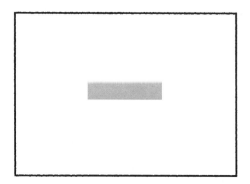

SHOT #2

When a single object, a gray rectangle, is placed in the frame, a visual rhythm is created. It generates alternation, repetition, and tempo. But these subcomponents are invisible. We need a visual method of revealing the rhythm so we can understand how it works and how we can control it.

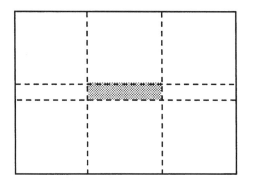

SHOT #3

If we extend the sides of the gray rectangle by adding dotted lines, we reveal how the gray rectangle has produced a visual rhythm. The dotted lines show how the gray rectangle has divided the frame into smaller areas. Each area becomes a visual beat. A beat creates rhythm. Some of these beats produced by the gray rectangle are accented and some are unaccented, which creates alternation.

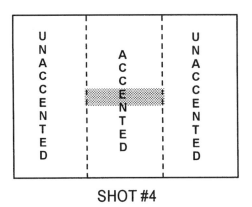

SHOT #4

If we examine the vertical lines created by the gray rectangle, the frame has been divided into thirds. There is alternation between these thirds. The center third is an accented beat because it contains the gray rectangle. The thirds on the left and right are unaccented because they don't contain any objects. Just as sound rhythm alternates between sound and silence, Shot #4 illustrates how the visual rhythm alternates between accented and unaccented beats. Sometimes the term "positive space" is used for accented areas and "negative space" is used for unaccented areas of the frame.

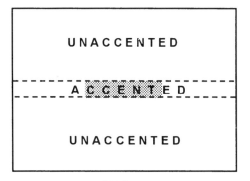

SHOT #5

There is also alternation in the horizontal divisions created by the gray rectangle. The narrow accented band in the center alternates with the larger unaccented areas above and below it.

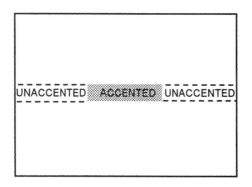

SHOT #6

The narrow center band can be divided into alternating thirds. The gray rectangle and the narrow bands to its left and right create alternation. The gray rectangle is accented and the two side areas are unaccented.

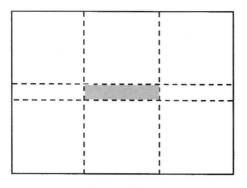

SHOT #7

The gray rectangle has also created repetition. The dotted lines show how the gray rectangle has divided the frame into many smaller areas. The recurrence of these areas creates repetition.

Dividing the frame has also created tempo. Our eye scans the entire frame and makes several instantaneous measurements. We measure the distance between the gray rectangle and the frame lines, and we measure the size and proportion of the divided areas of the frame. As the number of areas increases, the tempo speeds up. The tempo in Shot #7 is slow. If the frame were divided into more parts, the tempo would increase.

The three stationary ovals in Shot #8 represent a moderate rhythm.

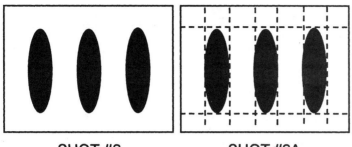

SHOT #8   SHOT #8A

When we add dotted lines between the ovals, the alternation, repetition, and tempo are revealed. There is alternation between the ovals and the space around them. There is repetition in the ovals themselves, and there is a faster tempo created by the number of frame divisions.

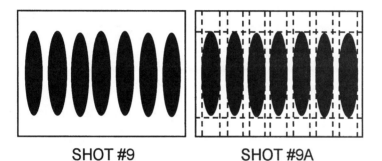

SHOT #9   SHOT #9A

Shot #9 illustrates alternation and repetition, and the tempo is even faster because there are more ovals that divide the frame into more parts.

But we don't make films or videos about rectangles and ovals, so we need to relate these rhythm concepts back to the real world.

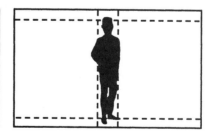

SHOT #10   SHOT #10A

In Shot #10, the ovals have been replaced by an actor, but as you can see, the subcomponents of visual rhythm are still present. If we draw dotted lines (Shot #10A) around the actor, the frame is once again divided into separate areas.

There is alternation. The actor becomes the accent surrounded by unaccented areas. There is repetition, because the frame is divided into more than one area, and the tempo is slow, because there are so few divisions within the frame.

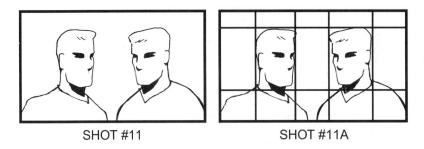

SHOT #11   SHOT #11A

Shot #11 is a "two-shot." Adding dotted lines reveals the shot's alternation, repetition, and tempo.

SHOT #12   SHOT #12A

Shot #12 is also a two-shot, but it's composed differently. Adding dotted lines between the heads reveals how the visual rhythm has been effected.

There is alternation and repetition, but the divided areas of the frame are unequal so there is a changing tempo as the viewer looks around the frame.

You can examine any shot and determine the visual rhythm of the stationary objects in the frame. Applying the Principle of Contrast and Affinity to rhythm will help you structure the composition of your shots.

RHYTHM OF MOVING OBJECTS

An object must move in relation to the frame line to create movement. If the object and the camera are moving together so that the object remains stationary in the frame, there is no visually useful movement. If, however, the object is actually moving in relation to the frame, we have movement that may produce a visual rhythm, although movement will not necessarily create rhythm.

There are two types of rhythm in moving objects: primary and secondary. A primary rhythm is created by the movement of a whole object. When a part of the whole object moves independently, a secondary rhythm can be created.

PRIMARY RHYTHM

There are four ways a moving object can create a primary visual rhythm:

1. Entering and exiting the frame.
2. Moving in front of or behind another object.

3. Starting and stopping.
4. Changing direction.

Let's use the movement of a soccer ball to define these four methods of creating primary visual rhythm.

1. *Entering and Exiting the Frame.* When an object crosses the frame line, a single visual beat is created.

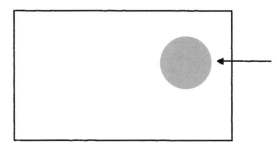

SHOT #13

But the ball entering the frame cannot create rhythm because a single beat lacks alternation, repetition, and tempo.

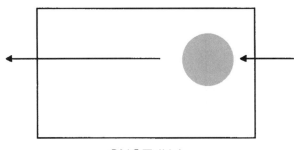

SHOT #14

If the ball enters and exits the frame, a rhythm may be created. Entering and exiting produces two beats, so now the moving ball has alternation.

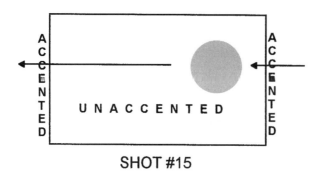

SHOT #15

The alternation is created because the frame lines act as visual accents in contrast to the frame area that is unaccented. Repetition is also produced because there are two frame lines and the ball crosses both of them. Tempo is also created because the viewer senses the amount of time it takes the ball to move from one frame line to the other.

If several objects enter or exit the frame, a more complicated visual rhythm can be created. Each object's entrance or exit produces an additional visual beat.

2. *Moving in Front of or Behind Another Object.* We can create visual beats when a moving object passes in front of or behind other objects.

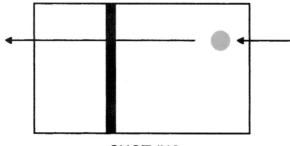

SHOT #16

The ball will enter frame, move past a FG object (drawn here as a pole), and exit the frame. As the ball passes the pole it will produce another visual beat like the ones created when the ball entered and exited the frame.

SHOT #17

Additional FG or BG objects, generate more alternation and repetition, and the tempo will increase because each new object will add a beat.

3. *Starting and Stopping.* If an object starts and stops moving in frame more than once, a visual rhythm is produced.

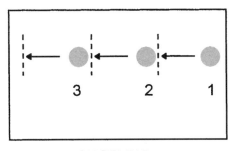

SHOT #18

The stopping and starting ball has alternation, repetition, and tempo, just like a metronome.

4. *Changing Direction.* A change in direction, if it happens more than once, will also create a visual rhythm.

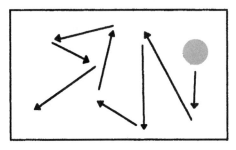

SHOT #19

Each change in the direction of the ball's movement will produce visual alternation, repetition, and tempo.

SECONDARY RHYTHM

A secondary rhythm is generated by the movement of part of an object that already generates a primary rhythm. Let's describe the secondary rhythms of some objects:

1. A walking person. The secondary rhythm is produced by the walker's moving legs.
2. Dancers. Different dance steps give a moving dancer's legs and feet a secondary rhythm.
3. A flying bird. The flapping wings will produce a secondary rhythm.
4. A drummer in a marching band. Here, two secondary rhythms can be created. One is the marching feet and the second is the moving drumsticks.

Let's examine the two rhythms produced by the movement of a walking person.

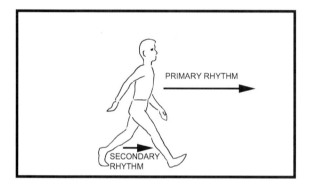

There is a primary rhythm as the person enters and exits frame, passes foreground objects, stops and starts or changes direction, but there is also a secondary rhythm produced by the person's moving legs and feet that has alternation, repetition, and tempo completely separate from the primary rhythm.

Secondary rhythms are often mistaken for primary rhythms. A running person may not have a primary rhythm at all, only a secondary rhythm created by his or her moving legs. Running in place creates a primary rhythm because the runner changes directions as he or she bounces up and down in place. The secondary rhythm is still created by the moving legs. A tap dancer's primary rhythm can be slow as the dancer moves past stationary objects, but the secondary rhythm, created by his or her moving feet, can be fast.

RHYTHM OF A MOVING CAMERA

Any camera movement is transferred to the objects in the frame. If we pan left, the objects in frame move to the right. This means that moving the camera produces object movement. If a camera movement causes an object to enter and exit frame, stop and start or change direction, the camera move has caused object movement to generate rhythm.

EDITORIAL RHYTHM

There is rhythm in editing. Every time the editor makes a cut, a new rhythmic beat is produced. Editorial rhythm has the same basic components of alternation, repetition and tempo. Editorial alternation occurs because the cut is an accent or beat. The greater the visual contrast in the visual components from shot to shot, the stronger the beat produced by the cut.

SHOT #21

SHOT #22

If we cut intercut Shots #21 and #22, the alternation will be intense (due to the tonal contrast), and a strong visual beat will be produced by the edit.

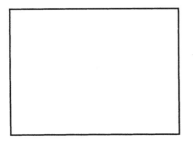
SHOT #23

SHOT #24

If we intercut Shots #23 and #24, the sense of alternation will be much weaker because of the tonal affinity, and the edit will create a less intense rhythmic beat.

Two kinds of visual repetition occur when a cut is made. The first type is *editorial repetition*. It occurs because a beat is produced by every cut or edit. With each cut, the pattern of repetition is continued.

The second type is *pictorial repetition*, which occurs when the same two shots are intercut more than once. If the editor is intercutting two close-ups in a conversation scene, an extremely visible repetition will occur because the audience is seeing two alternating shots repeated again and again. The more often the same shots are repeated, the more apparent the repetition becomes. In general, each time the same shot is repeated, the visual intensity diminishes.

Finally, there is *editorial tempo*. Any series of edits will have a tempo that remains constant, speeds up, or slows down. A sequence can have many quick cuts that generate a fast rhythm, or fewer cuts that create a slow rhythm. If the edits have a faster rhythm, it's easier for the audience to sense the tempo. As the time between cuts increases, the audience's sense of the editorial tempo diminishes. What is actually a slow tempo may be read as no tempo at all because the time length between cuts is too long for the alternation or repetition to be remembered.

Through editing, we can control the Principle of Contrast and Affinity. Editing will be our last chance to manipulate the structure of the story, the nature of the actor's performances, and the visual components before the production is completed. We'll see that the ultimate control of the Principle of Contrast and Affinity is in the hands of the editor, but an editor can only create within the confines of the footage that has been produced.

One hopes that the editor has the kinds of shots needed in the editing process to make the finished story successful and fulfill your visual goals. If we think of the story as a series of events, it will help us understand how to provide the footage you'll need during editing.

THE EVENT

A single action, a scene or a group of scenes can be called an event. This event can be simple (a hand opens a door) or complex (a person travels to the moon and returns). Any event can be broken down into a number of subevents.

Let's say the event is "a hand opens a door." Here are the subevents that make up that event:

1. The hand reaches for the knob.
2. The hand grasps the knob.
3. The hand turns the knob.
4. The door latch moves.
5. The door opens.
6. The hand releases the knob.

Listing the subevents allows us to understand each part of the overall event. We could diagram the event on a timeline like this:

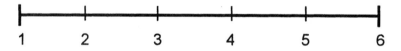

1   2   3   4   5   6

Each number on the timeline represents a subevent of "a hand opens a door." There are two ways to photograph this door event. As a continuous event or as a fragmented event.

THE CONTINUOUS EVENT

When we photograph an event in a continuous manner there will be no camera cuts. As we progress through the event, moving from one subevent to the next, the film, videotape, or digital recorder will be running continuously. The camera can remain stationary or the camera can move, but the event and all its subevents will be photographed in one continuous take. We can do as many takes as we want, but each one will record the complete event.

If we film the event continuously, editing will be unnecessary because the entire event has been photographed in one continuous piece. Our camera position may change during the event, but the entire event is captured in only one shot. The editor will not have control over the rhythm or anything else in the shot. The visual rhythm of the scene will be controlled as the event is being photographed.

THE FRAGMENTED EVENT

We can photograph a scene in a fragmented manner, which means the event is broken down into separate shots. Each subevent will be given its own shot or several shots. This is usually called shooting "coverage" and typically includes shots like a master shot, full shot, medium shots, close-ups, inserts, and cutaways which, when edited together, reconstruct the subevents into a single event.

The more visual component contrast occurring in the fragmented subevents the more intense the visual structure can become. If the fragmented events have visual component affinity, the visual intensity will be low. A skilled editor will understand the visual structure needed and pick the fragmented pieces most appropriate for the story.

Continuous and fragmented are opposites, and there are good reasons to use both techniques. Let's discuss the advantages:

1. *Visual Emphasis.* Fragmentation will have more emphasis when it has been preceded by a continuous sequence. Conversely, a continuously filmed sequence will gain emphasis if it has been preceded by a fragmented sequence.

2. *Contrast and Affinity Control.* When filming is continuous, the ability to change the visual components is limited because the camera can't stop. A fragmented sequence makes control of contrast and affinity easier. Since fragmenting allows an event to be broken down into a series of subevents or separate shots, the visual components can be rearranged for each new shot. This means that the director can create changes of contrast or affinity for every visual component in every shot. In postproduction, the editor can further arrange the fragmented shots to enhance either the visual contrast or affinity.

3. *Editorial Event Control.* When given a fragmented event, the editor can create a new arrangement for the order of the subevents. A continuously filmed scene will not permit editorial rearrangement.

4. *Editorial Rhythmic Control.* The rhythm of a scene can be altered when using a fragmented approach. The tempo of subevents can be increased or decreased through editing.

5. *Visual Variety.* Fragmentation or continuous shooting is an important factor in the overall visual variety of a production. If an audience is going to watch a two-hour film, how long can they watch something that's only fragmented? At what point will fragmenting lose its visual impact? Sometimes a visual structure needs continuous/fragmented variation just to keep the visuals from becoming dull.

6. *Directorial Choice.* The specific nature of a scene can suggest a fragmented or continuous approach. A scene that involves real time might be better played as a continuous shot. A scene involving complex action might best be filmed in a fragmented manner so that the physical complexities can be manipulated by the editor. Sometimes an event is so complicated that it can only be understood when the subevents are fragmented.

The decision to use a fragmented or continuous technique has no strict rules for its use. You must evaluate the nature of every scene and decide what technique will best serve the script.

RHYTHMIC PATTERNS

Different stories have different rhythms. It's possible to draw a flow-line to represent the rhythms of a story that can help you discover the visual rhythms for a production.

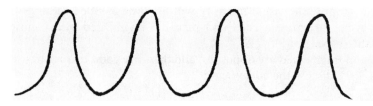

This flow-line represents the rhythms of stories that alternate between great rhythmic peaks and valleys. *The Godfather, Ran, Raging Bull, Lawrence of Arabia,* and *Citizen Kane* are examples of this type of overall visual rhythm.

This staccato rhythm represents a faster, more energetic rhythm often used in broad comedies. *A Night at the Opera, Bringing up Baby, Airplane,* and *Back to the Future* have visual rhythms suggested by this flow-line.

This slowly undulating flow-line has a slower rhythm that makes gradual, milder changes. *Howard's End, Hannah and Her Sisters, Wings of the Dove,* and *The Sixth Sense* follow this rhythmic pattern.

Any story, script, or visual concept will have a rhythmic flow-line pattern. It may be a combination of these examples or a different line altogether. Drawing a flow-line for the rhythm is an easy way to visualize the rhythmic contrast and affinities of your production.

In the days of silent films, orchestras sometimes played mood music during filming to help control the visual and dramatic rhythm of the scene. Today, because we record sound, the use of a metronome on the set is difficult, however it's possible to rehearse with a metronome.

Here are some standard metronome settings:

Metronome Setting	Number of Beats
240	4 per second
120	2 per second
60	1 per second
30	1 per 2 seconds

Using a metronome can help control the rhythm of dialogue, movement, or mood of a scene.

CONTRAST AND AFFINITY

There are several ways that rhythm can create contrast or affinity. Remember that contrast and affinity can occur within the shot, from shot to shot, and from sequence to sequence.

SLOW/FAST

A rhythm's tempo can range in speed from slow to fast. The tempo can be produced by stationary objects, moving objects, or the editor's cutting pattern.

Like line and shape, there are certain emotional values we sometimes attach to different tempos, although we can associate almost any meaning with any tempo. Sometimes a faster tempo communicates happiness, excitement, or comedy, and a slower rhythm suggests calm, sadness, or tragedy. Since visual tempo is produced by objects in the frame, we can assign different tempos to different objects or actors. What is the best tempo for an actor's walk or run? What kind of visual rhythm will best suit a character's personality?

The editor will create rhythm by cutting the fragmented scene together and by manipulating the rhythm of the scene itself. The editor can speed up or slow down either rhythm.

ACCELERATION/DECELERATION

A tempo does not have to remain constant: it can accelerate (speed up) or decelerate (slow down). The rate of acceleration/deceleration can be fast or slow.

As a rhythm increases in tempo it usually communicates an intensifying dynamic. As a tempo slows down it usually reduces the intensity.

REGULAR/IRREGULAR

We also classify rhythm in terms of being regular and irregular. When the tempo remains constant the rhythm is regular. If the tempo changes often enough, the rhythm can develop an irregular pattern.

Because regularity has a predictable pattern, we usually associate it with affinity or lack of intensity. An irregular rhythm generally increases the rhythmic contrast and produces greater visual intensity or dynamic.

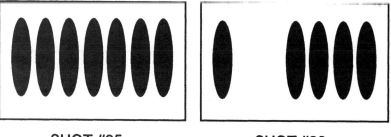

SHOT #25   SHOT #26

Shot #25 has a regular tempo and #26 has an irregular tempo. Shot #26 has more intensity because irregularity generates contrast.

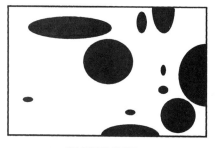

SHOT #27

Shot #27 has an extremely irregular tempo. The viewer's eye bounces around the frame, speeding up and slowing down because the distance between the ovals and their size is so irregular.

CONTINUOUS/FRAGMENTED

Although not a component of rhythm, this is an important method of controlling rhythm. If a scene is shot continuously, the rhythm cannot be controlled by the editor. However, a fragmented scene allows the editor to control rhythm by editing the fragments or subcomponents into a completed event or scene. The editor can control the tempo, tempo changes, and regularity of the scene's rhythm by the number of cuts or edits and by choosing which shots to include.

Fragmenting allows you to create jump cuts. Jump cuts occur when the continuity of an action is removed. The greater the jump cut the greater the visual intensity. The same thing happens when the camera jumps the stage line. Most of the time the camera remains on the same side of a stage line but when it jumps the line, additional contrast is created and the visual intensity increases.

FILMS TO WATCH

1. RHYTHMIC CONTROL
   Raging Bull (1980)
   Directed by Martin Scorsese
   Written by Paul Schrader and Mardik Martin
   Photographed by Michael Chapman
   Art Direction by Gene Rudolph
   Edited by Thelma Schoonmaker

   A Clockwork Orange (1971)
   Directed by Stanley Kubrick
   Written by Stanley Kubrick
   Photographed by John Alcott
   Production Design by John Barry
   Edited by William Butler

   Rumblefish (1983)
   Directed by Francis Ford Coppola
   Written by Francis Ford Coppola
   Photographed by Steve Burum
   Production Design by Dean Tavoularis
   Edited by Barry Malkin

   Visions of Eight (1972)
   Produced by David Wolper
   Various Directors, Cinematographers, Editors

   Barry Lyndon (1975)
   Directed by Stanley Kubrick
   Written by Stanley Kubrick
   Photographed by John Alcott
   Production Design by Ken Adam

   Rashomon (1951)
   Directed by Akira Kurosawa
   Written by Akira Kurosawa
   Photographed by Kazuo Matsuyama
   Art Direction by H. Motsumoto

   The Last Picture Show (1971)
   Directed by Peter Bogdanovich
   Written by Bogdanovich and Larry McMurtry
   Photographed by Robert Surtees
   Production Design by Polly Platt
   Edited by Don Cambern

2. THE CONTINUOUS AND FRAGMENTED EVENT
   Touch of Evil (1958)
   Directed by Orson Welles
   Written by Orson Welles
   Photographed by Russell Metty
   Art Direction by Robert Clatworthy
   Edited by Edward Curtiss

Goodfellas (1990)
    Directed by Martin Scorsese
    Written by Nicholas Pileggi
    Photographed by Michael Ballhaus
    Production Design by Christie Zea
    Edited by Thelma Schoonmaker

The Untouchables (1987)
    Directed by Brian DePalma
    Written by David Mamet
    Photographed by Steven Burum
    Production Design by Patrizia Von Brandenstein
    Edited by Jerry Greenberg

Rope (1948)
    Directed by Alfred Hitchcock
    Written by Hume Cronyn and Arthur Laurents
    Photographed by William Skall
    Art Direction by Perry Ferguson
    Edited by William H. Ziegler

Run, Lola, Run (1999)
    Directed by Tom Tykwer
    Written by Tom Tykwer
    Photographed by Frank Griebe
    Production Design by Alexander Manasse
    Edited by Mathilde Bonnefoy

JFK (1991)
    Directed by Oliver Stone
    Written by Stone and Zachary Sklar
    Photographed by Robert Richardson
    Production Design by Victor Kempster
    Edited by Joe Hutshing and Pietro Scalia

Jacob's Ladder (1990)
    Directed by Adrian Lyne
    Written by Bruce Joel Rubin
    Photographed by Jeffery Kimball
    Production Design by Brian Morris
    Edited by Tom Rolf

Election (1999)
    Directed by Alexander Payne
    Written by Alexander Payne
    Photographed by James Glennon
    Production Design by Jane Ann Stewart
    Edited by Kevin Tent

C H A P T E R 9

STORY AND VISUAL STRUCTURE

THE KEY RELATIONSHIP

We've finished defining the basic visual components. Now we're ready to control visual structure using the Principle of Contrast and Affinity. Almost ready. There's still one more subject to discuss. We must understand some basics about story structure.

We'll never be able to use visual structure correctly if we don't understand story structure. This chapter isn't going to explain story structure (there are dozens of other books for that) but instead define some story structure terms that will help us link story and visual structure together.

Let's discuss story structure. A story has three basic parts called the beginning (exposition), the middle (conflict), and the end (resolution). We must understand these three basic parts of any story structure before we can use visual structure.

EXPOSITION

The beginning of a story is called the exposition. We can define exposition as "the facts we need to begin the story." These facts include (but are not limited to) who the main characters are, what they're doing, and when and where they live. If the audience is not given the facts they need (or think they need), they can never become involved in the story because they're distracted trying to fill in the missing exposition.

The concept of exposition comes from theater. Although the fundamentals of exposition were first described and used by Aristotle in ancient Greece, we'll confine our examples to modern film. Over the years, writers have developed many different techniques to introduce exposition into their stories.

The exposition in *Casablanca* (1942) begins with a map of Europe and narration explaining why the city of Casablanca was so important. It continues with the police radio report about stolen passport papers and a quick montage of the corrupt characters who live among the tourists in Casablanca. Audiences knew little or nothing about Casablanca's political situation, so the exposition had to present a lot of facts to begin the story and avoid confusion.

Citizen Kane's (1941) exposition is the "News on the March" newsreel that shows highlights of Charles Foster Kane's life. Since Kane's story is a nonlinear flashback, the exposition is critical to understanding the chronology of the story.

Orson Welles narrated some of his films (a convention he brought from radio) as a way of giving the audience the facts they needed to begin the story. In the opening of *The Magnificent Ambersons* (1942), Welles speaks the exposition, telling the audience about the main characters and the social customs of the era. Sidney Lumet's *Network* (1976) uses a narrator to present the exposition about a television network with poor ratings.

Billy Wilder begins his film *The Apartment* (1960) with narration. The main character, C.C. Baxter, introduces the unethical situation involving his apartment and his bosses at work. Sometimes the narration continues throughout the story as in *Father of the Bride* (1991) and *Shawshank Redemption* (1994). In *Little Big Man* (1970), Dustin Hoffman first appears in the exposition as an old man. His voice becomes the narrator for the entire film, which is a flashback. The mad composer Salieri narrates *Amadeus* (1984) in the same way. The same structure (without the age change) is used with Fred MacMurray in *Double Indemnity* (1944). In *Ferris Bueller's Day Off* (1986), Ferris spends most of the movie talking directly to the camera, filling in exposition as well as his comments about the story's situation.

A longstanding expositional technique is the simple title card or crawl that opens a film. *The Searchers* (1956) has a title card that reads "Texas 1868." This is part of the exposition. It tells us when and where we are. Hollywood often uses the crawl to quickly explain expositions in films like *Airforce* (1943), *Boy's Town* (1938), and all of the *Star Wars* (1977) movies.

Sidney Lumet's *Murder on the Orient Express* (1974) has an elaborate expositional prologue that explains tragic events that occurred in the past. These events later prove important in revealing the true identity of the passengers on the train.

In the exposition of Sergio Leone's *The Good, the Bad, and the Ugly* (1966), each of the three main characters is presented in a freeze frame labeled "The Good," "The Bad," or "The Ugly." There's no doubt at the end of the exposition about who's who.

As a story develops, additional exposition is sometimes needed to introduce new characters, elaborate on new situations, or give the audience information that was withheld in the beginning exposition.

THE CONFLICT AND CLIMAX

The middle of a story is called the rising action or the conflict. When the story begins, there's usually little or no conflict. As the story develops, the conflict increases in intensity. The most intense part of the conflict is the climax where the conflict is resolved.

The nature of a conflict can be physical (involving external action) or intellectual (involving internal emotional struggle). Sometimes the conflict is both, but it always becomes more intense as the story progresses towards the climax.

In *Casablanca*, the conflict is both physical and intellectual. One conflict involves two stolen tickets of passage and the other involves Rick's love for Ilsa.

As the conflict intensifies, the two conflicts entwine. At the climax, Rick gives Ilsa and Victor the tickets and remains alone in Casablanca.

In *Citizen Kane* one conflict is the reporter's physical search trying to discover the meaning of Kane's last word: "rosebud." In his search, the reporter stumbles in and out of various intellectual conflicts between Kane and his wives, friends, and enemies.

The physical conflict in *Jaws* (1975) concerns a town and a shark. Can the shark be killed before it ruins the lucrative summer tourist trade? The climax is the final boat scene where the shark is finally destroyed.

C.C. Baxter's intellectual conflict in *The Apartment* involves personal integrity and true love. He finally realizes that he will never be able to satisfy himself and his bosses. Baxter must accept their lack of morality or regain his own sense of integrity.

Remains of the Day (1993) is about a butler who refuses to challenge ancient British custom. His intellectual conflict is the portrait of a man who spends his life hiding from a changing world. At the climax he decides not to change and remains locked in the archaic traditions of butlerhood.

Honesty and corruption form the conflicting intellectual elements in *Serpico* (1973). No matter what department Frank Serpico is transferred into, he discovers growing corruption on higher and higher levels. His conflict is trying to remain honest in a corrupt environment.

Richard Brooks' *In Cold Blood* (1967) is a conflict about a physical search for a pair of murderers and also an intellectual conflict about understanding their motivations. The climax of the film is not about finding the criminals (we already know they'll be found) but learning what motivated them to commit the crime.

In all of these story examples, the conflict increases in intensity as the story progresses. Each scene pushes the story towards the climax where the conflict must be resolved.

THE RESOLUTION

After the climax is over there may be details or secondary events and characters that need time to fully complete their story. The resolution wraps up these incomplete story elements and gives the audience time to recover from the intensity of the climax.

The resolution in *Casablanca* takes place at the airport once Rick has seen Ilsa and Victor fly safely away. Rick turns to the Police Chief and it's business as usual as they walk off into the darkness. The conflict is over.

The physical search in *Citizen Kane* ends without an answer to the mystery word "rosebud." The resolution shows the reporters packing up and leaving, but the audience gets to see the childhood sled inscribed with "rosebud" as it disappears into a trash furnace. It explains Kane and his lost childhood.

The resolution in *Jaws* is quick and simple. The shark has been killed and the police chief is reunited with the ichthyologist who had been hiding underwater. The dangerous shark is dead and the ocean is once again safe for swimmers. As the two men calmly swim to shore, birds fly around them in celebration of their victory and the ominous music that signaled the shark's approach is gone.

Hitchcock's *North by Northwest* (1959) has a twenty-second resolution. Thornhill kisses Kendall as they cuddle up onboard a train.

Sometimes a title card resolution is used telling the audience what happened to the characters as in *Animal House* (1978) and *American Graffiti* (1973) or a voiceover sums up the story's themes and ideas as in *Shawshank Redemption* (1994).

Bad storytelling ignores the resolution and makes an audience feel that a story didn't end, it just stopped suddenly. Poorly written stories may have problems with resolution because gaps in the plot aren't properly explained in the resolution.

Exposition, conflict/climax, and resolution have no exact relationship to act structure. Novices will incorrectly refer to Act I as the exposition, Act II as the conflict, and Act III as the resolution. Any specific rules about relating story structure to act structure can be misleading.

Every story, no matter how brief or long, will have an exposition, conflict, climax, and resolution. The story can be a joke, a poem, a commercial, a play, a television situation comedy, a feature-length film script, or a novel. It may have a good structure or it may have a bad structure, but it will have a structure. That structure will always include an exposition, a conflict, a climax, and a resolution.

When we read a story or script we become aware of its structure, but we need to bring that printed page to life on a screen. It's our job to produce a film or video that brings to the screen the structure that the writer put on the page.

Getting this story structure onto the screen isn't easy. The actors will play out the story and the music will add to the story's values. Now we can discuss doing the same thing with the visuals. We are ready to link story structure and visual structure together.

THE STORY STRUCTURE GRAPH

We can create a graph that diagrams the structure of a story's conflict or intensity.

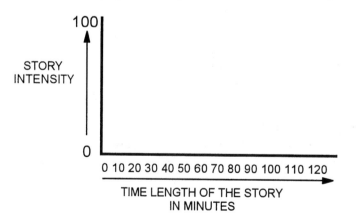

The horizontal axis of this graph indicates the time length of the story (120 minutes in this example). The vertical axis represents the intensity of the story. What does story intensity mean? It refers to the degree of conflict in the story. The "0" on the story intensity scale indicates that there's no intensity and "100" indicates great intensity.

GRAPH A

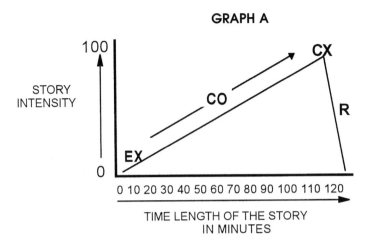

Now let's draw a line on the graph that represents the story's intensity. In Graph A, when the story begins at the exposition (EX), the story intensity is usually low or at "0" on the story intensity scale. As the story unfolds, the intensity begins to build and we enter the conflict (CO) of the story. The intensity of the conflict continues to increase until we reach the climax (CX), which is the most intense part of the story. After that, the story intensity diminishes as we enter the resolution (R) and the story ends.

This basic story structure will be our map for understanding the relationship between story structure and visual structure. We start with the expositional facts needed to begin the story, introduce a conflict that builds in intensity to a climax and then resolves into an ending. Later in this chapter we'll discuss variations on this story intensity structure graph.

GRAPH B

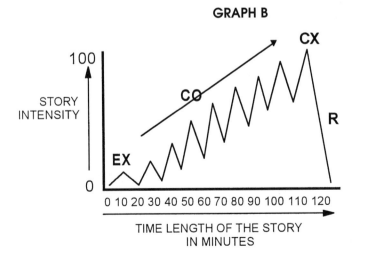

Graph B shows the same overall structure as Graph A, but the straight line representing the story intensity has been replaced by a jagged line. This jagged line more accurately represents the rises and falls in a story's intensity. Even though the line is jagged, its overall direction is uphill, and it will still peak at the most intense part of the story, the climax.

All good stories follow this uphill structure. Hitchcock's *North by Northwest* (1959) and Spielberg's *Raiders of the Lost Ark* (1981) are two excellent examples, because the build of intensifying events is extremely clear. Let's break these stories down into a list of sequences called a Story Sequence List. From this list we'll produce a graph that visually plots the story's intensity.

NORTH BY NORTHWEST

You must be familiar with *North by Northwest* to understand the following Story Sequence List. If you've not seen this film you should view it now. Even if you're familiar with the film, look at it again.

Each sequence in the story has been categorized as exposition, conflict, climax, or resolution and given a very brief description of its action.

EX = Exposition
CO = Conflict
CX = Climax
R = Resolution

North by Northwest **Story Sequence List**
1. EX: Roger Thornhill is a busy executive.
2. CO: Thornhill is kidnapped.
3. EX: Thornhill meets Vandamm at mansion.
4. CO: Drunk driving.
5. CO: Arrest, police station, return to mansion.
6. CO: Thornhill finds hotel room and escapes.
7. CO: United Nations.
8. EX: CIA Headquarters
9. CO: Grand Central Station.
10. CO: Thornhill meets Kendall on train.
11. CO: Chicago train station.
12. CO: Crop duster.
13. CO: Chicago hotel.
14. CO: Auction.
15. EX: CIA intervenes.
16. CO: Mt. Rushmore Visitor's Center.
17. CO: Kendall and Thornhill reunite.
18. CO: Thornhill in hospital.
19. CO: Vandamm's house.
20. CO: Vandamm's plane.
21. CX: Mt. Rushmore.
22. R: Thornhill and Kendall on the train.

GRAPH C: *NORTH BY NORTHWEST*

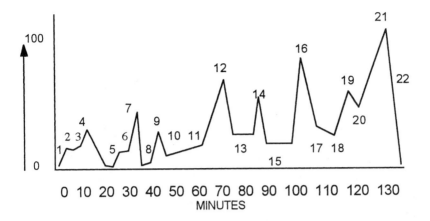

Making the Story Sequence List has given us the information we need to produce a graph. This graph shows the major intensity fluctuations in each sequence of *North by Northwest's* story. The numbers on the graph refer to the numbers in the Story Sequence List.

The story begins with no intensity at Story Sequence #1, which introduces Roger Thornhill. This is the start of the story's exposition. We learn that Thornhill is a self-involved executive. In Sequence #2 Thornhill is kidnapped and the intensity increases because the conflict has begun. In Sequence #3 the intensity continues to build as Thornhill realizes he's a prisoner. In Sequence #4 the conflict becomes even more intense as Thornhill, now drunk, drives along a dangerous mountain road. Finally, in Sequence #5 the intensity diminishes as Thornhill is unable to prove his story.

On the graph, each sequence on the Story Sequence List is represented by a rise or fall in the story intensity. As the sequences in the story gain intensity, they reach higher peaks on the graph. The most intense peak on the graph is the climax of the story at Mt. Rushmore (#21 on the Story Sequence List).

You may disagree with this version of the intensity builds in *North by Northwest*. Depending upon your ideas about story structure and character, you might locate the intensity rises and falls at different places in the story. That's fine. You can draw your graphs to plot the intensities in any way that you wish. What is recognized as intensities can differ from story to story, author to author, and director to director. The important concept here is to produce a graph and plot the story's intensities.

North by Northwest has three sequences: the Crop Duster (12), The Visitor's Center (16), and Mt. Rushmore (21), where the intensity is highest. The Crop Duster sequence, like every sequence in this film, has its own intensity build with an exposition, conflict/climax, and resolution. Let's examine the specifics of the Crop Duster Sequence and diagram its intensity structure.

CROP DUSTER SEQUENCE

EX = Exposition
CO = Conflict
CX = Climax
R = Resolution

Crop Duster Sequence List

1. EX: Thornhill arrives by bus.
2. CO: Two cars and a truck pass by.
3. CO: Man arrives and takes a bus.
4. CO: Plane attack #1.
5. CO: Plane attack #2 with machine guns.
6. CO: Thornhill tries to stop passing car.
7. CO: Plane attack #3 with machine guns.
8. CO: Plane attack #4. No guns.
9. CO: Plane attack #5 with crop-dusting chemicals.
10. CX: Plane hits tanker and explodes.
11. R: Thornhill steals truck and escapes.

GRAPH D: CROP DUSTER SEQUENCE

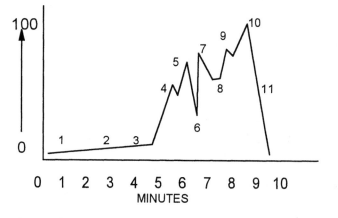

The numbers in Graph D refer to the numbers of the Crop Duster Sequence List. Notice how the structure starts at "0" intensity for about five minutes before the conflict begins to intensify with the attack of the plane. Each time the plane attacks the sequence builds in intensity towards the climax when the plane explodes. The brief resolution is Thornhill stealing the truck and driving away.

RAIDERS OF THE LOST ARK

Now let's break down the story sequences in *Raiders of the Lost Ark* and examine its intensity structure. You must already be familiar with the film to understand this list.

EX = Exposition

CO = Conflict

CX = Climax

R = Resolution

Raiders of the Lost Ark **Story Sequence List**

1. EX: Indy discovers idol and escapes.
2. EX: Indy teaches and is asked to locate the ark.
3. CO: Marion and tavern.
4. EX: Sallah in Cairo.
5. CO: Marketplace.
6. EX: Indy talks with Belloq.
7. CO: Medallion is analyzed.
8. CO: Map Room.
9. CO: Well of Souls; find ark.
10. CO: Well of Souls; escape.
11. CO: Airplane fight.
12. CO: Truck caravan chase.
13. CO: Ship and submarine.
14. CO: Indy follows the ark and surrenders.
15. CX: The ark is opened.
16. R: Washington; the ark is stored.

GRAPH E: *RAIDERS OF THE LOST ARK*

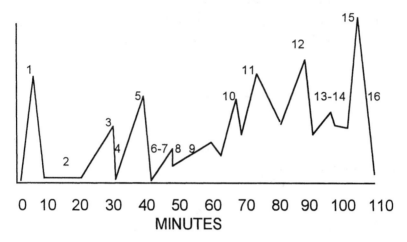

The numbers on the graph correspond to the numbers of the *Raiders* Story Sequence List. *Raiders* is a series of episodes that build in intensity to a final climax.

Note how Sequence #1 in the *Raiders* graph is very intense. This brief burst of intensity is called a spike. Even though Sequence #1 has a lot of intensity, it's also part of the exposition. After this opening intensity spike, the story exposition continues (but at "0" intensity) as Indy is approached by the United States government to find the missing ark. At that point the story intensity begins to build towards the climax, each sequence getting more intense than the one before it. The climax comes when the ark is opened and the conflict ends. The resolution shows Indy and Marion safely back in America and the ark is put into storage.

The opening spike in *Raiders* is exposition. It gives the audience facts they need to begin the story including the location, time period, Indy's job and personality, his fear of snakes, and who is the story's villain. In addition to being expositional, Sequence #1 is also a well-structured intensity build. Like the Crop Duster Sequence from *North by Northwest* it has an exposition, conflict, climax, and resolution all its own. Let's examine the story intensity structure of Sequence #1 in *Raider's of the Lost Ark.*

RAIDERS OF THE LOST ARK Sequence #1

EX = Exposition

CO = Conflict

CX = Climax

R = Resolution

Raiders of the Lost Ark Sequence #1 List

1. EX: Walk through jungle.
2. CO: Walk through cave.
3. CO: Indy takes Idol.

4. CO: Indy runs and exits cave.
5. EX: Belloq.
6. CX: Tribesmen chase Indy.
7. R: Escape on plane.

GRAPH F: SEQUENCE #1

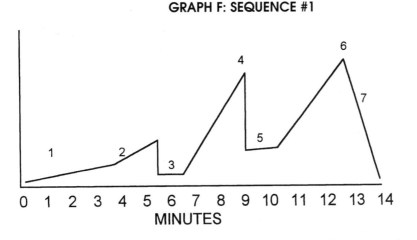

Sequences #1 and #2 (walking through the jungle and entering the cave) are expositional. The audience doesn't know Indiana Jones or anything about him. The first five minutes of the film allow us to meet him and learn a little about his character. The story intensity is low at this point. There is a lot of dramatic tension between Indy and his companions, but the conflict is just beginning so the overall intensity is low.

Once Indy steals the golden idol, all of the tomb's hidden traps come to life and he must run for his life. Suddenly there is great story intensity as Indy barely escapes the tomb. He exits the cave safely but is met by the story's villain Belloq. Belloq will appear much later in the film but he's cleverly introduced in the opening exposition. Indy must escape again, increasing the conflict and bringing us to the climax and resolution as he flies away into the sunset.

The main purpose of this twelve-minute opening sequence or prologue is expositional, yet it contains the basic structural components of exposition, conflict, climax, and resolution.

THE APARTMENT

Let's look at a story that doesn't have action sequences. We can examine Billy Wilder's *The Apartment*, plot its story structure, and produce a graph. You must be familiar with this film to understand the list.

EX = Exposition
CO = Conflict
CX = Climax
R = Resolution

The Apartment Story Sequence List

1. EX: C.C. Baxter and his apartment situation.
2. EX: Baxter likes Kubilick.
3. CO: Sheldrake wants a key.
4. CO: Baxter asks Kubilik out; she's dating Sheldrake.
5. CO: Baxter is promoted.
6. CO: Christmas party.
7. CO: Baxter in bar.
8. CO: Sheldrake and Kubilick in apartment.
9. CO: Kubilick overdoses.
10. CO: Kubilick recovers.
11. CO: Brother-in-law at office.
12. CO: Sheldrake fires Olson.
13. CO: Baxter and Kubilick prepare dinner.
14. CO: Brother-in-law hits Baxter.
15. CO: Sheldrake promotes Baxter and wants Kubilick.
16. CX: Baxter quits.
17. CX: New Year's Eve, Kubilick and Sheldrake.
18. R: Kubilick goes to Baxter.

GRAPH G: *THE APARTMENT*

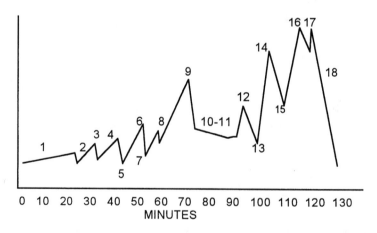

There are two separate conflicts in this story that intertwine. One conflict involves Baxter and Sheldrake, the other involves Kubilick and Sheldrake.

The conflict is already in motion when Baxter introduces himself and his situation (#1). He is continually taken advantage of by his dishonest bosses who use his apartment as a hideaway for their secret office romances. Although it's a terrible inconvenience, Baxter continues to allow them access to his apartment because his cooperation gets him promoted at work. The intensity decreases when Baxter tries to date Miss Kubilick (#2) and then increases when Kubilick's affair with Sheldrake is revealed (#4). Baxter becomes involved with Kubilick when she tries to commit suicide, and the conflict increases in intensity (#9). At the climax, Baxter quits his job (#16) and Kubilick leaves Sheldrake. In the resolution (#18), Baxter and Kubilick are united.

HOWARD'S END

Here is a breakdown of the story sequences in James Ivory's *Howard's End*. Again, you must be familiar with the film to understand the graph.

EX = Exposition

CO = Conflict

CX = Climax

R = Resolution

Howard's End **Story Sequence List**

1. EX: Correspondence about Helen's failed engagement.
2. EX: Stolen umbrella; Schlegel's home; Wilcox arrival.
3. EX: Bast apartment.
4. CO: Margaret Schlegel and Ruth Wilcox become friends.
5. CO: Ruth Wilcox dies; her will is read.
6. CO: Schlegels meet Leonard and Jackie Bast.
7. CO: Helen takes an interest in Leonard.
8. CO: Henry Wilcox is attracted to Margaret.
9. CO: Helen tries to help Leonard.
10. CO: Margaret arrives at Howard's End.
11. CO: Party; Henry was once involved with Jackie.
12. CO: Leonard and Helen in boat.
13. CO: Leonard refuses check.
14. CO: Helen returns from Germany.
15. CO: Helen wants to sleep at Howard's End.
16. CX: Charles confronts Leonard.
17. R: Schlegels live at Howard's End.

GRAPH H: *HOWARD'S END*

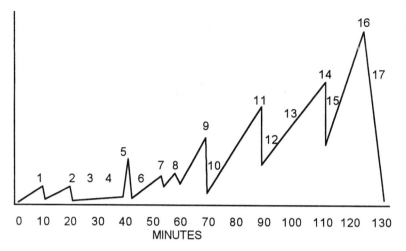

Howard's End is a portrait of three families in English society in the early 1900s. The problems of the morally bankrupt Wilcox family, the honorable Schlegel family, and the lower-class, victimized Bast family intertwine.

The story begins with very little conflict or intensity (#1 to #4). The large cast of characters is introduced and a series of coincidences brings the Schlegel, Wilcox, and Bast families together. The conflict begins to increase in intensity when Ruth Wilcox dies and her will is destroyed (#5). As the three families become more involved with each other the conflict continues to build. It reaches a higher point of intensity when Jackie reveals her past association with Henry Wilcox (#11). The conflict reaches its most intense moment when Charles kills Henry Bast (#16). In the story's resolution, the Schlegels reside at Howard's End, raise Helen's child, and the amoral Wilcox family is shattered.

Conflict in *Howard's End* is intellectual, not physical. The story is about the emotions of the characters rather than physical events like shark attacks or kidnapping. The intensity structure of the conflict in all the stories is the same, however.

VISUAL STRUCTURE

Now that you understand how to produce the graph for story intensity, let's create a graph for visual intensity. We can borrow the terms we use for story structure and apply them directly to visual structure.

VISUAL EXPOSITION

Just as there's story exposition, there's also visual exposition. In the story exposition the writer presents the facts needed to begin the story, including the characters, the basic plot, the location, and the time period. Exposition sets up the story's rules. We can do exactly the same thing with the visual exposition. We can set up our visual rules.

The director, cinematographer, and production designer can use visual exposition to introduce the visual components that will remain constant or change during the story. The visual exposition is the place to define the visual rules that will support the story.

A story begins: "Once upon a time there was a happy family." But we would add to that: "Once upon a time there was a happy family who lived in flat space." Now we have story and visual exposition. We have set a rule for photographing the family and we have given the audience a visual definition for "happy family." Although the audience can't define it, they will unconsciously recognize flat space and associate it with the happy family. The entire story will take place in flat space, or the space might change. We may assign deep space to an unhappy family in the story, which will be presented to the audience during the exposition for the unhappy family. Setting visual rules gives you a plan for photographing the families.

Ideally, the story and visual exposition should be revealed at the same time. In Steven Spielberg's *Jaws*, the story, musical, and visual exposition occur simultaneously. *Jaws* begins its exposition as a bloodthirsty shark devours an innocent swimmer. In the film's opening shot we hear the ominous musical notes that become the shark's theme song, and the handheld underwater camera that is the shark's point-of-view. Spielberg sets up his story, musical, and visual exposition in the opening sequence. We learn the rules for the shark's personality, music, and camera angle in this expository sequence. The audience now has all the facts they need to begin story.

In *Jaws*, the story, musical, and visual rules created in the exposition never change. The shark remains evil, the same music always accompanies the shark's appearance, and the shark's underwater view is always photographed in the same way. The audience associates the music and camera angle with the shark so completely that actually showing the shark becomes unnecessary. The exposition is so strong that the theme music or camera angle automatically triggers fear in the audience.

In the *story* exposition, we lay down the rules for the character's personalities, the plot of the story, and the time period. In the *visual* exposition, we lay down the rules for the basic visual components in the film. As a story progresses, the writer can develop the story's plot and characters and we can do exactly the same thing with our basic visual components.

The visual component rules presented during the exposition become the guidelines for everyone involved in the production. The structure you've picked for space, line, shape, tone, color, movement, and rhythm will help you find the correct lenses, camera angles, locations, wardrobe, and architectural elements for your production. The visual rules will give your production visual unity, style, and (through the use of contrast and affinity) visual structure.

VISUAL CONFLICT AND CLIMAX

A story structure has a middle that is often called the conflict and climax. In a story conflict, the intensity slowly builds until it reaches its most intense moment or climax.

In *Jaws*, the conflict involves killing the shark before it devours more inno-cent swimmers and ruins the summer tourist season. As the hunters close in on the shark, the conflict becomes more intense. Finally, at the story's climax, the most intense part of the conflict, the shark attacks, devours the fisherman, and is killed by the police chief.

The visual structure can build in intensity to a visual climax in the same way that the story's conflict builds to a climax. How?

The answer lies in using the Principle of Contrast and Affinity. Let's review this important concept:

> **The greater the contrast in a visual component,**
> **the more the visual intensity or dynamic *increases*.**
> **The greater the affinity in a visual component,**
> **the more the visual intensity or dynamic *decreases*.**
> More simply stated:
> **CONTRAST = GREATER VISUAL INTENSITY**
> **AFFINITY = LESS VISUAL INTENSITY**

This is why we spent so much time discussing each visual component. Now we can look at each visual component and consider how we can give it contrast or affinity to control the visual intensity and visual structure of our production.

A writer uses words to create *story* intensity. A musician uses notes to create *musical* intensity. Now we have space, line, shape, tone, color, movement, and rhythm to create *visual* intensity.

Once we understand the story's intensities, we can arrange the basic visual components to produce visual intensity (through contrast) or less intensity (through affinity). We can parallel the story's structure with the visual structure because we understand the basic visual components and how to use them.

THE VISUAL RESOLUTION

The end of a story is called the resolution, and visual structure has a resolution, too. In a story's resolution, the conflict is over and the story's intensity decreases. The visual intensity can also decrease by using the Principle of Contrast and Affinity. As the visual affinity increases, the visual intensity will decrease.

In *Jaws*, the final shot of the film is a long continuous wide shot as the sur-vivors paddle off to shore. If we compare the visual affinity of the resolution to the visual contrasts of the climax, we can see how Spielberg created affinity for the resolution.

Story structure and visual structure share the basic parts: exposition, conflict, climax, and resolution. Now we're ready to join story structure and visual struc-ture together.

THE VISUAL STRUCTURE GRAPH

GRAPH #1

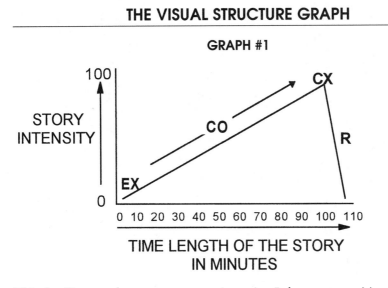

This familiar graph represents story intensity. It has an exposition, an intensifying conflict, a climax, and a resolution. It illustrates the general intensity build of the story. Not all stories follow this exact pattern, but we'll use it to explain the relationship between story and visual structure.

We can now add a second graph to represent the visual intensity in relation to the story intensity.

GRAPH #2

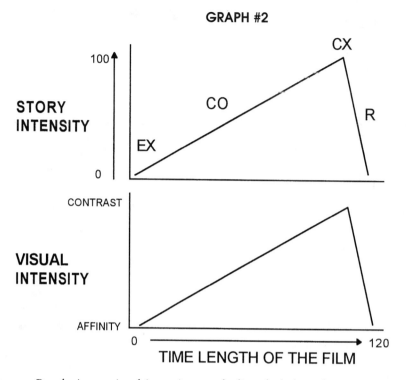

By placing a visual intensity graph directly below the story intensity graph, we can see their relationship to each other. The story intensity can increase or decrease from 0 to 100, but let's substitute "affinity" for 0 and "contrast" for 100 on the visual intensity graph.

We will create a visual structure that parallels the story structure. When the story structure gains intensity, the visual structure must do the same.

The structure begins with affinity of the visual components, and as the story intensity increases, the visual affinity will change to contrast. At the climax of the story we'll have maximum contrast of the visual components, and in the story resolution the visual contrasts will change to affinity. By lining up the visual intensity graph directly under the story intensity graph, we can see how much visual contrast or affinity is being used at any point in the story.

This is an extremely simple example of how visual structure works in relation to the story structure. Let's look at some other examples.

GRAPH #3

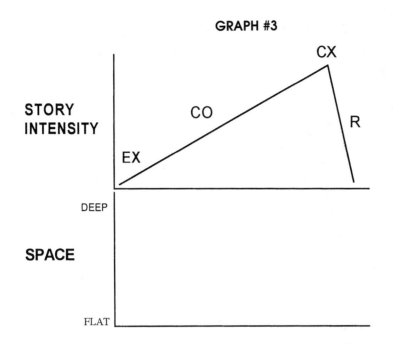

STORY
INTENSITY

CX

CO

R

EX

DEEP

SPACE

FLAT

Keeping the story intensity graph the same, we can make a second, more specific graph. Instead of graphing the general contrast and affinity of the visual structure, we can use the second graph to diagram space. Let's label the second graph "flat" and "deep." Now we can specifically graph what kind of spatial structure we want in our production.

There are three variations in the way we can graph a visual component:

1. As a constant.
2. As a progression.
3. As contrast or affinity.

VARIATION #1: THE CONSTANT

As a constant, we'll control a visual component by keeping it the same through-out the production.

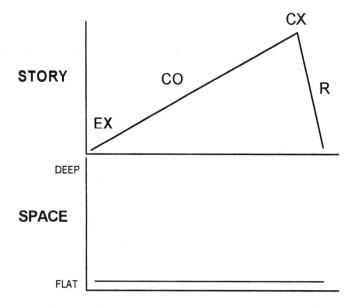

This graph indicates that the space will remain flat in every shot. There won't be any change in the visual space of the film at all. We have created affinity of space. Making such a specific choice will give the production tremendous visual unity. The project will have a specific look simply by choosing one type of space. This choice will be the spatial rule for the entire production. Every shot will be flat.

Why would we want to be so limiting? Why not? An entirely flat film might be perfect for a particular story. What if the story is about prisoners unsuccess-fully struggling to escape? Keeping the space flat throughout the film can help visualize their situation.

Perhaps the story is about a journey into the complex life of a reclusive bil-lionaire. Instead of flat space you decide deep space best visualizes the compli-cated, multidimensional life of this individual. You decide to make every shot in this film deep. To see how that film came out, watch *Citizen Kane*.

VARIATION #2: THE PROGRESSION

Instead of keeping a visual component constant for an entire film, it can make a slow change.

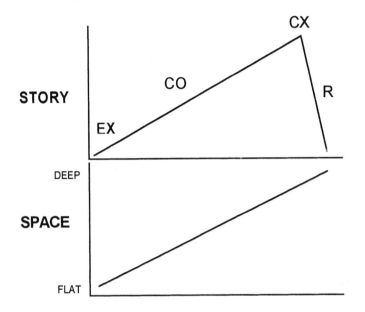

We're still using the same two graphs. The top one is Story and the bottom one is Space. In this variation, the space slowly progresses or changes from flat to deep.

Why would we choose this spatial structure? Because it's motivated by the story structure. We're always looking for a visual structure that will help tell the story.

Perhaps the story is about a couple who meet, hate each other, but end up falling in love. We'll assign flat space to hate and deep space to love. By the end of the film we'll have made two progressions, one from hate to love and another from flat to deep. The visual change parallels the relationship change. We're using the visual structure to help tell the story.

The story could be about a change from innocence (flat space) to knowledge (deep space), or from cowardice (flat space) to courage (deep space).

Remember, the types of space we're associating with these relationship changes are completely arbitrary. Who says flat means hate, innocence, or cowardice? Does deep space always mean love, knowledge, or courage? Of course not. It's arbitrary. You can associate any emotional quality, relationship change, mood, or idea with any type of space. You must define your space in the exposition and then it becomes your rule for the entire story. Deep, flat, and limited space can mean anything you want. Anything. You just have to decide, explain it to the audience in the exposition, and then abide by your rule.

VARIATION #3: CONTRAST AND AFFINITY

This is the most complex control we can use, but it allows us the most specific orchestration of the visual structure in relation to the story.

The story can be examined sequence by sequence, scene by scene, or shot by shot, and specific choices for controlling the visual components can be made. If a particular story sequence is more intense, we can make our visuals more intense. If another story sequence is less intense, we can make our visuals less intense. By using contrast and affinity we can design and control a visual structure that has a very specific relationship to the intensities of the story.

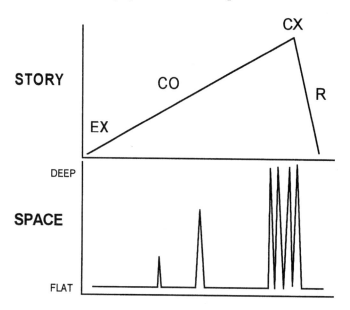

This graph uses contrast and affinity to create a visual intensity that parallels the story intensity.

According to the graph, the film is primarily flat space, then there's a spike of moderately deep space, another spike of even deeper space, and at the story's climax there is intercutting of flat and deep space from shot to shot. Then the space becomes flat for the resolution of the story. What is the justification for the visual spikes of deep space?

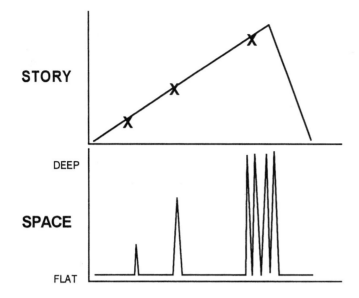

The visual spikes are motivated by something in the story. Perhaps this is a monster movie and the monster appears at three places in the story (indicated in the story graph with an X). The visual spikes coincide with the places in the story where the monster appears. To help make the monster's appearance more intense, we're going to use deep space. The contrast between this deep space and the usually flat space of the film will add visual intensity. The most intense part of the story is a climactic fight between the hero and the monster. To give that sequence the greatest intensity, we're going to alternate between deep and flat space from shot to shot. This will produce a visual structure that parallels the story structure. The story and visual intensities are now linked.

Spikes can also be used with nonphysical stories. The spikes can heighten intellectual or emotional moments in a story. Perhaps the story is about someone trying to remember his or her past, and the spikes are used to make the memories more jarring or more soothing. The spikes don't have to add contrast, they can add affinity. The idea of the spikes is to generate a visual change and create contrast. Remember that the motivation for any visual change is always found in the structure of the story.

USING THE GRAPHS

Drawing graphs gives you a simple way to quickly plan how you'll use the visual components. Because the graphs are so easy to produce, you can quickly try different ideas and combinations of components to see which ones will work best for your production. The graphs will remind you to think about every component, and they'll also display how the visual components will work in relation to one another and to the story structure.

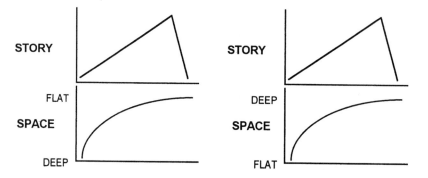

The space graph on the left shows a visual progression from deep to flat. The right space graph is identical, but the deep and flat labels have been switched. By changing two labels, the entire approach to the space in your production has been reversed. What could be simpler? The graphs allow you to quickly try, change, and organize your visual ideas while keeping the story structure in mind. The labels you put on the visual component graphs are arbitrary. You can set them up in whatever way works best for your production.

The story graph can illustrate the entire script or just a single sequence or scene. The visual component graphs can be used to plot changes in a visual component over the course of an entire story, or the graphs can illustrate visual changes that occur in one scene or even in a single shot.

The important thing to remember is that all visual component graphs must line up under the story graph so you can see the relationship between the two structures. Whenever you structure the visual components, you must always examine the story structure first because the visual component's job is to tell the story. Visual structure works best when it parallels the story structure.

Graphs are usually produced when you prepare your production. In post-production, new graphs can be created. An editor can remake the graphs once the actual footage has been evaluated for visual contrast and affinity. If you're having problems with a sequence, you can create a graph and analyze the edited visual structure to help you find a solution to the problem.

Let's look at other graph examples based on the constant, progression, and contrast/affinity concepts.

EXAMPLE #1

The graphs can be used to diagram the structure of any visual component. The component name you write on the left side of the graph forces you to consider that visual component's contribution to the visual structure.

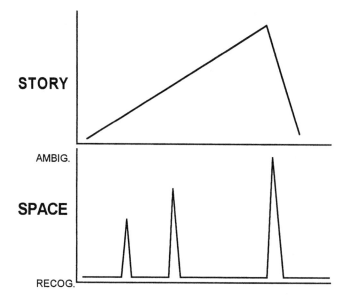

This graph indicates how ambiguous and recognizable space will be used. In this example, ambiguous space will pop into the film three times.

This story is about someone who sees a ghost. The ambiguous space will be used whenever the ghost appears. Just as Spielberg used the ominous music for the shark in *Jaws*, we can use ambiguous space for the ghost.

Notice how the ambiguous space becomes more extreme as the story progresses. The most ambiguous space will occur at the most intense part of the story's conflict, the climax. Remember, we're linking story structure and visual structure together so the visual contrast will grow as the story intensity increases.

EXAMPLE #2

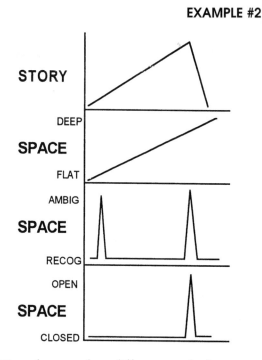

Now there are three different graphs for space, each linked to the story structure. The graphs show that the production's spatial structure is a visual progression from flat to deep space; ambiguous space appears twice (once at the start and again at the climax); and there is one moment of open space at the story's climax.

These visual decisions are based on an analysis of the story structure. Suppose this film is a comedy about falling in love. Flat space symbolizes loneliness and deep space means a happy relationship. The couple meet at a wild party (ambiguous space), and at the film's climax get married at a similar crazy party (ambiguous space again). The final party turns into a wild celebration (open space). The goal is to find a spatial structure that brings the story structure to visual life.

Making this graph forces you to think about each subcomponent of space. How can you use space to create a visual structure that tells your story, gives the film visual unity, and makes it unique?

Let's look at line, shape, color, tone, and rhythm in the same way.

EXAMPLE #3

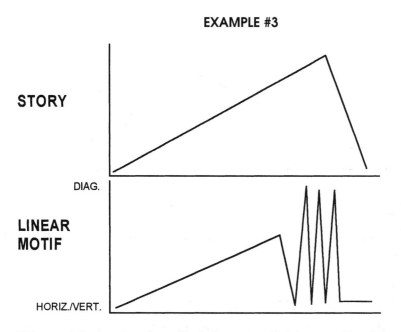

STORY

DIAG.

LINEAR
MOTIF

HORIZ./VERT.

This graph is the plan for a film's linear motif. It's a combination of a progression and contrast/affinity. The linear motif begins with horizontal/vertical, and as the story unfolds, the linear motif begins a progression towards diagonal lines. Near the climax of the story, the motif alternates between horizontal/vertical and diagonal lines. In the resolution, all of the lines become horizontal/vertical again.

Perhaps this is an action story. As it increases in intensity, the linear motif becomes diagonal to give the story's action sequences an increasing dynamic. To make the climax even more intense, the visual structure returns to horizontal/vertical before the climax, so the sudden use of extreme diagonals during the climax has even greater visual contrast and intensity.

We have now given the visual component of line a structure that is based on our understanding of the story intensity. We're now using the visual component of line to help tell the story.

EXAMPLE #4

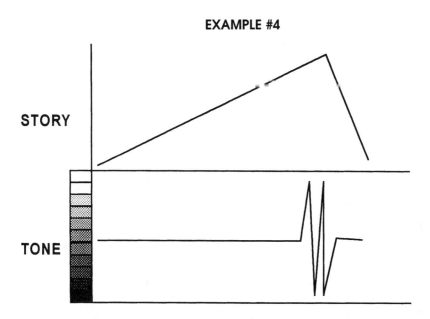

This graph plots the contrast and affinity of tone or the brightness range of the shots in our production. Instead of labeling the graph "black" and "white" this graph actually presents the gray scale. In this example, the production will have affinity of middle grays until the climax, where the tonal structure will change to contrast. During the story resolution, the tonal range will return to affinity in the middle range of grays.

Perhaps this story is about conformity (affinity of tone): the hero tries unsuccessfully to break out (contrast of tone) and fails (return to affinity of tone).

This tone graph plots the same structure as the one above.

EXAMPLE #5

The graphing for color is complex because there are so many aspects of color to consider.

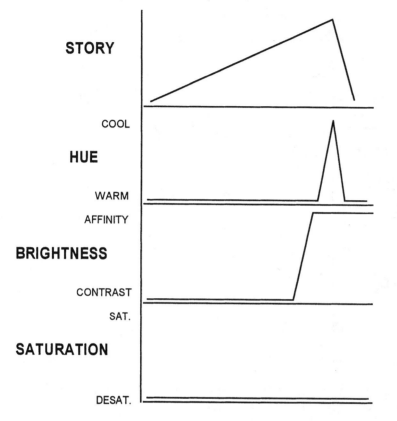

According to these graphs, color will be structured in the following way:

1. All warm colors that shift to cool at the climax.
2. Begin with contrast of brightness, which will change to affinity for the climax and resolution.
3. Remain desaturated throughout.

The terms "warm" and "cool" used in the hue graph are very general, so we could create a graph that gets more specific. The warm hues are red, orange, yellow, and red magenta, but we might only want to use red and orange hues in this production. Maybe the term "cool" is too general and we really want a cyan/yellow hue. It's easy to relabel the hue graph and make a more specific choice.

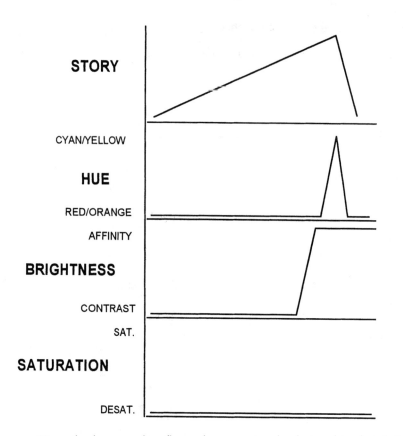

STORY

CYAN/YELLOW

HUE

RED/ORANGE

AFFINITY

BRIGHTNESS

CONTRAST

SAT.

SATURATION

DESAT.

Now the hue graph reflects the warm/cool relationship, but it is more hue specific.

A color graph can only be used as a general guide because you can't rely on words to describe specific colors. A color script is the best way to plan your color structure.

EXAMPLE #6

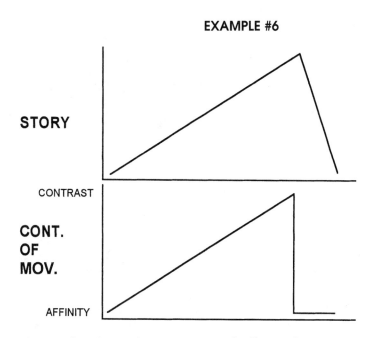

STORY

CONTRAST

**CONT.
OF
MOV.**

AFFINITY

This graph indicates how contrast and affinity of continuum of movement will be used. The film starts with affinity of continuum of movement but will slowly change towards contrast as the conflict intensifies. The climax will have maximum contrast of continuum of movement. The resolution of the film will return to affinity of continuum of movement.

Controlling the continuum of movement will effect how scenes are staged by the director, composed by the camera operator, and later assembled by the editor.

The continuum graph can be created when you plan your production. It may change when you shoot and again when the shots are edited together. A new plan for the continuum of movement often evolves in postproduction because most of continuum of movement depends on editing.

Suppose you've been editing an action sequence and the planned structure doesn't have a build in intensity. Perhaps it was shot wrong or the actors were weak. If you examine the edited footage and graph the contrasts and affinities, you can discover how the intensity was structured. If the sequence needs more intensity, you can regraph and then recut the footage to increase or decrease visual intensity as needed.

EXAMPLE #7

So far, all the examples show the visual intensity paralleling the story intensity. The most contrasting visuals have occurred at the most intense parts of the story. But it doesn't have to work that way. You can choose to link the story and visual intensities so they move together or you can slip them out of synchronizing with each other.

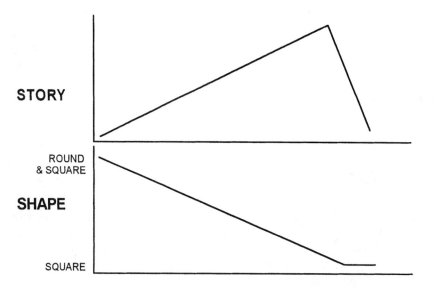

This graph deals with the general shape of objects in the frame. The visual plan here is to start the film with contrast between round and square shapes, and as the film progresses, the round shapes are removed from the shots. By the end of the story all the shapes are square.

Although the contrast occurs early in the film and the affinity is used at the climax, this may not be bad structure. Again, we're only trying to tell the story visually. Some stories may have aspects of the plot or character relationships where the visual components should develop affinity.

This story could be about two people who are separate and different. As the story unfolds, they learn to share. Shape's visual progression from contrast to affinity illustrates the character's behavioral changes. Choosing this visual structure for shape will help us make choices for set dressing, props, and lighting schemes.

The story structure graph still builds to a climax in the conventional manner, so we'll need contrast in other visual components to make the visual intensity parallel the story intensity.

EXAMPLE #8

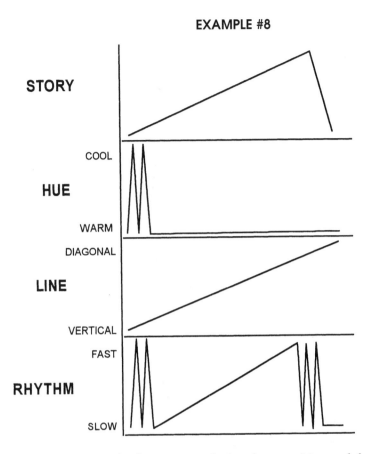

In this structure, color has contrast during the exposition and then remains warm throughout the rest of the production. But the story still builds to a climax. To keep the overall visual structure parallel with the story structure, line and rhythm gain contrast as the story reaches its climax.

An analysis of the script is the key to discovering the best visual structure for the visual components. Perhaps this story begins with a flashback that is the motivation for the events that take place in the rest of the story. To give this flashback special emphasis, it will use warm and cool colors that will generate contrast with the rest of the film, which will be a warm. Even though color will have this contrast during the exposition, the other components will still support the story's traditional structure.

EXAMPLE #9

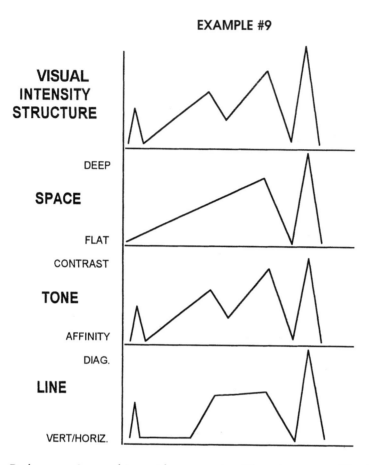

**VISUAL
INTENSITY
STRUCTURE**

DEEP

SPACE

FLAT

CONTRAST

TONE

AFFINITY

DIAG.

LINE

VERT/HORIZ.

Perhaps you're working without a script. There is no text. You have been asked to "make something visual" and later, music or sound effects will be added to your purely visual creation. Using the graphs, you can structure your visual ideas because you understand the Principle of Contrast and Affinity.

There isn't a story graph here because there isn't any script. Instead, there's a visual intensity graph that builds to a climax. How was this visual intensity structure created? It was arbitrarily generated, based on an understanding of the basic parts of any structure: exposition, conflict, climax, and resolution. If there isn't any script or text, a structure is still needed as a guide for controlling the visual components. Maybe this visual sequence is a dance, a montage, a nonverbal television commercial, or a ten-second corporate logo. The sequence is still going to need a structure.

Once the visual intensity structure is set, it becomes easy to create graphs for each visual component, and then, using the Principle of Contrast and Affinity, to organize the basic visual components to support the Visual Structure graph.

Examine the space, tone, and line graphs and see how they contribute to generating the visual intensity dictated by the Visual Intensity Structure graph. When the visual intensity graph indicates a change in intensity, the visual components of space, tone, and line gain affinity or contrast to support the visual structure.

EXAMPLE #10

There are also situations where the visual structure must be based upon certain preexisting visual elements like stock footage or established art work. In these cases you must work backwards and analyze the basic visual components as they already appear in the existing material.

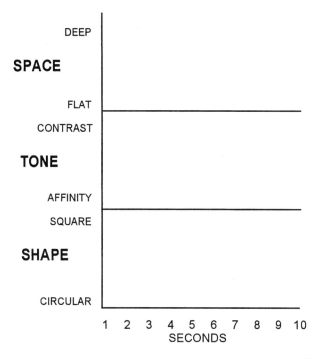

Notice that the story intensity graph is missing. This time we're going to create the visual component graphs first and use them to plot the structure for the space, tone, and shape in our existing visual material.

Let's assume we've been given a corporate logo. We've been asked to produce a ten-second sequence that ends with four seconds of the logo.

First we need to examine the existing logo. Is it flat, deep, limited, or ambiguous space? What are its tonal or brightness characteristics? What kind of shape does it have? The logo's visual component characteristics can be drawn into the visual component graphs.

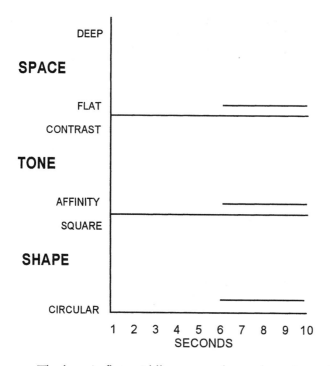

The logo is flat, middle gray, and round, so these visual characteristic have been drawn into the graphs.

Since the sequence ends with the logo and holds for four seconds, we can create a six-second structure that builds to the logo's appearance. What kind of structure will we use? How will we use the visual components? There are only three choices:

1. Constant
2. Progression
3. Contrast/Affinity

Let's draw some visual component structures into the first six seconds of the graphs.

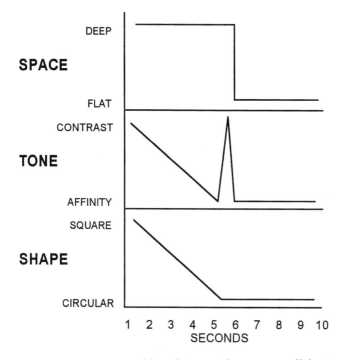

Here is one possible solution. The space will begin deep and become flat when the logo appears. The tone will begin with visual contrast, slowly gain affinity, and become contrasty just before the logo appears. The shapes on screen will begin square but progress into the circular logo.

What kind of overall visual structure does this combination of space, tone, and shape create? Let's add a visual intensity graph to the top of our other graphs and see what we've created.

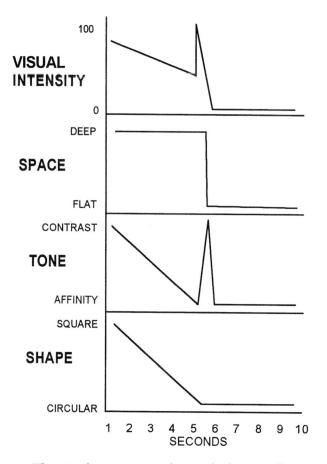

The visual intensity graph reveals the overall visual structure created by the visual component choices we've made. The climax or most intense part of the sequence is the appearance of the logo. The visual structure is now a graph, and we can refine or change it to make the structure better.

We could try other visual solutions with more contrast, add a spike at the exposition, or create a version that starts with great affinity and gains contrast just before the logo appears. The visual components will allow us to create whatever intensity or visual structure we feel is best suited for the ten-second logo.

EXAMPLE #11

This graph will take an extremely untraditional approach to visual structure. It will graph chaos, or an apparent lack of structure. Of course, even chaos has a structure; in fact, chaos is extremely difficult to achieve and maintain.

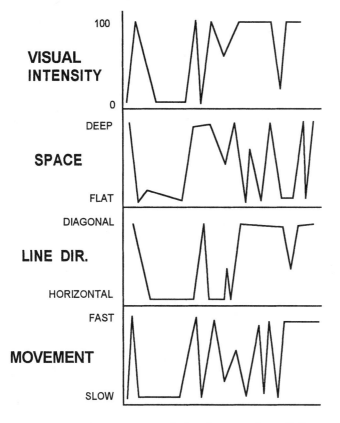

The visual intensity graph has large and small fluctuations in intensity that produce a random quality. Each visual component has been changed to contrast or affinity to parallel the chaotic structure of the visual intensity graph. The components alternate in a random pattern to keep the visual variety changing and unpredictable. Chaos demands unusual variety in it's structure, so that no pattern can be seen by the viewer.

EXAMPLE #12

Here are most of the visual components graphed in relation to the story intensity build. Due to page size, this run of graphs covers two pages. The story graph is repeated at the top of both pages.

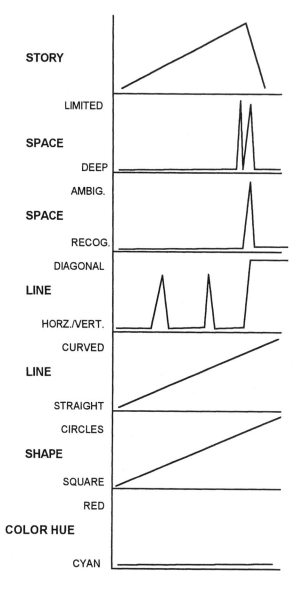

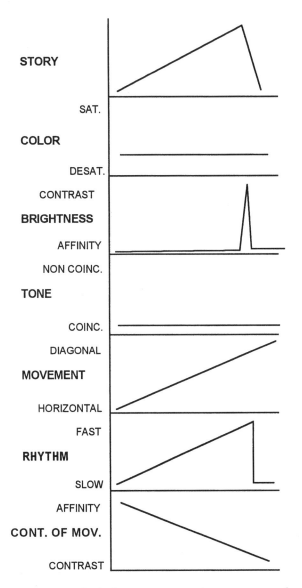

STORY

COLOR
- SAT.
- DESAT.

BRIGHTNESS
- CONTRAST
- AFFINITY

TONE
- NON COINC.
- COINC.

MOVEMENT
- DIAGONAL
- HORIZONTAL

RHYTHM
- FAST
- SLOW

CONT. OF MOV.
- AFFINITY
- CONTRAST

You can include as many graphs as your production requires. Each time you add a visual component graph under your story graph, you force yourself to answer questions about the visual structure of your production. The more questions you can answer, the easier it will be to choose locations, design sets, light your shots, place the camera, pick lenses, and stage your actors.

Although this set of graphs doesn't account for all of the subcomponents, it gives us a sense of the general visual possibilities available for any production. Here's a more comprehensive list:

1. STORY: Intensity
2. SPACE: Flat/deep
3. SPACE: Ambiguous/recognizable

4. SPACE: Open/closed
5. SPACE: Surface divisions
6. LINE: Quality
7. LINE: Intensity
8. LINE: Direction
9. SHAPE: 2-D/3-D
10. SHAPE: Circle, square, triangle
11. COLOR: Hue
12. COLOR: Brightness (same as Tonal Range)
13. COLOR: Saturation
14. COLOR: Warm/cool
15. COLOR: Complimentary
16. TONE: Incident/reflectance
17. TONE: Coincidence/noncoincidence
18. MOVEMENT: (Object) Direction
19. MOVEMENT: (Object) Fast/slow
20. MOVEMENT: Continuum of movement
21. MOVEMENT: (Camera) 2-D/3-D
22. RHYTHM: (Stationary objects) Fast/slow
23. RHYTHM: (Stationary objects) Regular/irregular
24. RHYTHM: (Moving objects) Fast/slow
25. RHYTHM: (Moving objects) Regular/irregular
26. RHYTHM: (Moving objects) Accelerate/decelerate
27. RHYTHM: (Editorial) Fast/slow
28. RHYTHM: (Editorial) Regular/irregular
29. RHYTHM: (Editorial) Accelerate/decelerate
30. RHYTHM: Continuous/fragmented

Whenever you begin thinking about the visual component graphs, you must first consider the story. Since the visuals are being used to tell the story, you must begin by understanding and diagramming the story intensity.

The story graph in these examples has been left rather general on purpose. Your story should be graphed more carefully with the specific intensity rises and falls of the script drawn into the graph. Remember, too, that the story intensities can change during shooting and especially editing. Story situations may change dynamic once they are filmed. Scenes may also change intensity in postproduction once they have been edited together.

Since a story can be restructured in editing, its entire balance can change as scenes are moved, shortened, or removed from the story. Be ready to regraph the intensities of your story and visual components during postproduction. Deciding how to align the visual component's structure to your script can be a learning process as you discover more about the story and visual structure in postproduction.

CHAPTER 10

PRACTICE, NOT THEORY

Now that we've defined each visual component, explained contrast and affinity, and introduced the concept of graphing, it's time to put theory into practice. The most rewarding part is how well the theory works when you use it.

CHOOSING YOUR VISUAL RULES

You must begin with your idea, concept, story, or script. What are you trying to say to your audience? What group of visual components will communicate your ideas in the best possible way? There are plenty of solutions. It would be impossible to discuss all of the visual component variations available to you, so don't be constrained by the limits of this book.

You can invent your own type of space if you want. You don't have to confine your choices to flat, deep, limited, and ambiguous. Define your own space. Mix and match the deep and flat cues to create a space that best suits you and your story. Perhaps your new type of space uses all of the depth cues, but the colors are only cool and the lenses are always telephoto. Maybe you prefer limited space, but you like to use movement perpendicular to the picture plane. Fine. Use it. Make new visual rules that satisfy your requirements, but whatever you decide, stick to your rules or understand what will happen if you don't.

If you decide that your production will use flat space, you have made a sweeping decision that will radically affect the way you prepare and photograph your production. The choice of flat space will dictate where the camera is set for every shot. Actors will be staged in a specific manner to emphasize the flat space. Lenses and locations will be selected with flat space in mind, and lighting and color schemes will be adjusted to help create flat space. Suddenly your film will have a particular visual style because you've set down one rule. But don't stop there.

Find rules for the color, too. Although there are some traditional color schemes that work well, you can make up your own. Draw a subtractive color wheel and pick specific hues for your production. Don't limit yourself to warm, cool, or complementary color schemes. Read your script and pick the hues, brightnesses, and saturations that will tell the story as you see it.

Find rules for line, shape, and movement. Will there be any diagonal lines in your shots? If so, when will they appear and why? If you're photographing a series of chases, should they look identical or build in intensity? What visual rules can you create for movement to help make your visual structure support the story?

Visual rules will give your production visual unity. The actor's performances will have unity. The music will have unity. The visuals need unity, too. This doesn't mean that actor's performances, musical themes, or visual components can't change as the story progresses—they can. These changes are called an arc or progression. Any component can change as the story's plot develops.

You have three opportunities to create these rules: during preparation, during production, and during postproduction. The rules may change because the circumstances on the set are not what you had planned or you discover a better solution. In postproduction you might find that your original plan isn't working and a new visual structure must be created. Sometimes a reshoot is necessary. Understanding the problems in the existing visual structure is critical to developing a new structure that will solve the problems.

How do you go about finding the right visual rules? There are four ways: the arbitrary choice, the instinctual choice, the researched choice, and the analytic choice, or point of view.

THE ARBITRARY CHOICE

You may have absolutely no idea how to pick visual rules. Even though you understand the definition of every visual component, you can't decide what choice will be best. If this is the problem, then toss a coin in the air, throw darts at a list, or pick components out of a hat, but *choose something* and make that arbitrary choice the rule.

The worst thing you can do is to make no choice. Remember that if you choose not to control the visual components, they will structure themselves anyway and the audience will react to that structure. The resulting uncontrolled structure will probably work against the telling of your story.

Making an arbitrary choice forces you to confront each visual component. In working with arbitrary visual component choices, you usually discover something that works better and you can then adjust and refine your choices.

THE INSTINCTUAL CHOICE

There are many directors, designers, and photographers who control visual structure using instinct or "raw talent" (an overused term at best). Instinct is a fine way to get the ball rolling, or, if you work alone and have plenty of time and money to spend in a lifetime. Great instincts are unexplainable, coming from a unique inner voice that offers solutions to visual structure problems.

When you first read a script or prepare with your cast and crew, there are moments of inspiration where your instincts suggest ideas. That's when instincts are great. Use them. You may never understand why your instincts were correct, but when you see the final product you'll realize you made the right decision.

But sometimes instincts are incomplete, unreliable, or wrong. Instinctual choices may represent old habits or underdeveloped ideas that sound good but are ultimately disappointing. Sometimes our instincts are "of the moment" and later appear meaningless. "If you had been there, it seemed to work" is a lame explanation for a poor instinctual choice. Instincts can be great, but they're not always reliable.

When you understand the visual components and visual structure you can elaborate on your instincts and make better use of your ideas. When your instincts collapse, knowledge of visual structure and the visual components can keep you moving forward.

THE RESEARCHED CHOICE

When you prepare a production, you're looking for the inspiration to guide you in choosing rules for the visual components. Obviously, you start by reading the script, but where do you go next? Here are some places:

1. *Look at pictures.* Find art books with drawings, paintings, and photographs from various periods in time (not just the period of your story) that look correct for the visuals in your production. Better yet, visit an art museum and look at the actual paintings. If the visual components in certain paintings or photographs appeal to you, ask yourself why. What is there about the space, line, shape, tone, and color that can work for your production? How can you recreate or elaborate on a borrowed visual structure? Make a scrapbook of pictures that have inspired your rules for the visual components. Give a copy of that scrapbook to your key crew members so they can see what you have in mind.

2. *Do research.* Go to a library and dig up everything you can find on the subject of your project. You'll discover words and pictures you never knew existed that will inspire you and give you new ideas about controlling visual structure.

3. *Look at old movies.* This includes movies from last year that you missed. There are thousands of movies you haven't seen. Do some exploring. Old films have millions of great visual ideas to borrow or enhance.

4. *Hire an artist to draw concept renderings.* Let visually creative people dream about how your production might look. Study their drawings because it can help you discover the visual structure for your production. In animation, dozens of artists create hundreds of conceptual drawings exploring possible visual styles. Experiment. Draw something, anything, and see how it looks.

ANALYTIC CHOICE: POINT OF VIEW

You can build a set of visual rules by analyzing the story or script and discovering both the author's and your own point of view.

The term *point of view* has a variety of meanings. Usually it refers to the angle of the camera, but in this book point of view refers to the way that you want the audience to feel about your subject or story.

For example, if you were a writer and your subject was a detective, you'd write your story with a particular point of view in mind. The point of view would dictate how you'd write the detective's character. Here are five possible point-of-view choices:

1. Detectives are intellectual geniuses.
2. Detectives are rough and barely above the law.
3. Detectives are witty, high-society alcoholics.
4. Detectives are incompetent.
5. Detectives are maniacs.

There's a huge difference in the writer's point of view about detectives when we compare Conan Doyle's intellectual Sherlock Holmes (played by Basil Rathbone), Hammett's rough Sam Spade (played by Humphrey Bogart), Hackett and Goodrich's Nick Charles (played by William Powell), Edwards and Richlin's incompetent Inspector Clousseau (played by Peter Sellers), and Bernstein and Shadyac's maniacal Ace Ventura (played by Jim Carrey). They're all detectives, but they're not alike because each was written with a different point of view.

In each case, the subject is a detective, but the way the audience is led to feel about that particular detective is different. A writer must know how they want the audience to feel about their detective, or they really won't know what to write. The more specific the point of view, the easier it will be to write appropriately. If the script is written properly the audience will understand the point of view about the subject.

Point of view sets up rules for the writer about plot, character, and dialogue. Point of view also sets up rules for the director, photographer, and production designer about the visuals. If you know your point of view you can use the basic visual components to control how the audience feels about the subject. As you choose the rules for each visual component, you are making selections that communicate your point of view.

VISUAL COMPONENT CONTROL

You've read your script and developed a point of view. Now it's time to begin making visual component choices and find the visual rules for your production. A good way to begin is by listing the seven basic visual components:

1. SPACE
2. LINE
3. SHAPE
4. COLOR
5. TONE
6. MOVEMENT
7. RHYTHM

Now, what will you do with each one of them? Here are some ideas:

1. You can think of your production as a single continuous visual entity and set up visual rules that will remain constant throughout the production. As an example, let's give ourselves this set of components choices:

- SPACE—deep
- LINE—vertical and horizontal
- SHAPE—square
- COLOR—cool and desaturated
- TONE—mid-range
- MOVEMENT—moderate
- RHYTHM—moderate

This is an excellent approach. It will assure a unity to the visual structure, and it will become easy to control and maintain because the crew will become familiar with the techniques needed to achieve these simple visual goals.

2. You might want to try something more complex and have one visual component change or make a progression during your production. A progression is a slow change from one aspect to another. All of the other components will remain unchanged. Here's an example:

- SPACE—deep changes to flat
- LINE—vertical and horizontal
- SHAPE—square
- COLOR—cool and desaturated
- TONE—mid-range
- MOVEMENT—moderate
- RHYTHM—moderate

Although we could pick any visual component for the change, in this example space is going to slowly progress from deep to flat. Any change in the visual components should be motivated by thematic or character changes in the story. In a story, a change or a progression is usually called an arc.

2a. *The Story Arc.* We can relate the visual component change to an arc in the overall theme of the story.

For example, the story situation might arc from calm to chaotic, or from dangerous to safe. A character may arc from sad to happy or from arrogant to humble. In each case, the story or characters progressively change, creating an arc. A change in a single visual component (in this example, space) can be used to illustrate this story or character arc. The space begins deep and, as the story arc progresses, the space will change to flat. The story arc and the visual progression are now linked together.

2b. *The Act Arc.* Longer scripts and stories are broken down into parts called acts. It's possible to make the visual components change with each new act.

Act One: flat space
Act Two: deep space
Act Three: flat space

Remember, there are also one-, two-, four-, five-, six-, and seven-act structures. A visual component arc can be arranged and distributed over any number of acts.

2c. *The Scene Arc.* A script is divided into sequences or scenes that allow us to create smaller or more complicated visual arcs. We can make a scene list and assign the visual component change to each sequence.

Scene 1-4: flat space
Scene 5: deep space
Scene 6-9: flat space
Scene 10: deep space
Scene 11-15: flat space
Scene 16: deep space

Of course, this organization is starting to feel like the graphs we produced in the last chapter, and a graph is an easier way to plan your visual controls.

This is exactly the same plan as the scene list, but it has been converted into a graph. The graph gives you a simple way to visualize your plan for any visual component. Note that the timeline has been replaced by scene numbers.

2d. *The Directorial Beat Arc.* We can also take any scene and break it down into beats. Beats divide a scene into small parts. Each beat indicates a change in the intentions or relationships between characters. Beats are defined more completely in Part H of the Appendix. A beat list can organize the basic visual components within a scene. This example uses the scene found in Part H of the Appendix.

Beat 1: flat space
Beat 2: flat space
Beat 3: deep space
Beat 4: deep space
Beat 5: flat space

Instead of a list, we could draw a graph that shows the visual component changes in relation to the beats.

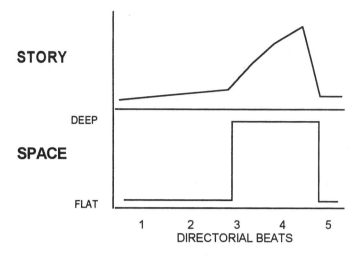

Notice that the timeline has been replaced by the directorial beats.

3. The next level of complexity is to make more than one visual component change. We're still going to start with our basic list of the visual components:

- SPACE—deep changes to flat
- LINE—vertical and horizontal
- SHAPE—square
- COLOR—cool changes to warm
- TONE—mid-range
- MOVEMENT—moderate
- RHYTHM—moderate

Notice that color is going to make a change from cool to warm. We could make changes in as many basic visual components as necessary.

4. Now our visual scheme is going to become fairly complicated. Let's expand the list of basic visual components to include some of the subcomponents. The list is longer, but the basis for making choices is still understanding the story and having a point of view.

- SPACE—deep changes to flat
- LINE—
    a. curved changes to straight
    b. vertical and horizontal
- SHAPE—circle changes to square
- COLOR—
    a. hue: red, orange, green
    b. brightness: dark
    c. saturation: desaturated
- TONE—
    a. dark
    b. coincidence
- MOVEMENT—
    a. object: slow changes to fast
    b. camera: none to fast

- RHYTHM—
  a. editorial: moderate to fast

Ask yourself which components should stay the same and which components should change. Remember that changes can occur within a shot, from shot to shot, and from sequence to sequence. Your choices create rules that will give your production visual structure. Draw graphs and see what you like best.

Making decisions about the visual components is essential to controlling the visual structure of your production. Different directors, cinematographers, and production designers work in different ways to solve the problem of finding a visual structure. Here are some suggestions for finding a method that works for you:

1. *You can wait until the day of shooting and work out the scene's structure that morning with the actors and the crew.* This works well if you're fast and clever. You can move through each scene one day at a time. Ultimately, this gets difficult to maintain because you get worn down or forget things. On the one hand, there's nothing more exciting than the moment-to-moment collaboration of cast and crew, but there's nothing more potentially disastrous as well. Being unprepared and spending production time searching for answers can be a recipe for disaster. You can get a unique, spontaneous result making it up as you go along, but it's hard to maintain, difficult for the people working with you to follow, and, of course, expensive.

2. *Make notes, drawings, and maps of your plan before you get to the set.* Jot down ideas in your script about the meaning of a scene and how it can be communicated using the visual components. On the set, these notes will remind you of your ideas.

Make a little list of the basic visual components in your script. At the beginning of each scene, write down how the components will be controlled. If a component is going to change, write down a quick note to yourself about that change. Directors often write notes in their script about an actor's emotional state or the staging of a scene. Why not make notes about the visual components, too?

The earlier you begin this process the better. As you prepare, collaborate with your photographer and production designer about how to choose and control the visual components. Give yourself time to allow your visual ideas to mature.

3. *Approach the entire process like a stage play.* Bring in your actors, mark off the rehearsal room floor with the dimensions of your locations, and spend time rehearsing as if your production was a theater play. This will allow you to concentrate on the story and the actors. During this rehearsal period, you'll find the best actor staging and camera angles, discover the story's point of view, and refine your ideas for the control of the visual components.

Since you can rehearse your entire script in real time, you'll have a unique opportunity to see the story uninterrupted from beginning to end. You won't have this view of your production again until you're in the editing room. As you watch, think about how each visual component can work to help tell your story.

What aspects of the story and the actor's performances can be underscored by a visual component?

4. *You can create storyboards that are drawings of each camera angle.* A completed storyboard looks like a comic book version of the film. There are actually two times when storyboards come in handy. They can be drawn during preproduction so you know what to shoot, and they can be created in postproduction. Often the footage doesn't look like the storyboards, so generating new storyboards for the actual footage may help you find the best way to edit the footage together. Instead of drawing storyboards, you can use actual still frames made from a video printer.

What's the purpose of storyboarding? Storyboards illustrate a shot before you shoot it. Storyboards show you what is in the shot and the general composition. But storyboards are also a visual script that is almost as difficult to create as the script itself.

If storyboards are to be of any use, they can't be taken lightly. If you use storyboards, they should be as important a commitment as the script itself. You may need to redraw the storyboards again and again just like a writer must rewrite a script. Creating storyboards gives you the chance to visualize how you'll structure the basic visual components. Use storyboards to discover how you'll compose your shots, stage your actors, and use the visual components. See Part I of the Appendix for a further discussion about storyboards.

5. *Bring friends to your locations and take still photos that represent the shots you'll later shoot with your actors and crew.* A drawback to storyboards is that they often show camera angles that are impossible to create with a real camera. Shooting still photos with a camera in the actual location will give you an accurate idea of what the space, line, shape, and color will look like in your final production.

Try shooting various angles and decide which ones look best when the still photos are printed. Then take these still pictures and make them your storyboards. Now you have pictures that you can analyze in terms of the visual components. Do the visual components in the still photos work? If not, what should you change to make them work? Is there a problem with the camera angle, lens choice, lighting, color? Creating these still photos let's you see your visual component choices before you actually shoot.

6. *Bring actors to your locations and videotape the rehearsals.* Shoot all the necessary angles, edit them together, and see if you like the results. This is similar to using stills, but it gives you even more information about your final production. Video cameras are inexpensive and easy to use, so it's possible to produce a quick version of your entire production. Study this rough version of your production and see how the visual components are working.

The end result of this preparation process is always the same. You're looking for ways to find a visual structure that will tell your story and express your point of view.

VISUAL CONTROL FOR DIFFERENT PRODUCTIONS

In this book, most of the examples deal with longer stories usually found in television and theatrical features. But the principles of visual structure apply to any kind of production that appears on any kind of screen. Here are specific ways to approach visual structure depending on the kind of a production you're involved in.

THE ADVERTISEMENT

An ad can be a commercial on television, a pop-up banner on the Web, a billboard, or a magazine layout designed to make the consumer buy a product or service. Controlling visual structure is essential, because advertisements are brief and relatively expensive to produce.

A commercial, like any production must have a structure. It can have a traditional structure with a clearly defined expositional beginning, a middle with conflict and climax, and a resolution, or it may be less traditional, deleting or rearranging these structural elements. Even if the structure is "random," it will still have a structure, and the visual components must be employed to produce that random visual quality.

Commercials are often driven by technology. As soon as a new visual effect is created, it shows up in a commercial trying to be unique and eye-catching. These new tricks are always interesting, but you must remember that the result of any special effect is simply a new way to use or create the basic visual components and the Principle of Contrast and Affinity.

Commercials go through visual phases or fads. Over the years these have included rapid editing, multiple image layering, selective focus, color shifts in hue and saturation, soft-focus filters, morphing, typography movement, distortion lenses, letterboxing, stroboscopic photography, time lapse, split screens, slow or fast motion, and accelerating or decelerating movement. Visual fads in commercials are actually just new variations in the visual components. These new combinations will appear to have more visual contrast and intensity until that fad has been exploited, then there's a shift to a new set of visual components choices that become the next trendy visual fad.

Because a commercial is so short the visuals often take precedence over the story content. In fact, it's not uncommon for the visuals to become the content. This means that you have to structure the visuals even more carefully because it's not the visuals supporting a story, it's just visuals for the sake of visuals. Creating an intensity build for these visuals is the key to an interesting commercial.

THE DOCUMENTARY

Shooting a documentary is not an excuse to ignore controlling the visual components. You always have the ability to control the visual structure, even in situations where it seems impossible.

Let's talk about three basic types of documentary:

1. Using found footage.
2. Shooting in a controlled situation.
3. Shooting in an uncontrolled situation.

Found Footage

Found footage means that you will assemble your production using footage that is archival photographs or film and videotape that has already been shot by other people. Essentially you'll only need postproduction, because you are simply going to edit together visual material that already exists.

Finding the story structure and creating a visual structure that supports it is still the critical problem. What will your point of view be? How will you communicate it to the audience?

You can still plan and storyboard your production, but you'll do it based on the material you already have. Analyze it for space, line, shape, tone, color, movement, and rhythm and then use the editing process to structure the visual components.

Controlled Documentary

The controlled documentary situation allows you to create your own visuals. Even if your documentary is full of "talking heads," you have a lot of control. What kind of space will you place behind the people? What colors? What kind of lighting? What kind of lines and shapes? What lens will you use?

The answers to these questions lie in your script and your point of view. How do you want the audience to feel about the subject? What visual components will best communicate that feeling?

If your documentary is about a conflict, how can you make the opposing sides look different? If your documentary is informational, how do you want the audience to feel about the information they're getting? Should it be positive or negative? What is your point of view? It's impossible to ignore point of view. Even if you don't have one, the audience will find one. If you have no point of view, you'll have no way of knowing how to control any of the visual components in your shots because you won't know what to communicate to your audience.

Uncontrolled Documentary

Shooting a documentary in an uncontrolled situation is the toughest because you may not know what, if anything, is going to happen. The key is understanding your point of view. If something happens in your uncontrolled situation, how do you want the viewer to feel about it? You may need to have different visual plans in mind and have the ability to change plans quickly depending on the situation. If you have general rules for the visuals, it will help you make quick spontaneous decisions.

Examine your shooting location carefully before you begin and try to take advantage of the visuals that are already there. Can you control the space, color, or tone of your shots by moving your camera to a new position? Will certain lenses help to include or exclude certain visual components? The more you know about your subject and point of view, the easier it will be to photograph the pictures that communicate your ideas best.

THE TELEVISION ID

The television ID is not a commercial. It's simply a quick two-second reminder of something on television, usually the channel you're watching or the program's underwriter. Don't let the short time fool you. A lot can happen in just two seconds. The same rules of structure apply. There is still a beginning, middle, and an end. How can you move through that structure quickly and interestingly?

THE VIDEO GAME

The only difference between a traditional story and a video game story is that the viewer has some control over the plot. This, however, does not excuse the video-game creator from controlling the visual components.

Part of the experience of any video game is its structure and the progression in the journey or adventure that is the game. How can the structure of the game become more visually exciting as the game progresses? The answer is the Principle of Contrast and Affinity.

As a player advances to new levels, the game's intensifying conflict must be reflected in the visual structure. As a player gets closer to the completion (or climax) of each episode or level, the visuals should intensify or gain contrast.

All of the visual components are being used in any video game, and the game players will react to these components. Planning a visual structure, creating visual rules, and using them in a video game will greatly improve the gaming experience.

THE INTERNET

The Internet has given us a new avenue for watching our productions, but the computer is just another screen, and all of the visual components are still going to arrive on the screen every time you jump on the Web. It really doesn't matter if you're viewing a simple Web page or a video produced especially for the Internet. All of the visual structure ideas discussed in this book still apply. The Internet may be unique in its ability to send and receive images, but the structure of the images is still governed by the Principle of Contrast and Affinity.

MULTIPLE-CAMERA TELEVISION PROGRAMS

As long as the classic multicamera shooting style is used for situation comedies, daytime dramas, and talk shows, variations in the visual structure will be difficult. The space will remain flat, camera placement and lens choice will be limited, the lighting will be even, and the editing style will be motivated by close-ups. Those restrictions are acceptable, but most of these programs will look alike, as they do now. These visual limitations place almost all the emphasis on the actors, which is fine, but if you turn the sound off, you realize that all the content is being carried by the dialogue. Except for variations in set design and wardrobe, these shows have an identical visual style.

SINGLE-CAMERA TELEVISION PROGRAMS

Depending on your schedule and budget, there can be great variety in the visual structure of single-camera TV programs.

Quality single-camera television shows have tended to find very specific rules for the visual components and then exploit those rules to make their show look unique. Those choices usually involve color (limiting hue, brightness, and saturation), camera movement (using a dolly or going handheld), rhythm (traditional editing or unmotivated editorial styles), or space (limiting lens choices to either wide or telephoto lenses, and deliberate deep or flat staging of actors). The more specific the visual controls, the more visually individual the show becomes.

Very specific visual component rules work well for television shows that must shoot a lot of material quickly and change directors for each episode. The crew, which remains fairly constant, can maintain and refine the visual style. Because visual style is only a very specific set of basic visual components, finding one is not difficult.

FEATURE PRODUCTION

In a feature-length production, for television or movie theaters, the visual components should be explored from scratch. Each script should be approached with the idea that there is a unique set of visual components that will best communicate the story. The search for unique visual rules doesn't always happen. Directors, production designers, editors, and cinematographers may have visual styles that they repeat either because they have a fixed visual style that is their trademark, they're lazy, or because they're hired to duplicate another production. Cinematographers and Production Designers are often hired to repeat a style they created for another film. Some directors are hired for the same reason. Networks, producers, or studios may place limitations on visual choices by limiting budgets and shooting schedules. In an ideal situation, all of the choices for the visual components and contrast and affinity should be reconsidered each time a new project is started.

THE ANIMATED FILM

It doesn't matter if your animation is traditional or produced in a computer. Animation offers the greatest amount of visual control because everything in the shot must be created. It means that the number of visual control possibilities are far more complex because there are so many specific choices that must be made. There is no longer a gap between the live-action world and the animated world. Both share a common visual language.

Animation and computer-generated imagery is a visual area that has vast unexplored areas. We are just now beginning to see the visual ideas possible with these tools, which give us the chance to use the visual components in totally unique ways to tell stories.

DON'T GO CRAZY

It's easy to overthink and get bogged down in visual component control. Keep it simple. The clearer you can be about controlling the visual components, the easier it will be for your crew to help you and for the audience to sense the structure you had in mind. You need visual rules.

We give ourselves rules because it allows us to make choices easier. When there are no rules, no foundations for any decisions, then there's no right or wrong answer for any question. Even the most chaotic visual statement can be reduced to a set of rules.

Think about memorable or favorite pictures you've seen on a screen. Remember that a screen is a page in a book or magazine, a billboard, a canvas in a museum, a television or computer monitor, or a movie screen. At the foundation of all of those visuals, whether the creator knew it or not, are the visual components.

Some writers, directors, cinematographers, production designers, and editors cannot explain how they decided on certain visual ideas. Others know exactly why they did it. Actually, it doesn't matter at all. Whether it was accidental, instinctual, or carefully thought out, it made it to the screen and it had an effect on us, the audience.

Our purpose here is not to take other people's work and examine it one frame at a time. If you overthink the visual controls, you only see the leaves on the trees and you'll forget you're in a forest. You can become so concerned with minuscule details that the overall idea for your production becomes lost. Be careful. The audience is going to watch your production once, if you're lucky, and more than once if you're very, very lucky. Should we ignore detail and just go for the big picture? No. But there is a middle ground where we have to be able to balance practicality with reality.

We can learn from the past. We should watch old films and go to museums and see great photographs and paintings, but it's unnecessary to examine them with a microscope. At a certain point, it's better to go out and try it yourself.

What about spontaneity? Use it. Visual rules are a framework. You're not going to get arrested for breaking a visual rule, but you must keep in mind how it will affect the audience when a rule is broken. Don't strangle yourself with rules that make production unrealistic, but understand how and why visual structure communicates to the audience.

We set up rules because it helps the audience in two ways. First, they will respond to the visual unity of the film because it will become familiar to them. When you have rules and you stick to them, the production takes on its own specific look or visual style. Visual style, of course, is only a specific arrangement of the basic visual components.

Secondly, we can use the visual rules in conjunction with the Principle of Contrast and Affinity to control the visual structure of the film and give the audience a visual experience that parallels the story experience. An audience wants to be taken on a ride. When they sit down in front of a screen they want to be taken into a world that has structure. Even if what they watch only lasts ten seconds, they want it to have structure. Not just story structure but visual structure, too.

The Bicycle Thief, Citizen Kane, Die Hard, Cries and Whispers, The Godfather, Lawrence of Arabia, Manhattan, Saving Private Ryan, Rules of the Game, The Searchers, Yojimbo, and *8 1/2* each have a unique look because their visual rules are so strong. If you examine Alfred Hitchcock's films, you'll see how he refined his rules with each film. Ultimately this gave his lifetime of films a visual quality that was uniquely his.

If you spend too much time thinking about the visual components, you'll come up with a production that looks great and has no heart and soul. Remember that the job of the visual components is to support the story.

It's a person or a group of people in a situation. People get involved with other people or things that act like people. You must always start with your people, your personalities, and your story.

You must know your story and understand its structure. Then you can begin the exquisite journey into the world of visual structure.

APPENDIX

This appendix contains information that became too complex or lengthy to include in the main body of the book. Some of the subjects covered here are of a technical nature and may only be of interest to people with the appropriate background.

P A R T   A

NODAL POINT PHOTOGRAPHY

Nodal point panning and tilting occurs when the optical center of the lens is placed directly on axis with the pan and tilt movement of the camera.

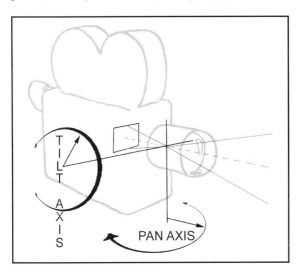

This keeps the optical center of the lens fixed as the camera is panned or tilted.

Originally developed for making camera moves in miniature and special effect photography, the nodal point tilt and pan will create absolutely no relative movement from FG to BG. Most conventional camera tripod heads are not set up for nodal point photography and will always create minor but perceptible levels of relative movement between the FG and BG.

P A R T   B

DEPTH OF FIELD: LENSES' EFFECTS ON SPACE

Even though wide-angle lenses have a greater depth of field, all lenses have the same depth of field when the image size of the subject is kept the same.

Here's an example:

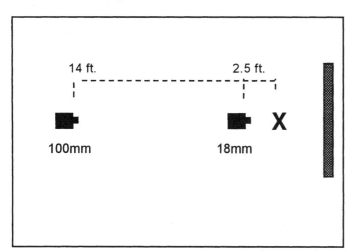

This is an overhead view or ground plan of a wall, an actor (indicated by the X), and a camera. The camera, with a 100mm telephoto lens, is set up 14 feet from an actor in front of a wall, but the wall is out of focus, and we want both the actor and the wall to be in focus. Without moving the camera, we switch to an 18mm wide-angle lens that we think "has a much greater depth of field."

Now the actor and wall are both in focus but they're too small in the frame, so we move the camera closer to get the same image size on the actor that we had with the 100mm telephoto lens.

When the camera is 2 $^{1}/_{2}$ feet in front of the actor, we have duplicated the image size we had with the 100mm lens, but the wall will be out of focus again. We'll see more of the wall because the 18mm lens' angle of view is so wide, but the wall will be as out of focus as it was with the 100mm telephoto lens at 14 feet. All lenses have the same depth of field given the same image size.

This does not mean that wide-angle lenses won't help in the creation of illusory depth. They will. But the wide-angle lens will help because it forces us to place objects closer to the camera.

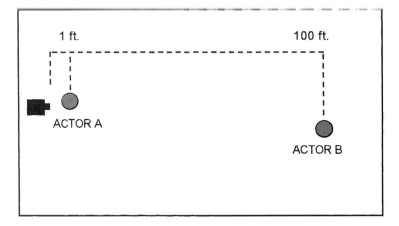

This is an overhead view or ground plan showing the camera and two actors. Note that ACTOR A is only 1 foot from the camera, and ACTOR B is 100 feet from the camera.

This scene, photographed with a 15mm wide angle lens, would look something like this:

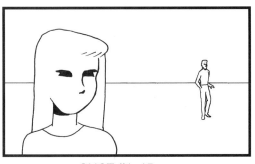

SHOT #1 15mm

The woman (Actor A) in the foreground will be extremely large in the frame, and we'd see lots of detail in her face and hair. The man (Actor B), 100 feet away in the distance, will be small in comparison and we would not see any details at all.

The woman looks biggest because she is only 1 foot from the camera. The man is 100 feet from the camera or 10,000% further away. No wonder he looks so small compared to the woman.

Keeping the camera in the exact same place, lets put a 500mm telephoto lens on the camera and look again.

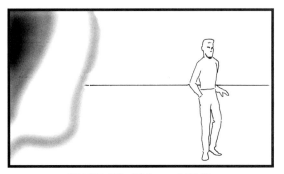

SHOT #2 500mm LENS

Shot #2 appears flat because there are no depth cues in the shot. Only one of the two actors will be in focus, and we know that once an object is out of focus it cannot be read as a depth cue. The woman is too close to the camera and will photograph as an out-of-focus shape.

Now keeping the actors in the same place, let's move our camera with the 500mm telephoto lens. We'll move back 2,500 feet (roughly half a mile) and we'll look at the two actors again.

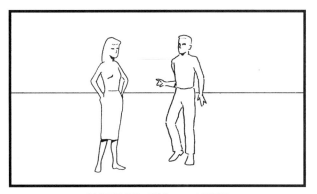

SHOT #3 500mm LENS

Shot #3 looks very flat. Both actors are in focus and appear almost the same size. Why? Because they're both nearly the same distance from the camera. The woman is 2,501 feet away and the man is 2,600 feet away. The man is only 4% further away than the woman. No wonder they look the same size. This shot appears flat because of the distance of the objects from the camera. A telephoto lens cannot compress the image. It has no magical powers to flatten, or squash things together. The telephoto lens can, however, *exclude* the depth cues.

Keeping the camera 2,500 feet away, we'll now switch to a 15mm wide-angle lens.

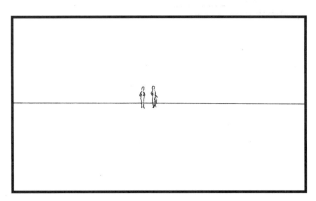

SHOT #4 15mm LENS

With this setup, we would only see two tiny, distant actors. But if you enlarged Shot #4 it would look exactly like Shot #3.

As we use longer telephoto lenses, we're forced to back the camera up in order to include and compose the objects in the frame. As we back up the camera, we gain more and more distance between the camera and the objects we're photographing. This forces all in-focus objects to remain at a greater distance from the lens. When this happens, the space, due to the distance of objects from the camera, appears to flatten, but it only looks flatter because everything is equally far from the camera.

The point here is that a lens can't "compress" or "deepen" a shot. Don't depend on wide-angle or telephoto lenses to create deep or flat space. The lens can help, but the creation of these two types of space will be due to the distance of objects from the camera and the lens's ability to get them into view.

Is it possible to shoot a deep space scene using a telephoto lens? Yes, although it might be easier with a wider-angle lens because the wider lens can include more depth cues.

Is it possible to shoot a flat space movie with wide-angle lenses? Yes, although it's sometimes easier to use a telephoto lens because it excludes the depth cues so quickly.

P A R T   C

ANAMORPHIC LENSES AND 70MM

Standard lenses are called spherical or "flat" lenses. They are used to photograph 1.33, 1.66, and 1.85 films and all of the television shows that you watch. Spherical or "flat" means that the lens' glass elements are round (not oblong or asymmetrical) and produce an image that is not distorted. (Spherical lenses are used on all still cameras.) In the early 1950s, Hollywood adopted a system that used aspherical or anamorphic lenses that purposely distorted the image. This system, first made famous by 20th Century Fox, was called Cinemascope.

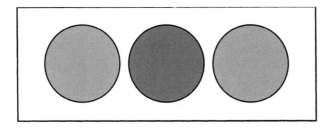

This is a 2.40:1 shot when seen through the camera's viewfinder. Using an anamorphic lens, the wide image would fit onto a standard 1.33:1 35mm film frame.

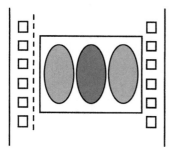

This is the same shot as it will appear on the 35mm film. The image has been squeezed by the camera's anamorphic lens to fit onto the standard 1.33:1 35mm film frame.

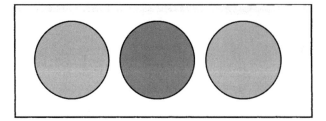

This is the same shot as it will appear on the theater screens. The squeezed up image on the film has been unsqueezed by another anamorphic lens on the projector.

There's another system that delivers a near 2.40:1 aspect ratio but it doesn't use anamorphic lenses. It uses 70mm film and delivers an aspect ratio of 2.2:1. Although a limited number of movies are still released in 70mm, there have never been any 70mm cameras in use. All of the cameras are 65mm and all of the projectors are 70mm. Why do the cameras use 65mm film and the theaters project 70mm? The release prints shown in theaters are 5mm wider to make room on the film for the sound track.

The standard aspect ratio for 65/70mm film is approximately 2.2:1. This is possible because the 65/70mm film is already so wide that a frame only five perforations high delivers a beautiful, wide-screen image. Most current films released in 70mm are originally shot in 35mm anamorphic or Super 35mm and enlarged to 70mm for a limited release.

PART D

THE GOLDEN SECTION

The golden section is a surface division that has long been used in fine art. Here are instructions for creating a golden section in a 2:1 aspect ratio frame.

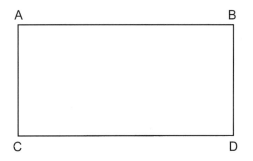

This is the frame that will be divided using the golden section.

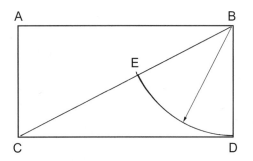

First, divide the frame in half with a diagonal line, CB. Then transfer the length of the frame's side BD onto the diagonal line, creating EB.

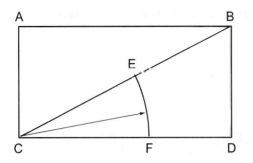

Now, transfer the length of CE down to the bottom of the frame, giving you point F.

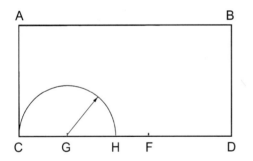

Transfer the length of FD across the bottom of the frame creating point G.

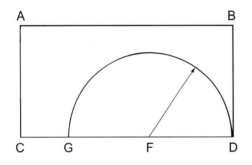

Transfer the length of CG across the bottom of the frame creating point H. Draw vertical lines from points G, H, and F.

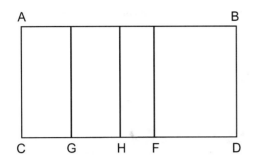

    This creates three divisions. The proportion of CF to FD is called the Golden Section. CG and CF have the same ratio as FD and CF. HF has the same ratio to GH as CG has to GF.

PART E

COLOR AND DEGREES KELVIN

Different light sources produce different colored light. We see all of these light sources as neutral or colorless but none of them produce white light. We can classify these various light sources with a system developed in the late 1800s by Lord William Kelvin and still in use today.

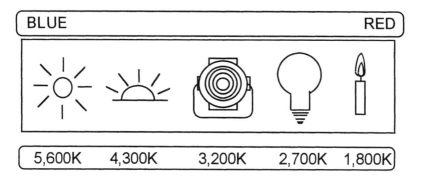

The Kelvin scale helps us describe and compare the color of light emitted from various sources. The lower the Kelvin number the redder the light, and the higher the Kelvin number the bluer the light. The scale is calibrated in degrees, although these degree numbers as we use them in lighting have nothing to do with thermal heat. A 5,600K light is not necessarily hotter than a 2,700K light.

Let's look more closely at each light source pictured on this Kelvin scale.

The *candle* at 1,800K appears fairly low on the Kelvin scale and emits a red-orange colored light. If we put candlelight through a prism, it would produce a rainbow, but the rainbow would have a predominance of red-orange light.

The *60-watt lightbulb* also produces an orange light, although not as orange as the candle. The bulb's color temperature is approximately 2,800K, which places it a bit closer to the blue end of the visible spectrum. A 40-watt bulb is redder (2,700K) and a 100-watt bulb is bluer (2,900K), although any common household bulb gets redder with use.

The *movie light* is manufactured to emit light at 3,200K. This is still on the redder side of the spectrum but not as red as the 60-watt bulb or the candle. The physical size or brightness of the light doesn't make any difference. If the light has been manufactured for film and video use, whether it be a 50-watt bulb or a 20,000-watt bulb, it will emit light at 3,200K. There's one exception noted under the upcoming *daylight* heading.

The *sunset* in this chart has been given an arbitrary color temperature of 4,300K. Average daylight is 5,600K, so as the sun sets the Kelvin number continually lowers (the light gets redder) as the sun gets closer to the horizon.

Daylight on an average day at noon is approximately 5,600K. Depending on the weather conditions, the direction your looking, and the time of year, this Kelvin reading will change. At higher altitudes where there's less atmosphere, the color temperature of skylight can get as high as 50,000K. Daylight's color temperature has a predominance of blue and violet light, although it still contains some red, yellow, and green as well. A special type of lamp was designed for film to closely simulate the color of daylight. Manufactured by a variety of companies but generically called HMI lights, they will produce a color temperature of light similar to daylight.

All of the light sources mentioned so far (the sun, stagelights, household lightbulbs, and candles) can be grouped together and called "continuous spectrum light sources" because each contains all of the wavelengths of visible light in various proportions. In other words, any continuous spectrum light source produces a complete visible spectrum or rainbow. The proportions of the colors will vary depending on the light source, but all the colors will be there. Fluorescent, neon, sodium vapor, and mercury vapor lights are called "discontinuous spectrum light sources" because they're missing certain wavelengths completely. For this reason, they cannot be classified on the Kelvin scale.

LIGHT AND FILM

When we compare candlelight to daylight there's a huge difference in brightness, but there's also a considerable difference in color. Imagine looking at a single lighted candle in a dark room. If you rush outside into the daylight, you'll notice that it's quite bright outdoors, but you probably won't notice that it's also very blue. Within seconds your eyes adjust to the brightness and color of the daylight and everything looks "normal." After a few minutes in the daylight return to the dark room with the lighted candle. The light from the candle will now appear unusually orange. Again, within seconds, your eyes will adjust and the darkness won't seem so dark and the orange candlelight will appear white.

Neither the daylight or the candlelight are neutral white light. The daylight is too blue and the candle is too orange. So why do both look neutral to us?

They appear neutral because our vision system has the extraordinary ability to adjust to the variations in brightness and color of most light sources. In fact, our brain wants to see white light so much so that it constantly makes adjustments to insure we think we're seeing neutral looking light. Imagine that our vision is a sophisticated color TV with dials that allow the brain to constantly correct the incoming light color and make it appear neutral. These adjustments happen automatically and constantly just like our breathing.

Film does not have our brain's ability to adjust. Motion picture films are manufactured to be compatible (or balanced) with only two light sources. There's indoor or tungsten-balanced film, which is manufactured to see 3,200K light as "normal," and there's outdoor or daylight-balanced film, which is manufactured to see 5,600K light as "normal." Any other combination of film and light source will change the color of the scene on film. To our eyes, both types of light look neutral because we can adjust, but film has no ability to adjust on its own. Let's examine some typical shooting situations and combinations of light source and film color temperatures.

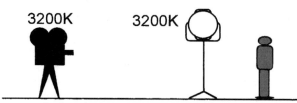

With the above arrangement, we'll have no color problem. The color temperature of the film in our camera matches or balances the color temperature of the light. The color rendering on film will look normal.

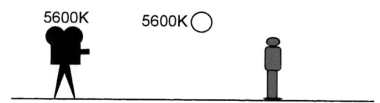

We'll have no problem here either because the film in the camera matches or balances the color temperature of the light source. The color rendering on film will be normal.

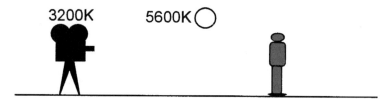

Here, we'll film an actor outdoors in 5,600K sunlight but with 3,200K film in the camera. What will happen to the color? The scene will appear too blue because the 5600K sunlight has a higher color temperature (bluer) than the 3,200K light that the film is manufactured to see as normal.

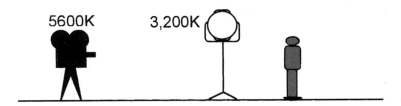

Now we've reversed the mismatch and we have 5,600K film in the camera and the light source is 3,200K. The result will be too orange because the light source has a color temperature lower (redder) than the color temperature of the film stock.

There's a simple solution to the mismatch of lighting and film color temperatures. A filter can be added to the camera lens or the light source. The filter will change the color temperature of the light that strikes the film. We'll discuss this in detail later in Part G.

Videotape has no color temperature rating but a video camera's electronics do. By activating the "white balance" on a camera, its electronics will compensate and make the incoming light appear neutral and white. Modern video cameras can automatically white balance by reading the ambient light coming into the lens and instantaneously adjust the video system's electronics.

Matching the color temperature of the film and light source is common practice, however there are many times when a mismatch of the two is intentional. You might want your pictures to be too blue or orange, and so a mismatch of light and film will quickly achieve your goal. Any color shift may be artistically correct even though it's a technical mismatch between the light source and the film's color temperature. The only correct color is the color you want for your final production.

Many cinematographers mix color temperatures on purpose to give a more natural or varied look to a scene. Remember, in the real world we mix color temperatures all the time. A room, for example, may have daylight coming in a window and a 60-watt lamp lighting a table at the same time. We may not notice the difference as quickly as we will on a screen, but two different color temperatures in one scene may produce the color scheme you want.

PART F

MIXING COLOR ON MONITORS

You probably think that television and computer screens also use the additive system. They don't. The color we see on television and computer screens is due to a system called *optical mixing*, which is similar to but different from the additive system. Examining television and computer screens with a magnifying glass reveals that the screen is comprised of hundreds of rows of tiny red, blue, and green dots or squares. These rows look roughly like this:

R	G	B	R	G	B	R	G	B
B	R	G	B	R	G	B	R	G

When a red color appears on screen, only the red dots light up. When a magenta color appears on the screen, both the red and blue dots brighten. When white appears on screen all the dots light up. The red, blue, and green dots are tightly packed together, but they do not overlap. The dots are so small that our eyes blend them together to produce color mixtures. The additive system requires colors to overlap when mixing. Since the three colors never overlap on a television or computer screen, we can't call this additive mixing; we call it optical mixing.

PART G

DEGREES KELVIN AND FILTERS

Let's reexamine the color mismatch problems between film and light source and see how filters, using the subtractive system, solve the problem.

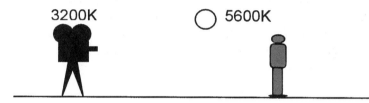

We're ready to film an actor outdoors in 5,600K sunlight, but we have 3,200K film in the camera. Shooting under these conditions will make the shot bluish, however we can use a filter to correct the problem. Since the sunlight is too blue, we need a filter to remove some of that blue. On the subtractive color wheel, yellow is opposite blue. Placing an orangish-yellow filter (commonly called an 85B filter) over the camera lens will absorb the complementary color (the unwanted blue light) and effectively lower the color temperature of the light to 3,200K.

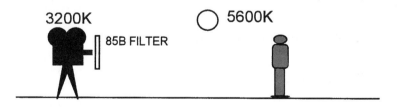

This will give us the proper balance between the light source and the film. Because a filter is subtractive (it absorbs wavelengths of light) we'll have to compensate for this absorbing or loss of light. When using an 85B filter, we'll open the lens up $2/3$ of a stop for proper exposure.

P A R T   H

THE DIRECTORIAL BEAT

The *beat* (a term developed in theater) sounds like the term describing rhythm, but it isn't. A directorial beat can be defined as a relationship or basic situation in a scene. A scene can be divided into many directorial beats. Each new beat signals a change in the character relationships or story situations within the scene.

Here's a scene we'll use to illustrate directorial beats. The scene takes place backstage at a theater where Jim Schreiber, a college student, looks for a rock singer named Maisy Adams.

BEAT #1:..

INT. THEATER DRESSING ROOM
Jim stands in the dressing room and looks around. Maisy enters.

> MAISY
>
> Who are you . . . ?!
>
> JIM
>
> I . . .uh . . . came to see Miss Adams. Uh . . . the door was open.
>
> MAISY
>
> It still is. Close it on your way out.
>
> JIM
>
> Who're you?
>
> MAISY
>
> Her hairdresser. Now do I have to call the cops?

Jim starts to leave, stops and closes the door.

BEAT #2:..

> JIM
>
> I can't leave until she honors her commitment.

MAISY

What?

JIM

I have to tell Miss Adams: (reciting from memory) You were scheduled to do a concert at our university's Homecoming, then your manager canceled. Maybe you've received a more financially remunerative offer, but we've already advanced $7,500 for the arena and the printing of tickets. The student body and faculty are counting on me to come through. I have a responsibility to them.

MAISY

Well, you've got a real problem, kid. What makes you think I'll help you out?

BEAT #3:...

Jim realizes she's Maisy Adams without her trademark green hair.

JIM

You're Maisy Adams?

MAISY

Right. Listen, I've got a show to do.

JIM

But what about the hair?

MAISY

I'm not a natural green. Look, why did you think I'd help you, anyway?

JIM

Desperation . . . and your lyrics. They're about treating people with love and respect and honesty. I figured you were sensitive and could understand that a decent human being could die.

MAISY

Who?

JIM

Me!

BEAT #4: ....

MAISY

Look, uh . . .

JIM

Jim. Jim Schreiber.

MAISY

You've got me feeling guilty if I sing at the other show. Then again, how do you think they'll feel if they're canceled?

JIM

I feel badly for them. But not as badly as I'd feel for myself.

MAISY

I suppose my manager could handle it. He's great in a mess; especially one he's created. You got a contract or what?

BEAT #5: . . . .

JIM

(removes contract from coat pocket)

I can't tell you how happy this makes me.

MAISY

Yeah, I picked up on those vibes.

He hands her a pen.

MAISY

You know they want me to keep my real identity secret from the public.

JIM

I won't tell a soul.

She signs the contract and returns it to Jim.

JIM

Well, I'll see you next week.

MAISY

Enjoy tonight's show.

JIM

I . . . uh . . . didn't have time to purchase a ticket.

MAISY

Then watch from the wings.

Maisy takes a backstage pass off the dressing table. Peels off the backing and smoothes the sticky side onto Jim's thigh.

Maisy smiles and Jim blushes.

END . . . .

This scene can be divided into five directorial beats. Each new beat indicates a change in the intention or relationship between Jim and Maisy.

BEAT #1: Jim is nervous and Maisy is hostile.
BEAT #2: Jim gains strength and stays.
BEAT #3: Maisy reveals her identity and Jim pleads his case.
BEAT #4: Maisy agrees; Jim is happy.
BEAT #5: Maisy flirts with Jim.

Beats are useful in a number of different ways. Writers use beats to organize a scene's plot and character relationship changes. Directors use beats to guide the actors. Beats are the key to understanding the structure of the story, the scenes, and the character relationships. Let's look at ways we can define directorial beats.

1. *Acting.* The way the actors deliver their lines, the expressions on their faces, and their body language can delineate the beat changes. We will understand a character's change in mood, needs, and feelings if each beat is properly performed by the actor. An actor can communicate the story's intention by understanding and acting with the directorial beat in mind.

2. *Staging.* Beats can also be delineated by the staging of the actors. Each time a beat changes, the actors will rearrange themselves to show how their relationship has changed. The director will move the actors into new positions (sitting, standing, walking, etc.) in relation to each other to help communicate to the audience that the relationships or intentions have changed. Theater relies heavily on this method of delineating beats.

3. *Camera.* The camera can be used to indicate beat changes by moving to a new position. Camera movement is usually linked to the movement of objects in the frame. The camera movement is accomplished by panning, tilting, dollying, or craning from one camera position to another. Whenever a new beat begins, the camera will move to a new location. Using this method, the camera does not cut; a scene is photographed continuously, so the camera movements are part of the shot.

4. *Camera/Editorial.* Assuming the scene has been fragmented, the editor is supplied with many different shots (master, two-shot, over-the-shoulder shots, close-ups, etc.) of the entire scene. This variety of shots is called "coverage." The editor examines the coverage and delineates the directorial beats by organizing the coverage.

The editor might start with a wide master for Beat #1. Beat #2 could use only the over-the-shoulder shots, and Beat #3 would only use the close-ups. There are many possible variations of the scene using this approach, since the scene has been photographed from so many different angles. The goal of the editor is to give the scene visual structure so that the beat changes are clear.

5. *Visual Component.* A beat change can be delineated by a change in a visual component. Changing the space from deep to flat for example, will help the audience sense the beat change.

In Beat #1 and #2, the dressing room might be photographed in flat space and cool colors. In Beat #3, Maisy might sit down at her dressing table and turn on the mirror lights calling attention to Jim's realization that she is the singer. At the same time the space might turn deep to help build visual conflict. Beat #5, the resolution, might have the actors move to a different area of the dressing room with a warmly colored wall in the background and a return to flat space. The more change in the visual components, the greater the intensity of the beat changes.

A director can choose one or any combination of these approaches to delineate the beat. If you delineate beats through acting and staging then you'll tend to shoot your films in a more continuous manner with fewer cuts and less coverage. If you fragment your scenes and shoot coverage, you can decide in postproduction how your beat changes will be handled.

Often the method of beat delineation is determined by the schedule or limitations of the production. Television daytime dramas must shoot so much each day that complex staging and camera work is prohibitive. They rely on the actors for the beat delineation because it's the least time-consuming.

Multicamera television sitcoms have more time to stage scenes but are limited by the camera's distance from the actors, the "live" shooting style, and the three walled sets. There's more actor staging to delineate the beats, but the camera angles are limited. In these situations the beats are usually delineated by the acting and the staging.

A one-camera television or theatrical film is limited only by its schedule and the talent of the production personnel in finding the best ways to control the beats.

Any production gains visual variety by using a constantly changing approach to the delineation of the beats. Ignoring the beats turns a scene into long, run-on sequences that have no shape. Delineating the beats gives a scene structure, which helps the audience understand the scene.

P A R T   I

STORYBOARDS

Suppose someone handed you a script with a gold cover. Does the gold cover mean the script is great? Of course not. You'd have to read the script to determine if it is any good. A script with a gold cover doesn't mean the script is as good as gold, but this is exactly what happens when most people look at storyboards. They are seduced by the quality of the drawings. The better the drawings, the better they think the storyboards must be. That's unfortunate, because great drawings do not necessarily create great storyboards.

Storyboards should be used to remind you of things that need to happen in the shot. If you're creating special effects, storyboards are necessary because they are the only way to visualize something that will be added in postproduction. But storyboards can also be used for conventional production.

How attractive the drawings look has very little to do with the usefulness of the storyboard. You are simply trying to find a way to remember what you need to do for a shot. The storyboards are not going to be seen by the audience. Storyboards are a working tool just like the script. Don't be embarrassed by poor drawing techniques when you use storyboards. Here are some examples of storyboards.

This panel is a well-drawn shot that tells you a lot about the composition and dramatic requirements of the shot.

Although this is a cruder sketch, it has the same basic information as the first drawing. Notice that some of the information is written instead of drawn.

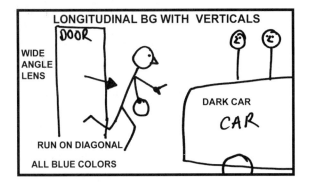

This drawing is even simpler but it still contains the information needed on the set. This storyboard also includes information about some of the visual components.

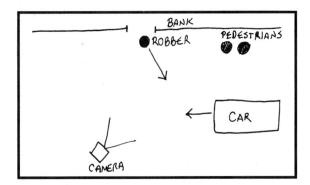

This drawing is only a map of the shot, but it still tells you the same type of information.

A storyboard is a reminder, not the finished production. Often, too much time is spent creating storyboards that look good, but don't tell the story properly. Storyboards can indicate the general composition of a shot but they can also remind you what to do with the visual components.

BIBLIOGRAPHY

Albers, Josef. *The Interaction of Color*. New Haven, CT: Yale University Press, 1963.

Alton John. *Painting with Light*. New York: Macmillan & Co., 1949.

Arnheim, Rudolph. *Visual Thinking*. Berkeley, CA: University of California Press, 1969.

Arnheim, Rudolph. *Art and Visual Perception*. Berkeley, CA: University of California Press, 1954.

Barda, Yon. *Eisenstein: The Growth of a Cinematic Genius*. Bloomington, IN: Indiana University Press, 1973.

Bloomer, Carolyn M. *Principles of Visual Perception*. New York: Design Press, 1976.

Bouleau, Charles. *The Painter's Secret Geometry*. New York: Harcourt Brace & World, 1963.

Campbell, Joseph. *The Hero with a Thousand Faces*. New York: Pantheon Books, 1949.

Charlot, Jean. Unpublished lectures given at the Disney Studios, 1938, collection of the Disney Studio Archives.

Dean, Alexander, and Carra, Lawrence. *Fundamentals of Play Directing*. New York: Holt Reinhart, Winston, 1947.

Dewey, John. *Art as Experience*. New York: Putnam, 1958.

Dewey, John. *Experience and Nature*. London: Allen & Unwin, 1929.

Dewey, John. *How We Think*. Boston: D.C. Heath, 1919.

Eisenstein, Sergei. *Notes of a Film Director*. London: Lawrence & Wishart, 1959.

Eisenstein, Sergei. *Film Form*. New York: Harcourt Brace & World, 1949.

Eisenstein, Sergei. *The Film Sense*. New York: Harcourt Brace & World, 1947.

Evans, Ralph. *An Introduction to Color*. London: John Wiley & Sons, 1948.

Evans, Ralph M. *Eye, Film, and Camera in Color Photography*. London: John Wiley & Sons, 1959.

Gibson, James J. *Perception of the Visual World*. Boston: Houghton Mifflin Co., 1950.

Gombrich, E.H. *The Image and the Eye*. Oxford: Phaedon Press, 1981.

Gombrich, E.H. *Art and Illusion*. Princeton, NJ: Princeton University Press, 1969.

Graham, Donald. *Composing Pictures*. New York: Van Reinhold Co., 1970.

Itten, Johannes. *The Art of Color*. New York: Van Nostrand Reinholt Co., 1961.

Kandinsky, Wassily. *The Art of Spiritual Harmony*. London: Constable and Co., 1914.

Katz, David. *The World of Colour*. London: Kegan Paul, Trench, Trubner & Co., 1935.

Kepes, Gyorgy, editor. *Module, Proportion, Symmetry, Rhythm*. New York: George Brazillier, 1966.

Kepes, Gyorgy, editor. *The Nature of Art and Motion*. New York: George Brazillier, 1965.

Klee, Paul. *The Thinking Eye*. New York: Wittenbourn, 1956.

Kuppers, Harald. *Color*. New York: Van Nostrand Reinhold, 1972.

Langer, Suzanne. *Problems of Art*. New York: Simon & Schuster, 1957.

Lumet, Sidney. *Making Movies*. New York: Alfred A. Knopf, 1995.

Manoogian, Haig P. *The Film-Maker's Art*. New York: Basic Books, 1966.

Merleau-Ponty, M. *Phenomenology of Perception*. London: Routledge & Kegan Paul, 1962.

Munsell Book of Color. Glossy & Matte editions, Munsell Corporation, 1976.

Munsell, A.H. *A Color Notation*. Boston: G.H. Elis Co., 1905.

Nilsen, Vladimir. *The Cinema as a Graphic Art*. London: George Newnes Ltd, 1936.

Nizhny, Vladimir. *Lessons with Eisenstein*. London: Allen & Unwin, 1962.

Ostwald, Wilhelm. *Colour Science*. London: Windsor & Newton, 1933.

Plochere, Gustov, and Plochere, Gladys. *Plochere Color System*. Los Angeles, 1948.

Scharf, Aaron. *Art and Photography*. London: Jarrold & Sons Ltd., 1968.

Scientific American editors. *Recent Progress in Perception*. San Francisco: W.H. Freeman and Co., 1976.

Scientific American editors. *Image, Object, and Illusion*. San Francisco: W.H. Freeman and Co., 1974.

Scientific American editors. *Communication*. San Francisco: W.H. Freeman, 1972.

Scientific American editors. *Perception: Mechanisms and Models*. San Francisco: W.H. Freeman and Co., 1972.

Seton, Marie. *Sergei M. Eisenstein*. New York: A.A. Wyn Inc.

Truffaut, Francois. *Hitchcock: A Definitive Study*. New York: Simon & Schuster, 1967.

Vernon, M.D. *A Further Study of Visual Perception*. Cambridge: Cambridge University Press, 1952.

Vorkapich, Slavko. Audio recordings of lectures, 1968-1972, collection of University of Southern California Library.

Vorkapich, Slavko. Unpublished notes, 1950-1972, collection of University of Southern California Library.

White, John. *The Birth and Rebirth of Pictorial Space*. Boston: Boston Books, 1967.

INDEX